When I Grow Up

Moya Sarner is a psychodynamic psychotherapist and
award-winning freelance journalist based in London.
She has written for *The Times*, *The Guardian*,
New Scientist, *Stylist*, and other publications.
When I Grow Up is her first book.

When I Grow Up

conversations
with adults in search
of adulthood

Moya Sarner

SCRIBE

Melbourne • London

Scribe Publications
2 John St, Clerkenwell, London, WC1N 2ES, United Kingdom
18–20 Edward St, Brunswick, Victoria 3056, Australia
3754 Pleasant Ave, Suite 100, Minneapolis, Minnesota 55409, USA

Published by Scribe 2022

Typeset in Adobe Caslon Pro by the publishers

Printed and bound in the UK by CPI Group (UK) Ltd, Croydon CR0 4YY

Scribe is committed to the sustainable use of natural resources and the use of paper products made responsibly from those resources.

978 1 957363 14 1 (US edition)
978 1 925849 88 2 (Australian edition)
978 1 913348 00 7 (UK edition)
978 1 922586 36 0 (ebook)

Catalogue records for this book are available from the National Library of Australia and the British Library.

scribepublications.com
scribepublications.com.au
scribepublications.co.uk

'Of all the hateful possibilities, growth and maturation are feared and detested most frequently.'

Wilfred Bion

Contents

Introduction
Beginnings

'Train in the Distance'
Song by Paul Simon

When I was a baby, just starting to crawl, my grandpa helped me learn by crouching down on the floor in my parents' home and dangling his keys in front of me. He would shuffle backwards as I wobbled towards him, all knees and arms. I was entranced by him and his keys, their jangle and shine; and he was besotted with me, grinning with delight at my development, at my beginning to grow up. I have no memory of this scene taking place, but I do remember very clearly, as a child of five or so, sitting on the sofa, watching baby me on the shaky home video taken by my mother with her hand-held camcorder. My grandpa died when I was in my early teens, more than 20 years ago now, so he never got to see me as an adult with a husband and a home of our own. Or I should say, he never got to see me as a supposed adult. Because long after I was old enough to be a grown-up, it felt to me like I was still reaching after that jangle and shine; as if he had held the keys to growing up in front of me when I was a babe, and no matter how many faltering steps I took, adulthood was always just out of my grasp.

I needed to write this book because I did not feel like a grown-up.

To outside observers, I was an adult. And there were times, such as at work as a journalist or cooking dinner for friends, where I did feel like a mature, capable, responsible grown-up woman in her 30s. But at apparently random moments, my non-adultness would pop out — like the time I opened my kitchen bin to find the underside of the lid thick and throbbing with squiggly maggots, and immediately texted my mother to ask what to do. It was as if I had no mind of my own, Google had never been invented, and I had no capacity or nous to rely on. More often, though, this feeling was nebulous, not so pin-downable. I carried around this weight of something delayed, something under-developed, something I needed but did not have. Although I had passed my driving test, I had not actually driven for years because I was afraid of crashing; I had a licence that said I was a driver — but I knew that deep down, I wasn't one.

So what to make of this hybrid, both-and-neither, not-quite-grown-up state? As I began writing this book, friends, relatives, and strangers confessed that, like me, they didn't feel like adults. Some called it imposter syndrome, or faking it 'til you make it, some spoke of feeling that something wasn't quite right in their sense of themselves. Sometimes they seemed to imply that I should take my feelings and theirs less seriously because they are so widespread, so normal.

I think the opposite.

The traditional milestones that we have relied upon to define adulthood are under pressure as never before. People in Western nations seem to be growing up later and later, as the accepted social landmarks of adulthood drift — or are pulled — further and further from our grasp, like my grandpa with his keys. Research by the Office for National Statistics (ONS) shows that the age of the average first-time home buyer in the UK has risen by seven years over the last five decades — and for many, home ownership remains unrealistic.[1] People are getting married older: in the US in 2019, the average age at first marriage for men was 30, for women, 28; an increase of eight years over the last six decades.[2] In Australia, the proportion of women having their first child over the age of 30 has more than doubled over 25 years,[3] and in the UK in 2015, the number of women giving birth over 40 outstripped the number of women giving birth under 20 for the first time since World War II.[4] And many more Americans may not become parents at all: in 2019, America saw the lowest number of babies born in three decades.[5] But it is not just these traditional measures of adulthood that are under pressure: it is the young people who feel like failures for not hitting them.

These statistics left me hungry, dissatisfied, searching for something more meaningful — because they didn't tell me what a grown-up really was. They were the seductively easy answers, but they didn't take me much closer to the truth. During my research, I heard about a quiz from a 1930s magazine titled, 'Are you an adult?' Readers were instructed to tick the boxes that best represented their responses, and then turn to page 87 to find out the results. I laughed when I heard about this, at the ridiculous idea that adulthood could be determined by a quiz in a magazine — but I know I would have been one of the suckers who could not resist the draw of page 87. I think this magazine quiz, tick-box approach to adulthood is crucial to understanding what we get wrong, as a culture and as individuals, about growing up.

It was the sociologist Harry Blatterer, a senior lecturer at Macquarie University, Australia, who told me about that quiz, when I asked him why he thought so many of us don't feel like adults. He explained to me how our own self-perception relies on recognition by others, which we might seek through achieving the social markers of full-time work, home ownership, a relationship, parenthood. In that sense, adulthood is a 'cultural artefact'. In the aftermath of World War II, with the rise of youth culture in the 50s and 60s (think James Dean in *Rebel Without a Cause*), there developed this idea, he said, that 'at the end of adolescence, you settle down to become an adult': the woman stays at home and has kids, the man goes out to work for the same company for 35 years then retires with a pension. As a child brought up in a middle-class British Jewish heteronormative family in the 1980s, I realised I had exactly that picture of an adult in my mind: someone standing in a doorway of a house holding a briefcase or a baby. That suburban image of American and English life is one of security and stability, one in which people can achieve milestones, tick boxes, and feel validated, Blatterer told me, 'and it's all very hetero'. To some, this will sound old-fashioned now, because our lives, and our societies, have undergone significant changes since then, and for many of my generation and those following, work, sexuality, relationships, and (non)parenthood can take very different shapes. But I wondered how profound these changes really were; some parts of society may seem more open and less rigid than in the past, but many of us are still stuck, whether we like it or not, with the image of adulthood our parents and grandparents were raised with.

For as long as I can remember, probably since I gazed up adoringly at my grandpa and his keys, I have wanted to be a grown-up. And when I began writing this book, I did seem to be living an adult life, having achieved most of the ONS-approved milestones — except for the baby, which still felt far too grown up for me. I had a career, a home, and a husband; an accountant, a pension, and a tax return; I had deliberated over and purchased a dishwasher, a washing machine, and a fridge. Judge me by my white goods, and I ticked almost all the boxes — I had the paperwork to prove I was the competent, confident adult I should be. But the more boxes I ticked, the more I realised how shaky, how tenuous, my own feeling of being-an-adult was. All this seemed only to emphasise the inadequacy of my childhood definition of adulthood, and of the statistics we imagine can measure it. I was a grown-up on paper, yes, but at times my adult skin felt paper-thin, and I experienced myself as a flattened version of the fleshed-out adult I was supposed to be. I had missed my deadline, and I was very cross with myself about it. But also curious. Perhaps, I thought, this crisis of adulthood that our society is facing, that I am facing personally, and that you may or may not be facing too in your own way, is also a chance for us to seek a more meaningful sense of what it is to be an adult. If a house and a spouse do not make a grown-up, then what does?

I wonder if in a peculiar way, I have been looking for answers to this question for longer than I realised. My first job as a journalist in my early 20s was at a women's magazine where my role was to find and interview women who had changed their lives for the better in some way. These changes might be small or they might be big; in the morning I might speak to one woman who had discovered a love of cycling after her divorce, in the afternoon I might speak to another woman who been through the horrific ordeal of losing a child and who had, somehow, found the internal resources to channel her pain and grief into setting up a charity to support other bereaved parents. I was good at my job, and I loved it. As I interviewed these women, as I gave them space to speak and tried to help them put their feelings into words, I began to understand how powerful it can be to have another human listen to your story, how powerful it can be to listen. At that time, my recollection is of having a clear sense of identity, and feeling quite confident in who I was: a young woman who worked hard and did well. But still, I didn't feel like an adult. Looking back now, I wonder if I had unconsciously managed to wangle myself a job in which I could legitimately ask people about how they had developed and grown from their experiences — how they became the people they are — without letting on, to them or to my editor or to myself, that I wasn't just doing it because it was my job, but because I needed to know.

When I eventually left that women's magazine, I went on to work for a national newspaper, and then decided to become a freelance journalist, pitching articles to different newspapers and magazines. Suddenly I had no editor telling me what to write about — no grown-up telling me what to do. My husband would leave the flat to go to his office every morning and I would sit, alone, at my desk, open a fresh

Word document on my laptop and quietly panic. That sense of identity started to feel a little shaky as I sat there, trying to come up with ideas for articles and convince myself that I did actually know what I was doing. So I decided to develop a specialism. I guess I felt a bit scared and lost and unknowing, and my way out of that was to try to know something. The specialism I was most interested in was mental health, so I signed up to an introductory course to learn about how the human mind develops, based on the ideas of psychoanalysis.

It didn't quite work out the way I thought it would.

That short introductory course soon took over my mind, my work, my whole life. It became the first of five years of psychotherapy training, and before long I was also a patient in psychoanalysis.

As I began writing this book, I was in the thick of this training: there were lectures, seminars, supervisions, sessions with patients, lunch with classmates in the cafeteria — all of that. By the time it went to the printers, I had qualified. The kind of therapy I am studying — psychodynamic psychotherapy — is based on the theories of psychoanalysis. When I began, I really didn't know anything about it — I just sort of fell into it (or perhaps my unconscious took me to where I needed to be). The word made me think of self-indulgent, rich American film stars with too much money and time on their hands — that was my prejudice. But the truth is psychoanalysis is the most powerful, exciting, outrageous, horrifying, beautiful, and painful mess of ideas I have ever let into my life. From my first lecture, it was as if a mighty storm had charged through my insides, blowing back the curtains, knocking over the chairs and vases, upsetting all the furniture of my mind. Take the unconscious; before, it was just a word to me. An everyday, mundane, uncontroversial word I would slip into conversation without really thinking about its meaning. But if we do stop and think about what 'the unconscious' truly means, we have to see that it is shocking, scandalous — terrifying! The unconscious means we are not who we think ourselves to be. It means there are things about ourselves that we cannot bear to know, that we push underground, into the dark, so we don't have to see; so that we can believe ourselves to be the person we want to be. It is a terrible shock to face up to this.

At the same time as studying the theories of psychoanalysis in the classroom, I became a patient of psychoanalysis in the consulting room. So as I learned about the unconscious in an intellectual way, I also began to see something of my own unconscious, and the stories I have told myself to get away from it. And that was extremely uncomfortable.

To be in analysis is a very strange and quite other-worldly experience; I think it is the most different thing I have ever done. It feels totally unlike other forms of mental health treatment, like cognitive behavioural therapy or medication, which you are likely to be offered if you go to your GP and say you are feeling depressed or anxious. My psychoanalyst has never tried to take away the pain I'm feeling, or to give me solutions to my problems, or to reassure me when I've shared my insecurities. This may sound counter-intuitive, or even sadistic — after all, a person in psychological distress often just wants help to alleviate that distress; I know I did — but psychoanalysis works in a different way. It is not about getting rid of pain, but about growing the capacity to feel it. Trying to put it into words and understand where it comes from. I often think back to a moment during my first meeting with my analyst when I was telling her about how I had always used running and gym classes to successfully manage my anxiety, but that since I had injured my back I hadn't been able to. I don't recall her exact response, but I remember the unsettling, gut-clenching feeling it provoked, and the vague, burgeoning awareness that all this time I thought I had been managing my emotions, but in fact I had been running away from them.

Four mornings a week, I walk to my analyst's consulting room, I lie down on her couch, and there is a silence. I say whatever comes into my mind or 'free associate' — I talk of my feelings, my thoughts, my dreams — or I try to. She sits in a chair at the end of the couch where I cannot see her, sometimes silent, sometimes speaking, making interpretations about what she thinks is going on in my mind. It involves a kind of being with myself and with someone else that I have never known, and that I am still struggling with. Something happens in the space created by her attitude that is not possible for me to put into words — a flaw, I realise, in a writer. And so, as I often do when my voice fails, I will seek solace in someone else's, like a child hiding in an adult: the brilliant psychoanalyst Thomas H. Ogden wrote that, for the patient or analysand, 'the consulting room is a profoundly quiet place as he realizes that he must find a voice with which to tell his story. This voice is the sound of his thoughts, which he may never have heard before. (The analysand may find he does not have a voice that feels like his own. This discovery may then serve as the starting point of the analysis.)'[6] This discovery was also the starting point of this book. I am in search of a voice that feels like my own.

What I can say in my own voice is that my analyst listens to me in a way that I have never been listened to before. She listens to the part of me that I cannot hear — that I do not want to hear. She listens to my unconscious. And through this experience, I am coming to see that while I thought I knew myself, I do not. For example, if I say something I think is positive, she might tell me that she thinks that in fact I feel the opposite, or that I am feeling envious of her, or that I am angry with her. Sometimes this feels like such a relief, such a profound moment of non-judgement and of truth. At others, it feels awful, really awful. Making painful contact with my own envy, my own aggression, my own longings, my own need to be in control; seeing that many of the stories I tell about myself may be comforting to believe, but they are not true in any meaningful sense. My so-called identity was totally hollow. 'Someone who works hard' is not an identity; 'good' is not an identity; 'doing what you are told' is not an identity. For me these were all just ways to try to feel okay about not being in touch with who I really am. As Ogden wrote: 'All that has been most obvious to the patient will no longer be treated as self-evident: rather, the familiar is to be worried about, to be puzzled over.'[7] I think it's about time we gave adulthood — or whatever it is that we have come to call adulthood — the same treatment.

It soon became very clear that this training and therapy was not really about developing a journalistic specialism in mental health. Now I see that narrative for what it was: a nice story, the one I needed to tell to get myself to where I needed to be. I was doing something much more uncomfortable than developing a specialism, like the difference between trying to know something, and trying to face up to the reality that almost everything I thought I knew was in question. The carefully constructed identity I had unknowingly crafted for myself had to come tumbling down. And that meant accepting that not only did I not feel like an adult — I did not even know what one was.

So that is where I found myself as I set off on this quest to learn something about what it means to grow up. My aim in this book is to take you, my reader, on this search with me. As we take our first steps, there are three important ideas you need to know about. The unconscious, which we have touched upon, is the first. The second is the lifelong endurance of infancy. Psychoanalysis shows that, although we must pass through infancy, childhood, and adolescence to reach adulthood, we never quite leave those psychological stages for good, no matter what age we reach. The experiences of the infant in the first year of life are understood to shape the adult he or she or they will become — whether we know about them or not. I have been undertaking an infant observation, a historic part of the psychotherapy training in Britain, introduced by Esther Bick in 1948.[8] For one hour every week, for more than seven decades, trainees have been sitting quietly, observing a new mother and her infant, watching that baby developing in real time, seeing how the infant bonds with their parents, how the baby manages the mother's absences, how the spaces between feeds grow longer, and how the baby engages more and more with the world. Just like all these trainees, I have thought about what might be going on in that baby's mind, what their cries might be trying to express, what it feels like to be fed, to be hungry, to be held. Love, loss, growth, pain, dependency and independence — surviving all this is what it means to grow up for a baby, and perhaps it is not so different for the rest of us. That is why, in every chapter of this book, whether it is about teenagers, young adults, middle-aged, or older people, you will also find it is about infancy, as I link every life stage back to our earliest weeks and months. Understanding how things begin will, I hope, help us to expand our understanding of how things end up the way they do, and how we can get stuck along the way.

The third idea is what I am calling a grow-up. I have learnt through psychoanalysis that we don't just grow up once; we have to keep growing up — or attempting to — over and over again. As I see it, at every stage we encounter challenges that require us to make a psychological leap, whether that is accepting as a child that your possessions must be shared, or losing your parents in your 50s and feeling like an orphan, or realising, as a 30-something-year-old, that you are far from the adult you expected yourself to be. If we avoid or bypass these leaps, we remain stuck in one place, unable to develop — unable to grow. It is only by facing up to them, meeting them squarely, and surviving them that we can hope to find some movement, even if we encounter that challenge again in the future, and are required to survive it again. My name for this kind of leap is a grow-up. It is only by making our way through countless grow-ups, some big and some small, and by making it through the same grow-ups over and over again, that we can hope to come closer to a truer sense of who we are, a kind of freedom of adulthood, and a way of living that feels real.

Although I did not have a map for the search on which I embarked, I did have a plan. That plan was to listen. To have conversations with the most interesting people I could find, both academic experts and so-called ordinary people, from different ages and stages of adulthood, about the grow-ups they've faced — whether they made it through, or whether they're still stuck, unable to make the leap. I got back in touch with people I met through journalism who have had fascinating lives and loves and losses, and who I thought had something important to share about growing up in whatever life stage they happened to be in. People like Boru, a young man who suffered from drug-induced psychosis at the age of 18, and was the youngest on his adult psychiatric ward. And Roxy Legane, a young woman who started the organisation Kids of Colour, who spoke about how she thinks racism affects people growing up — including herself. And Hemal, a father of two, who told me about how losing his mother and his brother in childhood has affected him as he has grown into a parent himself. And Alex, who talked about how it felt to survive into middle age, growing older than the age his father was when he killed himself. And Sheila, who continued growing up after finding love again, later in life. And Pog, who is still waiting to feel like an adult, age 90. I also spoke with academics from fields as varied as neuroscience and zoology, language and history, as well as a children's author, two rabbis, and, of course, some psychoanalysts; to anyone I could find who has dedicated their life to understanding something about what it means to develop, to grow up. And as I listened to all these people, I thought about my own experiences, as a patient and as a therapist in training, and wondered if any of this could help me to make sense of what it means to become an adult — or not.

Although I did not know what I would find when I started those conversations, I had already begun to develop a sense of something out there which might be called adulthood; less a set of achievements or social markers, and more a texture of life, a complex state that emerges gradually, continuously shape-shifting. Something to do with a feeling of solidity, a sense of the boundaries between myself and others. Growing up, I was coming to see in my analysis, involved developing a capacity to bear emotional pain, rather than running away from it; to accept difference from others, rather than repelling or denying those differences; and to see oneself as separate from one's loved ones. It means tolerating imperfection and uncertainty and feeling excluded. It also means enjoying our more childlike sides, and being able to dance and play and laugh so much you lose control. As the psychoanalyst and psychiatrist Carine Minne told me, 'You can't grow up if you don't have the capacity to healthily grow down regularly.'

Your and my experiences of this journey will be very different. My task has involved finding my way through conversations with fascinating people, through my training and through my analysis; getting lost, stuck and, unstuck again along the way. It has meant trying to find my own voice, bringing together the different parts of myself — the first-time author, the therapist in training, the struggling patient, the not-quite grown-up. Yours may be completely different — but perhaps no less challenging, shaped by your unique infancy, childhood, adolescence, and experiences in adulthood. For you this journey will hopefully involve encountering new ideas, some of which might have immediate meaning and value, others which might seem dubious or far-fetched, difficult or disturbing. Perhaps all of us, somewhere, are afraid we are about to open up something very messy, and find ourselves holding a dustbin-lid of maggots. I think if we can all open our minds to the abundance of different ways into adulthood — to take in and think about these ideas and roll them around in our minds without immediately accepting or rejecting them — we might, with good fortune, come to learn something about the very human struggle towards the freedom that comes from beginning to know oneself. This is the struggle that has been painted and sung, performed and written throughout human history, from the first flying bird scrawled on the wall of a cave, to Shakespeare's Lear who 'hath ever but slenderly known himself',[9] to the first prayer set to music, to the dancing teens of TikTok. Perhaps, by the end of the book, we will finally hold the key to adulthood in our hands — or perhaps we will still be grasping after it as it hovers above us, always out of reach.

Chapter One
The weird limbo

'I'm Not a Girl, Not Yet a Woman'
Sung by Britney Spears,
written by Max Martin / Rami Yacoub / Dido Armstrong

A baby is being born. She is leaving her mother's body, the only home she has ever known, and entering the world in a new way. A movement from inside to outside. She takes a breath — her first breath — and she cries — desperate, animal cries, the instinctual cries of new life. For the first time, she experiences the feeling of cool air on her skin; the feeling of warm skin on her skin; the feeling of having her own skin. She is placed on her mother's body and she clings and cries. They are as close as they can be and more separate than they have ever been.

The umbilical cord is cut. She has become a separate person.

Or has she?

An adult is 'someone who's got their shit sorted out', according to Boru; a definition that is the typical mix of wry wit, longing, and on-the-nose observation that I have come to think of as 'Boruvian'. He is 20 years old, and looks too tall for my small flat, his bleached blond hair tied in a low ponytail, the straps of his white dungarees dropping down below his black-and-white jacket, black polish patchy on his fingernails. There is a kind of peeling off of layers as he carefully removes the serious-looking camera hanging from his shoulder, then his jacket and then his hoody. He sits down, seeming to fold himself into the sofa, and speaks so quietly it is difficult for me to catch everything he says. His soft responses are punctuated by thoughtful, comfortable silences, and he has a gentle and tender way about him that makes me want to listen, not to miss a word.

I first interviewed Boru for a newspaper when he was 19 and back then, he seemed to me to be pretty grown-up.[1] He had survived and recovered from severe mental health problems, was in a serious relationship with a young woman he loved, and was working hard as a cycling instructor, a job he cared about. He had been through, as he would put it, a lot of shit, but he had sorted it out, and the experience seemed to have left him with a kind of radical maturity; he gave off a sense of absolute self-reliance. One year on, he comes to my home to be interviewed for this book and everything has changed — he seems vulnerable, shy, young. When we begin, his responses to my questions are politely monosyllabic, or close to it. Is he still in that long-term relationship? 'No,' with a soft smile. So is he single? 'Yeah.' Does he still work as a cycling instructor? 'No, I left quite recently.' So, what is he doing? He gives a quiet laugh as if to himself. 'Nothing. Trying to figure out what to do.' When I ask him if he is a grown-up, he says, 'No. No. Umm … yes and no … I felt like I was. And then I felt like I wasn't.' His hesitant, stumbling speech seems to give voice to that sense of uncertainty, of ricocheting between adult and not adult, of being both and neither and lost in between, that makes the first chapter of adult life so confusing and destabilising, even when it goes well.

For Boru, it did not go well.

He grew up in Greenwich, the youngest of three, and remembers arguments and conflict, not feeling close to his family. His mental health had already been deteriorating for some years when, at 17, it started to collapse. His mind was like a table on which there are lots of pieces of paper, he explains; some of the pieces are light like tissue paper, but others are heavy like cardboard, and the pile grew so high and heavy that the weight was too much for his table's legs, and they broke. 'The whole experience of it just weighed on me. My legs were too weak, and it all came crashing down.' He refused to go to school, would not eat, became addicted to drugs, attempted suicide. Still age 17, he was admitted as an inpatient to the adolescent unit of a psychiatric hospital and stayed there for several months, with later readmissions for brief periods. There, he received the help he desperately needed — he saw a psychotherapist, took part in creative group activities, and felt taken care of. He began to see a way forward for himself. He was recovering.

Then he turned 18.

What is an adult? There is an easy answer to this question for most of the world, according to Google: anyone who is 18 or older. But as Boru and I know in our bones, becoming an adult is not that simple. If it was, this would be a very short book.

If I had to choose the most profoundly underwhelming, comically inadequate, and frankly cruel answer for when we become adults, it would be at age 18. I don't think anybody really believes it. Unfortunately, it seems to be the definition with the most influence in our society and our institutions, the one that determines the treatment of so many young people, whether that be in voting booths or in bars, in court rooms or in mental health services. The reality, of course, is that the shift into adulthood is much less black and white, defined, and definitive than an arbitrary number suggests.

I was relieved to discover in my research that the UK's legal structures have evolved to recognise this to some degree. The blurry, messy, always-unfinished business of growing up can be read between the lines of the laws that make space for adulthood in young people before their 18th birthday, and for childhood after it. The judge Lord Scarman ruled in 1985 that, 'If the law should impose upon the process of "growing up" fixed limits where nature knows only a continuous process, the price would be artificiality and a lack of realism in an area where law must be sensitive to human development and social change.'[2] This is the basis of the legal concept that lawyers, judges, and clinicians use to assess whether or not children under 16 have the capacity to make adult decisions for themselves, called 'Gillick competence'. It stems from a famous case: Victoria Gillick, a religious Catholic and mother of 10, went to court to prevent doctors prescribing contraception to children under 16 without the consent of a parent, arguing that GPs were encouraging promiscuity in young people. Lord Scarman sitting in the Court of Appeal ruled that a child can make their own decisions about medical treatment 'if and when the child achieves a sufficient understanding and intelligence to enable him or her to understand fully what is proposed',[3] and this became the test to reflect the transition, in some respects at least, for a child into adulthood. On the older side of the 18th birthday, there is still more grey. In one of the most explicit acknowledgements that 18-year-olds are not cut-and-dried grown-ups, the Children Act 1989 requires social services to recognise that people who have grown up in care cannot be expected to fend for themselves at 18: the local authority is legally obliged to continue to provide help to a young person in this situation, in the words of the statute, 'to the extent that his welfare requires it'.[4]

When I first came across that phrase, 'to the extent that his welfare requires it',[5] I felt strangely moved, and I still feel that every time I read it. I think it's because the formality of the language masks the profound compassion and understanding in those words; the appreciation that young people will need more or less support on their journey to adulthood based on who they are as individuals and what experiences they've had, and that it is the responsibility of the state to provide this support. Not according to the council's convenience or budget, but according to the needs of that young person, to the extent that their welfare requires it — in theory at least. But that kind of sensitivity and nuance can get lost in the way our society and its institutions relate to adulthood. It certainly did for Boru.

For as inadequate as the age-based definition of adulthood may seem, this is the one that determines a young person's path through most mental health services in England: the majority of patients being treated by Child and Adolescent Mental Health Services will have to transition, when they turn 18, to Adult Mental Health Services. While there are some services that treat young people up to the age of 25, this is not the norm, and was not the case for Boru. As he approached his 18th birthday, he was told he could not continue to see the same therapists he had come to know and trust, could not return to the same hospital he had begun to feel safe in. He had to start again; to wait four months for a first meeting with a new adult psychotherapist, which was postponed, then postponed again. He recalls, 'I was being told, "You are an adult now, and we're going to treat you as such." That was scary. I didn't enjoy that.' It doesn't make any sense, he says: 'At 18, at 19, at 20, yes, I am more mature and grown-up than at 17, but if you look at how long my life expectancy will be, I'm less than one third in. I'm not an adult — or I am, but I'm not at the same time. I'm in the middle ground.' Any hope of finding understanding for this was crushed by the services which were supposed to be helping him. As his friends were getting their offers for university, Boru, having missed his A levels, was beginning to understand that his life was going to look very different from theirs. He got lost in the gap between child and adult, dropped in the 'middle ground' as his drug use intensified and his mind fragmented into more and more pieces of paper. At 18 he was diagnosed with drug-induced psychosis and admitted again to a psychiatric hospital — this time in the adult department. He was more ill than ever before, and it was terrifying. He says, 'I was shitting myself. Everyone's older than you, and you're the little kid.'

I find this painful to listen to — and I don't think it's just because I care for Boru and I don't want him to have had to have such distressing, disturbing experiences. I think it is also because of this feeling he conveys of being treated like an adult when he so clearly wasn't one

— when he felt more like the 'little kid'. I have never gone through anything like what Boru describes, but that feeling of finding yourself in the adult department before you're ready is something I can relate to. I think many of us can relate to it. From my early childhood, my father had some serious health problems, and I worried a lot about him. It is only since being in psychoanalysis that I have started to see just how heavy that worry was to carry, and how I twisted myself into all sorts of shapes to try and cope with it. I think I came to believe — unconsciously — that it was my job to worry about him, rather than his job as my parent to worry about me; I promoted myself to the adult department, to the role of parent, when I was still a child. Looking back now, I can understand why it might have felt safer for me to pretend to myself that I was the parent — to pretend to myself that I was in control of a situation that felt so overwhelming and scary because I was so helpless, when my father, who was supposed to be in control, was instead lying in a hospital, also helpless. I wonder how that might have got in the way of my growing up. And I wonder how things might have been for Boru if, instead of being treated like an adult, he had been treated like the young person in distress he was.

Boru spent a total of two weeks on that adult ward before being discharged with no therapy, despite asking for it. He has not returned to a psychiatric hospital since — he believes his then girlfriend and job were a big part of his recovery. As a result of these experiences, if he ever feels his mental health deteriorating again, he tells me he won't seek help from professionals. He sounds traumatised not just by what happened inside his mind, but by the failures of the services that were supposed to take care of him. If he feels his legs buckling again, he says, 'I think I'd just face it alone.' I wince when I hear this. The way personal experience and psychological insight is wrung out of our institutions has had a devastating impact on Boru — and he is not the only one. There have, tragically, been cases of suicide by young people around the transition from Child and Adolescent Mental Health Services.[6] The psychological boundaries of adulthood are soft and fudgy, but when they are enacted by our institutions and our society, they are painfully sharp. I don't yet know when we grow up, but surely it is better not to know than to reach for the easy answer of 18.

I ask Boru when he thinks he will be an adult. 'I couldn't put a time on it. You said yourself you sometimes don't feel like an adult at all. It might not happen, and I'll feel like I do right now, for ever. I think just having the term grown-up is separating things that don't need to be separated; everyone is at their own stage, everyone's doing different things. Someone might feel it — someone else might not,' he replies. His old job as a cycling instructor reinforced this view of things, as he worked with children of four who seem so advanced for their age — like the little boy who approached him and showed him how he had also painted his nails, and they chatted together. 'The gap between us was made smaller. It wasn't like he was younger or I was older, we were just people, just humans. I guess that sounds very idealistic, but it's true.'

It does sound idealistic, and it is — but you could argue that Boru's approach has more of a scientific basis than the idea that we all become adults at age 18. When I speak to Sarah-Jayne Blakemore, Professor of Psychology and Cognitive Neuroscience at the University of Cambridge and author of *Inventing Ourselves: The Secret Life of the Teenage Brain*,[7] I presume she will be able to provide a clear demarcation of adult and non-adult, at least when it comes to the brain. But no: 'We know quite a lot about brain development, but we neuroscientists wouldn't recognise an adult brain if we saw one. We don't really know what one looks like,' she tells me. I had been comfortably imagining that she could see and know when adulthood begins with her scanner — but the disconcerting truth is that, in neuroscience too, things are less separate.

Blakemore and I talk on the phone, and I immediately feel in the safe hands of a world expert; she is articulate and clear, communicating complex ideas in a way that I — no neuroscientist — can understand (at least, after I've read through the transcript a few times). She speaks in a voice that conveys confidence, an unapologetic awareness of what she knows and cannot know, and an enlivening fascination for her subject. I ask her if she has grown up, and her answer shows how personal development mirrors brain development — or is it vice versa? She replies: 'Hmm ... We are constantly evolving and learning and adapting and changing, and that doesn't ever stop. This is true from what we know about the brain — the brain is constantly changing, it's plastic throughout life and there's no age limit to learning. But I also feel this in my own life; that you don't just reach a steady state at some age in your late teens or 20s. You're constantly emerging and discovering new things about yourself.' I wonder, given her adventures and explorations of the adolescent brain, how she would define an adult, but she has no clear answer for me: 'It sounds simple, but that's actually such a complex question.' We might want to look in the brain to find these answers, but to be an adult isn't just about the state of our brain, she says; it's about our progress through life and our different experiences. 'They are all embedded in your brain, your brain processes them — but that is a very different thing from when your brain becomes mature.'

So when does the brain becomes mature? Thanks to the work of Blakemore and others, we now know that much of what she was taught about this at university in the 1990s was wrong. Back then, the textbooks said that most brain development occurs in the first few years of life, and that it stops in mid- to late-childhood — there was no field called adolescent brain development, and when she first submitted grant applications to explore this area, they were rejected. Reviewers told her, 'If you want to study how the brain develops, why would you study adolescence? You need to study children or babies.' A lot has changed in the last two decades: 'Now, my goodness — no one would argue that.' It's not that early development is not important, but that which follows had been grossly underestimated. This is now a lively, thriving, critical area of research, with scientists worldwide following Blakemore in dedicating their careers to furthering our understanding of the teenage brain.

One factor that changed everything was the development of magnetic resonance imaging, MRI, which shows what is happening inside real, living, growing brains. This kind of brain scanning meant neuroscientists like Blakemore could track changes in the structure of the brain and how it functions throughout the whole lifespan. What she and colleagues found is that the brain — especially the cortex, the surface layers — does not stop developing in childhood — far from it. Not the prefrontal cortex, the area right at the front of the brain, which is bigger in humans than almost any other animal and plays a key role in tasks from decision-making to planning, understanding other people, self-awareness, and risk-taking. Not the temporal cortex, involved in language, memory, and social understanding. Nor the parietal cortex, the locus for planning movements and spatial navigation. All of these regions, which together process the tasks and characteristics that make up who we are, can still be developing through to the late 20s. That is long past 18, and this should seriously challenge our assumptions about adulthood and when it begins.

When we talk about a brain growing up, we are talking about the developments taking place in the white matter and grey matter — terms which describe how the different brain cells and fibres look on an MRI scan. Grey matter includes brain cells — neurons — and the spaces that connect them, known as synapses, as well as blood vessels, while white matter is made up of long fibres called axons which transmit electrical signals between these neurons, and which are covered in a fatty substance called myelin, which appears white on the scan.

As we grow up into adults, grey matter volume decreases. The brain of a one-year-old child is estimated to contain around double the synapses of the brain of an adult, due to a process known as 'synaptic pruning', in which synapses that are used and useful are kept and strengthened, and those that are not used are eliminated. Blakemore compares this to pruning a rose bush; we prune the weaker branches so the remaining ones can grow stronger. This process of pruning continues throughout adolescence, only levelling off somewhere in the mid- to late-20s, perhaps even into the 30s. White matter, in contrast, increases in volume as we grow up — this continues throughout childhood, adolescence, the 20s, and even into the 30s and possibly 40s. This is associated with the speeding up of signal transmission, meaning your brain becomes faster at processing information, and continues to develop throughout these decades.

In fact, Blakemore tells me, my question of when the brain becomes adult 'doesn't make any sense from a neuroscience perspective'. To start, 'The idea that the brain suddenly becomes mature isn't true.' The brain is not a uniform piece of tissue, but made up of lots of different regions that are all developing at different rates. Even if your visual cortex, an area at the back of the brain that processes vision, matures at 14, your prefrontal cortex, right at the front, which processes decision-making among other things, might continue developing for one or two decades after that. Added to that, your visual cortex might develop at 14, mine at 15, and Blakemore's prefrontal cortex might develop five years earlier than both of ours: 'There are huge individual differences.' And, significantly, throughout life, every time you have a new experience — every time you see a new face or do something for the first time — your brain develops, a phenomenon known as 'neuroplasticity'. 'Neuroplasticity is a baseline state in your brain at all ages. There is no age limit to plasticity.' I have a feeling that everything she says about the development of our brains might also be true about our own development to and through adulthood.

So when do we grow up? My conversation with Blakemore reminds me that as a journalist, I am used to asking an expert for any answers I can't find on the internet. Perhaps that is part of why I chose that career — so that I could either know the answers, or ask other people who know the answers to tell me them. It is so much harder to accept that the right answer might not exist, and that maturing involves accepting that state of uncertainty and not knowing. This is something that, I think, Boru has already accepted; perhaps in some respects that makes him more grown up than me. I have felt this capacity in me growing, though, throughout my training to become a psychotherapist. For the psychoanalyst Wilfred Bion, the responsibility of the therapist is not to turn away from uncertainty, not to blot it out with answers, but to attempt to tolerate it, to stay with it, to work in the state of mind the poet Keats called 'negative capability':[8] 'being in uncertainties, Mysteries, doubts, without any irritable reaching after fact and reason'.[9] This is a psychological discipline that I am still working on. So although I feel even less clear about the answer to the question of when we grow up than before I spoke to Blakemore, I can also see this is a strange kind of progress, as coming to know something about growing up must first involve unknowing some of the false certainties we relied upon before. Like the neuroscientists who rejected Blakemore's grant applications and told her to study infancy instead, we also have to unlearn some of the things we thought we knew, before we can begin to understand what adulthood really involves. I have always thought that adults knew things, but I am feeling more and more that growing up, for me at least, is about accepting just how much I cannot know.

One thing we can say for sure is that contrary to what Google tells us, to what the law tells us, to what NHS mental health services tell us, and to what many of us grow up expecting, you aren't crowned an adult on your 18th birthday. In fact, according to the child and adolescent psychotherapist Ariel Nathanson, the social landmark of turning 18 'has nothing whatsoever to do with the development of adulthood. It is an arbitrary decision'. For him, 'The adult grows over time, over the duration of a lifespan, depending on states of mind.' It is a process, and that's important — a process with plenty of opportunity for things to go awry. That's where Nathanson comes in. I ask if he has grown up, and he gives a throaty chuckle: 'I'm a part-time adult, which I think is the most I can expect.'

We are in his consulting room at the Portman Clinic, and he sits loosely in his chair, laid-back but scrupulous in his explanations, his voice a languid, low-pitched thrum. I am in the seat usually occupied by his young patients, many of whom struggle with criminality, violence, addiction. For Nathanson, the late teens and early 20s are more usefully defined as late adolescence than adulthood — from the Latin *adolescere*, meaning 'to grow up'. This life stage is characterised by exactly the 'middle ground' feeling Boru describes, of being both adult and not, of being in between, and it is made up of particular grow-ups unique to these years: finishing school or college, separating from parents or guardians and siblings, entering bars and clubs for the first time (legally). These grow-ups mark both an ending and a beginning: an ending to secondary education and the structure it provided, and the beginning of a new kind of freedom, or, at least, a promise of freedom; a promise which may be broken or fulfilled by training or undergraduate study, by employment or the struggle to find it, by staying home or leaving home.

To understand this transitional life stage and the process that governs it, we have to go back its roots, to the transfer to secondary school, says Nathanson: 'The minute a kid takes their first steps in senior school, they see all these other big characters moping about, and suddenly they have a very concrete idea that childhood is not going to last forever, that this body will change.' This is 'an onslaught of changes and difficulties and bigness' — changes a child understands somehow as already unfolding within them, knowing that their bodies and minds will be transformed, in time. This knowledge can provoke a feeling of dangerous acceleration in young people; they can feel like they are strapped into the passenger seat of a driverless car, hurtling over the edge of a cliff, towards a place where stability will no longer exist and a time when 'Mum and Dad are not going to be there any more, and you need to make your own way. It's very frightening.' This is why people in their late teens can oscillate between feeling independent and capable and like they don't need their parents at all, to being absolutely desperate for their help and comfort, feeling like a small child. And that is totally normal. It is anxiety-provoking, bewildering, and distressing — and totally normal.

On hearing this, I am troubled by how much I can relate to this sense of oscillation between adult and child, given how long it's been since I was at secondary school. But then I think about my experiences of training to become a psychotherapist; how I was thrust into this new arena, full of fellow students, teachers, homework, new ideas to learn. How my relationships with my supervisors, while in many ways very different from the ones I had with my schoolteachers, do share some characteristics — how I have felt at times so desperate for my supervisor's help, and at others like I just want to find my own way. How I have been feeling this sense of changes unfolding within me that are beyond my control, and how unsettling and discombobulating that has been. And still is.

As a teacher at a London state secondary school, Rebecca, 26, is very much at ease with this oscillation — she sees it in her classroom every day. In my favourite coffee shop near my flat, over a plate of moist lemon drizzle cake, she tells me how she has watched hundreds and hundreds of young people grow up into almost adults, and how her students, aged 11 to 18, can be both grown up and childlike from one moment to the next. She has a kind and open face, and when she speaks about her students and her job, the tone of her voice changes, growing deeper with pride and passion.

I am intrigued to know what it was like for Rebecca starting out, when she would have been barely older than those she was teaching — how did the divide between children and adult play out then? At age 22 on her first day in her first job after qualifying, she walked into a classroom of students who were resitting their GCSEs after failing the first time around. Some of them were just two years younger than she was. She remembers, 'That was really strange. I was teaching people older than my cousins, the same age as my brother, and I didn't really feel old enough.' But it was only when she focussed on the age gap that these doubts crept in, as she was always aware that she was, and that she felt, more adult than the pupils she was teaching. She had done her A levels; gone to university and qualified as a teacher; moved away from home; lived abroad; paid taxes: 'I was really confident in what I was teaching and that I knew how to teach them — and I knew that they had no idea how young and inexperienced I was, which really helped.' One even guessed her age as 42. She knew that she had the capability to help them pass their exams, and she did. 'It was a really wonderful feeling,' she says, and when she talks about helping her students to succeed, her eyes shine and the gap between teacher and student, between adult and adolescent, seems to shrink again: 'I feel like a child when I'm waiting for the results; I feel like they're my own.' She taught someone recently who lacked self-confidence and didn't believe they could do well, but after working closely with Rebecca, they got the top grade. 'I cried when I saw their result, then I watched them cry when they saw it. When children who've had a really tough year, or who have doubted themselves, work hard for something and then do better than they thought they would ... It's the best feeling in the world.'

There are some experiences built into the UK education system which trigger a growing up process of sorts, she explains. Pupils have had to take some big decisions by the time they turn 18, which include picking vocational qualifications or GCSEs at 13 and A Levels at 16, choosing whether or not to do an apprenticeship or go to university, which one and what to study. These choices require that young people think about what they want from the rest of their life, and 'those are really big asks', says Rebecca. As they climb up through the school years, she treats them in more adult ways, both to meet their developing adult selves and to stimulate that development, putting more onus on them. She gives them tasks that take longer and are more difficult and require more self-direction, that she wants them to think about and struggle with, 'because that's when we learn and when we grow'. This is how she prepares them to go out into the adult world, whether that's the world of work as it was for Boru, or to university, as it was for Victoria.

'Are you an adult?' I ask Victoria. It is a question that she has been asking herself more and more over the last year and a bit, since she turned 18. She sits straight-backed on my sofa, taking up no more space than necessary, her dark hair tied back with two strands framing her face, and I am struck by how self-contained she seems. The vegan brownie I bought her sits on a plate on her knees and slowly, precisely, she lifts another forkful to her mouth. In a voice that is soft and reflective but with an edge of vibrant intelligence, she talks me through what this question means to her, and why she feels she cannot settle on an answer — how she both is and is not grown up at the same time; 'I'm in a weird situation where you're expected to be quite grown-up, but you're not quite grown-up. I still feel immature in a lot of ways, but in some ways I do feel mature. It's a weird limbo.' Or, as Britney Spears sang in 1991, when she was the age Victoria is now: 'I'm not a girl, not yet a woman'. As a child, Victoria didn't think she would, at this age, still be wrestling with these questions. 'I thought, oh, at 18, I'm going to be so grown-up. And then I got to 18, and I was just the same. Now I'm 19, and 21 is coming up, and I'm thinking, will I be an adult then?' It is unsettling to hear her say this, to describe so exactly my own experience of waiting for adulthood to come, at 14 years younger than me. Victoria is one of the first people I am interviewing for this book; the deadline for my first draft falls in the month that she turns 21 and I turn 35, ages that feel like significant markers in the journey to and through adulthood. I wonder if we will both have grown up by then — or if we will both still be waiting, stuck in this weird limbo.

Victoria grew up in East Sussex with her two younger siblings and parents who divorced amicably when she was eight, and she describes a happy, stable childhood with family she knew would take care of her, and who still do. What I find fascinating (and relatable) is how, even with a supportive family and a privileged upbringing, the most basic steps in the transition to adult life are nevertheless fraught with struggles and difficulties. She says, 'Moving out was really hard, because I was so homesick. I was suddenly in this place where I didn't know anyone, where you're expected to do all these things for yourself that you've never done before.' She describes feeling overwhelmed by the practical grow-ups that come with building an independent life at university in London, from paying household bills to organising how she spends her time; she is not complaining about this, it seems to me, but still reeling from the change. The move from school to university is going well for Victoria, with no major crises or disasters — we meet many months before the pandemic throws the lives of students into even more chaos — but speaking to her, it really hits me just how extraordinarily profound this shift can be. When Victoria lived at home, she would return from school to a warm, busy kitchen and dinner made by her mother for her whole family; in her first year at university, she says quietly, 'I'd go into the kitchen and there'd be no one there. I'd sit and eat on my own. It was a weird feeling.' There is a moment of silence, and I am reflecting on how there is a lot of meaning in that word, 'weird', which comes up again and again. It seems to carry a sense of loneliness and sad resignation. I look at her and feel a stab of realisation that every grow-up is an achievement, but it is also, necessarily, a loss.

Then suddenly her tone changes, her voice lifting, and we are into the next phase of the oscillation: 'Then I got used to it, and I started to actually enjoy it. It was quite nice being able to cook what I wanted for myself. I made changes, I went vegan.' The sense of loss sits alongside the chance to discover the adult she is becoming, and the two experiences can overlap in ambiguous ways. That's what she discovered when the summer break came around, and it was time for her to move back to the family home. She was so looking forward to it, but 'I found that I had grown up a bit during that year and changed, and then when I moved home it was quite infantilising.' She couldn't fit herself straight back into the space she'd left, like an immutable piece in the jigsaw puzzle of family life, because the time away had changed her shape, redrawn her edges. Andrew Fuligni, Professor at the UCLA Semel Institute for Neuroscience and Human Behavior, studies the adolescent years and the transition to adulthood. He says part of what makes things complicated for families when a child moves back home after living away is that 'the parents still see the child as they were before they left; but when they come back, they're a very different person. Just two months of living away from one's family can be transformative — a person can grow up a lot in that time.' There are well-established patterns of interaction, and when the child returns, the parents want to continue engaging in those interactions as they always have done. When he says, 'You have to learn a different way of interacting with the child, and I think that's very challenging,' it reminds me of Victoria's words: 'It's hard going back to how it used to be, because I've changed. And it's quite a big change.'

To understand the significance of this grow-up and the dramatic change that leaving home can catalyse, I think we have to go back. Back to before university, to before secondary school and primary school, to a much earlier kind of leaving home. The first one.

'The first thing that happens, at birth, is the baby becomes separate. And that's terrible! That's a very anxiety-provoking, extreme state,' says Nathanson. When I give myself over to his words, when I roll the idea around in my mind and examine it from all angles, I realise it is just the most extraordinary thing. The baby has never had the experience of being a physically separate individual, until that moment when one becomes two. What Victoria is living through now — this renegotiation of borders and boundaries, of sameness and separateness, which characterises adolescent experience — is an echo of what goes on in the first seconds and months of life. In infancy as in adolescence, the process of growing up is one of separation. It may sound bizarre to you to compare the experiences of post-pubescent not-quite-adults to those of a tiny newborn; it never would have occurred to me before I began training as a psychodynamic psychotherapist. But the more I've read about it during my training, the more I have come to understand how these first experiences of separation in the early days, weeks, and months of life function like a stone plopping in the pond of our minds, creating ripples for all the decades to come. Whatever life stage we find ourselves in, our feelings and anxieties will be linked in our unconscious with our earliest experiences. No matter how many years have passed, any major separation can act like a powerful magnet whose attracting force reaches deep into our minds to traces of memories we don't even know we've forgotten. This pull draws out our earliest patterns of response, so we experience reverberations of our birth, infancy, and childhood through this feeling of separation and separateness again and again throughout our lives. We feel it at times of movement, of bereavement, of heartbreak and other forms of leaving and loss — and we feel it in those moments of isolation, when we walk into a cold, empty kitchen and feel so far from home.

After birth, the moment of physical separation comes with the cutting of the cord, but the experience of psychological separateness is more ambiguous. The disentangling of the mother's mind from the baby's and of the baby's mind from the mother's is gradual, incomplete, and painful. Psychoanalysts have disagreed bitterly over when and how it happens, and I, along with every therapist in training, am in a process of trying to make some sense of these differing ideas and find my own way through.

Some compelling images and theories around this phase of life come from the psychoanalyst Donald W. Winnicott, a paediatrician and psychiatrist who worked for four decades in Paddington Green Hospital in a deprived area of London. He was among the very first cohorts of trainee psychoanalysts, qualifying in 1934, and was the first man to qualify as a child analyst. He went on to record 50 radio programmes about motherhood for BBC radio over 20 years from 1943, and through these popular broadcasts, he brought the ideas of psychoanalysis from the lecture theatre and the consulting room into people's homes, giving listeners a new way into thinking about their minds.

Winnicott's writings[10] vividly portray the minds of baby and mother as existing in what the psychoanalyst Ogden called a state of 'invisible oneness'.[11] In the womb and in the first months of life, there is no clear dividing line between them; as the baby's body has been growing inside the mother's body, nurtured by her physically, the baby's mind has been growing inside the mother's mind, nurtured by her psychologically. Over the course of early infancy, the baby will begin to shift, Winnicott wrote, 'from a state of being merged with the mother to a state of being in relation to the mother as something outside and separate'. This can only happen in what he called a 'good enough' situation, where an infant can trust that their mother can care for them. This is one way of thinking about the story that unfolds infant observations. This is why it is such a precious privilege for me to observe an infant as part of my training for an hour every week, to witness the incredibly normal and yet completely miraculous happening as, moment by moment and month by month, a baby begins to work out where they end and where their parents begin.

We have all seen how in the beginning, when a new baby cries for milk, in a healthy family situation their parents rush to feed them, understanding intuitively that a screaming baby is desperate to be fed immediately, and cannot bear to wait even 10 minutes. There is a conscious need in most parents to minimise the pain of hunger the baby is feeling for the first time, and Winnicott theorised there may also be another need, perhaps less conscious, to minimise the pain of difference and distance between mother and baby, as if to perpetuate the illusion that, as in the womb, there is still no separateness and no separation. But this is not a totally merged state, because Winnicott believed it was at the same time — and here's the paradox — absolutely crucial for parents to hold in mind the space for their baby's 'potential individuality' (as Ogden described it). Because as time pushes forward, as babies grow and get stronger, developing physically and psychologically, they are able to manage a bit more of a gap — a gap between wanting a feed and getting one, a gap between themselves and others. And these gaps are critical for development: they enable the infant to learn, gradually, to tolerate frustration and to bear hunger, to develop the capacity to think and to trust that food will come. As this gap grows between parent and baby, a space opens up which allows the infant to develop a personality of their own, to become an individual, to differentiate and separate, to play and begin to engage with the world. This is what Winnicott called the 'potential space', a paradoxical and intermediate area of experience between subject and object, a space in which imagination and play can flourish. This is one story of how a baby begins, gradually, to grow up into themselves.

It is also the story of how adolescents begin, gradually, to grow up into adults, as a more mature iteration of this physical and psychological gap opens up between themselves and their families and they begin to lead more separate lives. This is the gap in which Victoria has found a new capacity to explore, to experiment creatively with different recipes for self-expression, and to feed herself, in more than one way. Her reasons for turning vegan, she explains, are a mixture of environmental and ethical, but the timing — in her first year living away from home — is all about having the freedom and space to think for herself and make her own choices. When she speaks of the hours she spends at the stove, trying out different recipes and inventing her own, it sounds to me like she has transformed that empty, lonely kitchen into an adolescent version of the 'potential space', where she can find opportunities for adventure and discovery. A place warmed with the love and spirit of her mother, where the comforting smells of the home she grew up in intermingle with the exciting smells of the home she is creating for herself. She has found a new, grown-up way to play.

I was absolutely delighted when I first learnt during my training that, for psychoanalysts, playing is an extremely serious business. It was so unexpected, but it does make sense now I think about it — play involves developing the capacity to let the mind wonder and wander, to think, discover and create and grow. Sustaining this capacity during childhood, but also into adolescence and throughout adulthood, is understood by psychoanalysts as a vital psychological achievement, as nothing less than what enables a person to live a satisfying, fulfilling, healthy life. Without playing, we may get older, but we cannot grow up in any meaningful way. As Winnicott wrote, 'It is good to remember always that playing is itself a therapy.'[12]

At some moments in our lives, playing may feel like the most natural and easy thing in the world — I guess that's what we mean by child's play. As for Victoria and her cooking at 19, so too for Boru and his Sunday bike rides at 17. Back then, he felt that there was nothing better than 'just going out on your bike into the country lanes, getting the miles into your legs, looking at the fields, the pheasants and cows, just letting your mind wander to the road surface, the hedgerows or the potholes and gutter on the side of the road'. But it can also be more complex, as play and the growing up process can be interrupted, distorted. We will all find ourselves more or less able to play at different times in our lives. At periods of great anxiety, the instinct to enliven our minds with playful creativity and new experiences meets within us another urge: the drive to kill off the curious, thinking, and feeling parts of our minds, to kill off time — to kill off growth.

Boru knows something about this. 'The first time I took coke is a massive, significant point in my life,' he tells me, his voice animated. 'It was when I was 16 or 17. It's fucking ridiculous — it was at lunch, in school. My mate had some, and I was like, yeah, one time won't hurt!' His voice and eyes drop: 'But it really did. It really did.' At the time, drugs served a purpose: 'I'd be in sixth form taking ket in the school toilets, because I was like, fuck this and fuck that, and I was really angry.' Drugs gave him a way out of the anger of fuck this and fuck that, back to a time before the table of his mind grew so overloaded and there weren't any pieces of paper weighing him down, to a younger version of himself when his legs were stronger. At least, that's what he used to tell himself. 'And now, I just don't know if that idyllic time ever really existed. I don't know if this Happy-Go-Boru was ever, like, a thing. It feels like so long ago, I can't even recognise that feeling.' He has given up cycling, he says, no longer finding pleasure in those country lanes. I feel a deep sadness when I hear this; it feels like in giving up cycling, he has given up playing, and given up on himself.

He feels his drug use is intimately bound up with the least adult, least mature part of himself. Starting work straight after school made him feel hyper-mature, unlike his friends at university who he'd see on social media, doing what freshers do — what he thought of as 'childish stuff'. He'd see that and think, 'I'm grown up now.' But then he'd take cocaine. 'And it made me feel childish — like that was the one thing I have not got sorted. I said earlier that being an adult is having your shit sorted — and I did not and do not have that shit sorted.' He feels cocaine has limited his choices, gobbling up the money he worked hard to earn, that he could have saved for travelling. Unable to work through this grow-up, he feels stuck, powerless to move forward in his life, his development stunted. I can hear the regret and frustration in his voice when he says, 'It's just had such a grip on my life.'

Nathanson has treated young people with a range of different addictions, from drugs to pornography to video games. For him, many addictions in adolescence can be understood as a symptom of the breakdown of the ongoing process of maturation and separation that is growing up — that process he described so vividly as a driverless car accelerating towards the cliff edge. 'Adolescents can take refuge in these experiences that seem to stop time. And in doing that, they are all of a sudden in control of what is happening to them. Nobody is pushing them out; they are the boss,' he says. It is a solution, in the moment, for managing the anxiety of sitting in the passenger seat of that speeding driverless car. Or rather, it is a solution for *not* managing the anxiety, in the sense of simply turning it off, rather than growing the capacity to survive the feeling, to think what it might be about, and to feel able to contain it. It seems to me that if growing up means enduring the pain of separation and separateness, addictions provide an escape route from all of that — an escape route that becomes a trap.

The latest scientific research into addiction helps to show just how powerful that experience of escaping the passing of time can be, through the concept of immersion. Immersion is characterised by the absorbing experience of entering 'the zone', where time does not pass and troubling thoughts are kept at bay, through a kind of hyper-focus which does not — which cannot — waver. In my research I read about one gambler who was so immersed in her slot machine, she failed to notice the player nearby was having a heart attack.[13] Luke Clark, director of the University of British Columbia's Centre for Gambling Research, investigated the relationship between addiction and immersion in a recent study using his casino laboratory — complete with dim lighting, casino-style carpeting, and comfortable stools.[14] He had gamblers use specially adapted slot machines, with panels of flashing coloured lights attached to the sides, to measure their awareness of their immediate environment. What this research found was that problem gamblers are far more likely than casual gamblers to describe being 'in a trance' while playing, and they are measurably less aware of their surroundings and of time passing.[15] The image of the addict's world shrinking is not just a metaphor; their field of vision literally narrows, as external concerns are edged out of their awareness, until the focus of their addiction is all that can be seen. They are so immersed in the game it becomes a part of themselves, or they become a part of it. It is a very effective way of blocking out the anxiety of being separate. It can ruin your life, but it is effective.

Something like 0.7 per cent of people who gamble will develop something close to an addiction,[16] but I wonder if many more of us develop problematic habits while trying to manage — or rather, trying to avoid — the anxiety and pain of separation, change, growth. I have never used a slot machine, but I do recognise that feeling of being so absorbed that I cannot look away; of staring so intently at the screen in front of me that I block out everything else.

If you are currently in this 'weird limbo' life stage, you will not remember a time before mobile phones, the internet, and social media. It gives me a sense of vertigo to acknowledge that I do remember this. Victoria was born in the year 2000 and is part of what the generations researcher Jean Twenge has termed iGen, the first cohort to grow up with smartphones. Twenge reports that 2012 — the year Victoria joined Instagram, aged 12 — was also the year in which smartphones hit critical mass in the US, with more than half of America owning at least one.[17] Victoria doesn't talk about her phone and social media as something separate from herself. 'I feel like part of me, my identity, has been made through social media — which sounds like a really tragic thing to say,' she says, laughing — but she seems serious. 'I don't think that I would be who I am without it.' She has an ambivalent relationship with it: 'In some ways I like social media because I've learnt a lot about the environment, but then I'll be checking my phone and suddenly realise, "Oh my God, why am I spending so much time on this?" — and I don't really like it much.' At these times, it feels like an addiction.

This is certainly an experience I recognise — no matter how much I try to stop using my phone as an escape, the temptation is always there. In a recent study by Kings College London, researchers looked at 41 studies involving 41,871 young people across Europe, Asia, and America, and found that almost a quarter used their smartphone in ways 'consistent with behavioural addiction'.[18] Young women of Victoria's age were at highest risk of showing addicted patterns of behaviour and emotion, which the researchers have given the anodyne name of 'problematic smartphone use'. It is strange to think about what this phrase 'problematic smartphone use' might mean, given how normal it has become; the extent to which so many of us — of all ages and stages of adulthood — have become so viscerally attached to our devices both psychologically and physically. We are, all of us, 'psychologically cyborgs'[19] now, according to Richard Graham, a child and adolescent psychiatrist who ran the Tech Addiction Service at London's private Nightingale Hospital. 'In what feels like a very short amount of time in terms of human history, the smartphone and being connected to the internet in different forms has become something we expect, as much as we expect to breathe oxygen and drink water, almost on the level of a natural phenomenon,' he says. He recalls the words of Chief Justice Roberts of the US Supreme Court who, in a ruling protecting the privacy of smartphones, wrote that these devices have become 'such a pervasive and insistent part of daily life that the proverbial visitor from Mars might conclude they were an important feature of human anatomy'.[20] Graham agrees: 'We have incorporated these devices into our being.' We have outsourced our memory to reminder apps; we look down as the transport app updates instead of up to see if a bus is coming down the street; we follow the blue dot as we make our way along Google Maps instead of taking in the world around us. Once I even checked a weather app to see if I needed to take an umbrella to the shops, only to then look out the window and see the rain falling.

I am curious about this relentless, continuous, insidious relationship we have with the internet, and how it shapes us as adolescents and adults, how it might get in the way of growing up. Graham tells me about one young person he came across who uses Yubo — a social media app used mostly by teenagers to livestream with friends. She was connected for more than 200 hours in a 20-day period, leaving it turned on almost like a baby monitor. I make this comparison not with judgement or condescension, but with a compassion for what I understand as this young woman's powerful need to feel technologically connected to her friends in their physical absence, in order to feel safe and secure. I do not know what was going on for her, but I wonder if her experience might teach us something about the temptation to use the internet in this way, because at times we simply cannot bear to sit and be on our own.

Graham says, 'These devices make it more challenging to be separate; this ordinary need in development to become independent is challenged by the possibility of never needing to be alone.' We don't know if this young woman is being helped by Yubo, or if it is a maladaptive coping strategy that is holding back her progression; if, as Graham puts it, 'she's tied to the device in a way that is a necessity, rather than a tool to be used as and when'.

Necessity or tool. This is the question that haunts so many of us in our relationship with technology, regardless of our life stage. I try hard not to look at my phone too much, but still I would not like to count up the number of hours I have wasted, staring emptily at news headlines on Twitter, scrolling, vacant-eyed, before stumbling off to bed, wondering where the time has gone and why I was so unable to look away. Wondering why it felt so *necessary*, why I seemed to have no other option. At those moments it feels like I've lost myself. Perhaps, as Nathanson described, I am killing off my anxiety rather than thinking about where it comes from.

Victoria uses social media in many ways that enhance her life, but she also speaks of a similar experience of losing track of time and of herself, scrolling through other peoples' lives and lies on Instagram, liking their pictures, 'being like, wow, they've gone to uni, they're doing all these things, that's amazing'. This kind of socially acceptable voyeurism does strange things to our minds, and many of us will recognise the disconcerting experience Victoria describes, of knowingly buying into someone else's perfected portrayal of life online, even as you suspect it must be a fiction: 'You look at someone's life and you think that they have it together, you think, oh wow, that's really good. And you know that they're probably a mess, they're probably just the same as everyone else, but you still think, oh, maybe I should try and be a bit more like that,' she says. Clinical psychologist Rachel Andrew has found this dissonance among many patients, younger as well as older; when I was researching an article about envy[21] she told me she has noticed that most of us intellectually understand that the images and narratives we see on social media platforms aren't real, we can talk about that and rationalise it — 'but on an emotional level, it's still pushing buttons. If those images or narratives tap into what we aspire to, but what we don't have, then it becomes very powerful'. We lose our capacity to feel the difference between something real and something false.

But it is not just our sense of others that is skewed and twisted by social media. 'We have something even more pernicious, I think,' the renowned social psychologist Sherry Turkle told me over email, as I researched that envy article. 'We look at the lives we have constructed online in which we only show the best of ourselves, and we feel a fear of missing out in relation to our own lives. We don't measure up to the lives we tell others we are living, and we look at the self as though it were an other, and feel envious of it.' This provokes a strange, alienating split inside of ourselves, cleaving a difference and a distance between any true sense we have of ourselves and the fictional character we perform. This kind of 'self-envy' of the image we portray, she wrote, can leave us feeling 'inauthentic, curiously envious of our own avatars'. Nathanson tells me he has noticed that in contemporary society, people seem to talk about themselves as if they have a kind of internal marketing director, developing their personal brand, 'constantly marketing something, constantly selling something'. It is as if we have what he calls a 'bullshit artist' inside us, whispering in our own ear and tweeting, Snapchatting, and Instagramming in everyone else's, 'I can be whatever you want me to be.' It seems to me that being whatever someone else wants us to be is the exact opposite of growing up into our own adult selves.

I don't think this personal branding, bullshit artist, self-marketing phenomenon has been caused by the internet — I think it is far older than that. I think it is a psychological experience that most people of different generations will recognise to a greater or lesser degree, one that social media very effectively taps into. An important part of my analysis so far has been a process of coming to recognise that I thought I knew who I was, when actually, I don't. I have no idea. It is quite a terrifying thing to get to your early 30s and realise that you have absolutely no idea who you really are, of what is going on underneath. Instead, I think I became very good at guessing who other people want me to be — hard-working, doing what I'm told, a good person, a good wife, a good daughter, a good friend, all of that — and I became very comfortable trying, unconsciously, to be that person instead. It was comfortable, but it was dangerous — a different kind of escape route / trap. I used to have a strange and impressive party trick: I could fold myself into peculiar shapes because I was so flexible. I was told that I was in fact hyper-mobile, that my joints have an unusually large range of movement, which could sometimes result in back pain. I find this very meaningful — I wonder if it could be a bodily manifestation of a psychological state which was too flexible; I was not rooted in myself but in the impressions of others, and that left me untethered, so malleable I could fold myself into the shape that others wanted me to be. I may find this more comfortable than being true to myself (given I do not yet understand what that actually means) — but it also causes me pain. For me, psychoanalysis has been crucial in helping me to see that I was doing this, as I try to sit with not knowing who I am, rather than twisting myself in some hyper-mobile way into being somebody else.

It all makes me think of Winnicott's concept of the 'False Self'.[22] The first time I heard that phrase during my training, I remember feeling that here was an idea I had been looking for, waiting to discover — as if I knew what it meant before I read his paper. But when I did get around to reading it, I realised that Winnicott used this phrase in a different way from what I was expecting, to refer to something quite specific and a little counter-intuitive: he believed the origin of the most extreme version of a False Self was to be found in infancy (where else). A baby girl might be ravenous, cold, in pain, uncomfortable, enraged at being kept waiting — full of spontaneous bodily and psychological experiences which she needs her parents to understand and help with.

But if her parents are struggling and cannot manage the emotional force of such intense demands, Winnicott theorised, their baby might intuitively sense their desperation, and unconsciously override her spontaneous and true needs in order to comply with what she senses they can provide. This sets the False Self in motion: characterised by compliance, imitation, and acting, the False Self appears as the infant unconsciously tries to be the baby, then child, then adolescent, and then the adult, that she thinks is wanted, that she feels can be managed, rather than the one she truly, spontaneously is. In the most extreme cases, a False Self can take over, and leave a person without any True Self to speak of, and she could end up feeling that she does not really exist because nothing real has been allowed to grow. There are less extreme cases though, and Winnicott writes that we probably all experience a False Self to differing degrees; in a healthy situation, where parents can meet their child's demands in what he called a 'good enough' way, a False Self might take the shape of 'a healthy polite aspect of the self' which allows a person to function in society, rather than, say, demanding to be fed whenever she is hungry, before her colleagues queuing up in the work canteen.

Until I started my training, I always thought of pretending as being a very active, conscious choice. For example, sometimes I might knowingly decide to pretend to a friend that I don't mind meeting in their neighbourhood, because they have a child and I know it will be much easier for them, even though I might privately acknowledge to myself that I'd much rather meet in my neighbourhood, because I'm tired and don't want to get on the bus. Perhaps we could think of that as a 'healthy polite' kind of False Self, one that I'm aware of. But Winnicott's description of the more extreme version takes us towards an entirely different kind of pretending that we don't even know we're doing; an unconscious reshaping of our wants and needs that is totally dependent on the expectations or wishes of others, leaving a sense of emptiness where something real could be. This way of thinking about things — this interplay of something false emerging unconsciously to cover up something real — seems significant; useful for our questions about adulthood. For me, reaching for an awareness of the interplay of these forces, the false and the real, and coming to recognise the pressures that pull me and push me one way or the other, has been a crucial set of grow-ups. Before beginning my analysis, I had no idea there was anything false about me, not about my trying so hard to be good, nor about my often putting other peoples' needs before my own. I never really thought about it, because I assumed that this was just who I was — that I was 'caring', 'thoughtful'. It is only now that I am asking myself why I am like that — what all that might be covering up — that I am finally able to begin to interrogate the false and the real within myself. I'm not there yet, but my sense is that a meaningful kind of adulthood must involve reaching (or trying to reach) a balance between these two poles: not being so false that none of your needs or wants are met and nothing real can grow, and at the same time not being so real that your needs and wants overwhelm everything and everyone else. That is how a real and rooted kind of care and thoughtfulness can develop — but you can't get anywhere near there without working out where the true ends and the false begins.

Developing a sense of what is false and what is real within oneself, it seems, is fundamental to growing up — something to add to the definition we are building. Victoria described to me how she came to recognise something not quite real in her self-portrayal on social media — and how this helped her decide to step away from it. When she was younger, she would take a lot of time and care, thinking and planning exactly when and what to publish, to 'make sure I had a good post that looked cool, that I was doing something unique, and that I didn't post twice in one day'. She is aware that at times, she got caught up in the social media trap of what I call 'performative adulthood': she would post an Instagram story with pictures of the dinner she'd just cooked, and followers would comment, 'Wow, how do you do that?' She reflects with honesty, 'Obviously, like, that's me sort of showing off that I can do adult things.' But that is changing; 'I think a part of growing up is realising that things like that aren't so important. Now I just post random things on my accounts, because I try to take it way less seriously.' This year, she adds, 'I've realised that if I want to do things, I can't just sit scrolling through social media.' She tries to set limits using an app to restrict her use of Instagram, Snapchat, Twitter, and Facebook to a fixed amount of time each day. Sometimes, when she reaches the end of her half hour allotted for Instagram, she goes over it, because she has worked out how to unblock herself — but this is still a form of progress: 'Before, I didn't really think about it, I didn't care. But recently, I've really tried to control myself with social media. I think it's an important growing up step, to be able to limit yourself. You've got to, if you want to get things done.'

I feel like Victoria is way ahead of the game — 15 years ahead of me — because I have only just had this same realisation. When I am working on this book and I come across something difficult or painful and my mind wanders, I often find my fingers have taken me to Twitter before I've realised what I am typing. Suddenly 20 minutes have scrolled by and my mind is deadened and lazy. So I have downloaded an app ironically called SelfControl — a variation of the one Victoria uses — which blocks certain websites for a period of time. It is ironic because, of course, I am not using real self-control; I am giving all my self-control over to this app. Every time I find myself tripping over a tweet, following it to somewhere I really don't need to be, I try to wrench myself back, and turn on SelfControl for an hour or two. At these moments, it feels like the adult part of me is going down into that hole to get the less adult part of me out — with more or less success. Like Victoria, I also feel that getting a grip on my 'problematic' relationship with the internet is an important part of my growing up — and that I've got to do that if I want to get things done. I wonder if my only hope of finishing this book lies in my limited technical knowhow; unlike Victoria, I haven't worked out a way to unblock myself, and I hope I never do.

Speaking of unblocking ... I keep coming back to Boru's definition of adulthood as having your shit sorted. I think it might be more meaningful than he realised. Psychoanalysts are very interested in shit. Melanie Klein and her colleagues theorised that every bodily function has a psychological correlate — eating is paired unconsciously with the psychological act of taking something in; shitting with the psychological act of getting rid of something from one's mind — getting it out. This is how, as babies, we respond to feeling bad, we shit or we scream or we move our bodies to get rid of the bad thing. Even before we are born — when we are in the process of being born — doctors are constantly monitoring and on the lookout for meconium (*i.e.*, baby shit) during labour, because it means the baby is in distress and needs help, potentially an emergency C-section. From our earliest moments, there is this connection between feeling scared or in pain, and shitting. The hope is that as we grow up, as we develop a more mature means to digest our feelings, we are able to get our shit — and our emotions — sorted out inside us, rather than expelling it all immediately, either by taking our feelings out on someone else, or getting rid of our feelings by killing off our minds with coke or Instagram or Netflix. Developing this capacity is a critical part of the growing up process, I think, and it is something that many of us so-called adults need but do not have.

Sam tells me that as a child in Nigeria he was very involved in the church, and from the age of eight years old, everyone called him Pastor. I can see why. He has a way of speaking with energy and poetry which cuts right to the truth of how he feels about things. His braids are tied back in a short ponytail, a neat beard frames his face, and an open, confident smile seems to warm the atmosphere around him, drawing me in. He has a charisma about him that makes me think, this man is going to be somebody. I later imagine myself showing off to someone that when he was 19 years old, he once sat on my sofa and ate a chocolate cookie I gave him, before he was famous.

Sam does not like the thought of being an adult — although he sounds like one to me. He has lived independently since the age of 16, including living alone in the family home in Manchester while his father worked away wherever he could find it. 'I ran the house,' he tells me. He took a year out to work and pay the bills: 'I didn't have to pay them, but I made it mandatory because I'm my own individual. I don't want anyone else making decisions or helping with anything, because that stunts your growth.' Clearly, I think to myself, this is a man who has his shit together — an obvious grown-up — but Sam tells me he feels anything but. 'I guess technically I am an adult, but I don't feel like one. The whole idea of being an adult is just … it's frightening, it's foreign.' He laughs and says, 'I love cartoons too much to call myself an adult.' Being a grown-up, for Sam, means being responsible for somebody else — a partner or a child. 'It's the heaviness of the intensity of responsibility of taxes and knowledge of certain things. I think of a guy with a beard driving a car home to his little child and his partner and … not watching cartoons.'

I wonder if these things — a beard, a car, a partner, and a kid, Sam's version of my figure in a doorway with a briefcase or a baby — will one day make him feel grown up, but he tells me he doesn't think he will ever say the words, 'I'm an adult.' He will never take on that mantle. Why? What does he dread so much about adulthood? 'Because I'm going to forever live purely, in a manner that makes me feel like there's so much untapped potential in life, and that I should enjoy everything. Because I don't feel like adults do that — at least, people who self-identify as adults.' For him, adulthood brings with it a distorted sense of realism, of rules and constraints and reasons why things are not possible. This is where his objections to adulthood lie. 'When people tell me, "be realistic" — I have a major problem with that, because there's nothing realistic about the world we live in.' The scientific advances we have seen, from mobile phones to planes — none of this is realistic he says, and as he speaks his eyes shine, and I feel like I'm listening to poetry: 'The understanding of what is realistic or not is open to those who can dream. And I believe children offer that purity, that love, that enthusiasm and imagination. And adulthood doesn't. And that's why I don't think I'm ever going to grow up, because that realm of possibilities is always going to be open to me.' His own experiences with the UK's immigration system have taught him about how the adult system works, how it's constructed. 'That knowledge is painful, and it kills ambition and it takes away purity. It stunts people's ability to dream to the fullest potential, to see the impossible as possible; that's something that being a child allows you to do.'

But much as he denies it, I think there is something very grown up about Sam. As he tells me about some of the grow-ups he has worked through, and those he hasn't, he seems to me to be entirely responsible for himself. He has just finished his first term studying politics at university in London for which he won a scholarship, and has been living in the UK for eight years after moving with his two brothers and his mother, later joined by his father. At first, they shared a bedroom in a cousin's house, until they got their own place in Manchester. He talks of leaving his life in Nigeria behind to move to the UK as one of the major grow-ups of his life: 'It's such an unusual experience, and it comes with a whole width of issues and challenges. How to say goodbye to people, or how to go and not say goodbye. And how does that make you feel? And what internal experience do you face?' We seem to be returning, again and again, to questions of separation and separateness. I ask him how he holds on to relationships with friends and family and he chuckles and shakes his head: 'I really don't let people go.' What keeps friends connected is 'being honest and true, and sharing parts of yourself. That allows them to share parts of themselves with you, and once you hold a part of someone, you can keep that flame going, and it's a lot harder to let go.'

He tells me about his mother who died from a heart condition when he was 13. She was 'the tank of the family', the youngest of seven siblings, an extremely talented woman who provided for everyone, giving herself to the church, to her family. When Sam found out about her heart condition as a child, he was determined to become a heart surgeon. He looks down as he says, 'This is one of the only promises I know that I failed to keep. It is a difficult memory to go back to.' He swore to her that he would be the one to save her, that he'd dedicate his life to understanding the cardiac system and cardiac surgery, to work out what was wrong with her heart and what he could do to cure her. 'And yeah, I failed. I severely failed, like I was nowhere close. And I don't intend to ever let anyone down like that again.'

When he got the phone call and was told that she had died, he could not believe the words he heard. It was only when he saw his little brother crying, and when he heard his older brother upstairs breaking doors and punching the bathroom tiles until they cracked — it was only when he saw the pain in his family that he cried himself. He was determined after that never to cry again, and other than the day of the funeral, he has cried on only one other occasion: 'I was playing the piano at home, and tears just started gushing out of my eyes, uncontrollably. I wasn't even crying, but tears were falling out. I was like, what the flip is going on right now? Cos you're not crying, but you're crying.' Ever since then, his eyes have stayed dry. It sounds to me like he is proud of that — but he quickly corrects my assumption. 'No, I think it's a very problematic thing. For a while, I was like yeah, that's great, I'm not in pain. But now I'm clearly struggling to feel at all. I feel like tears should be able to come out of these eyes, but they're not.' He is very protective of himself; he has never been to his mother's grave. I hear this and my heart aches for him — in that moment, I do not see an adult man, but a child who promised he would save his mother and blames himself for breaking that promise; a child who promised himself he would not cry, and now finds himself desperate but unable to break that promise. It sounds like this is a grow-up he cannot yet see his way through.

His mother brought him and his brothers to the UK on a Tier 1 Visa for those with desired skills. On the second anniversary of her death, Sam received a letter from the Home Office. He recalls it saying: you have 21 days to pack your bags and leave the country and you can't appeal from the UK. The lives of his family were thrown into chaos, and Sam rallied all the people he could to help them fight their corner — and there were many. People who run the Youth Parliament of which he was a member, representing the constituency of Manchester, the athletics organisation he used to run for and also helped to run, the various organisations he has volunteered with for young people of colour and young people who are working class and young carers. Everyone came together to support him, some even attending the court cases in which Sam's family sought to overturn the Home Office's decision. In court, a barrister asked him, 'A lot of people have lost their mum, what makes your situation so different?' His little brother started crying. Sam tells me, 'I was like, oh my gosh, you're such a douchebag, what is this? I didn't say that, obviously.' He sat and thought about how to respond to this question. He looked at the date and saw that it was 9 November 2018, and told that barrister, 'Exactly one year ago I sat in your Parliament, on those green benches that only MPs are allowed to sit on, as a member of the Youth Parliament. I sat there representing my constituents of Manchester. And I'd like to note that today I'm sat in this court trying to defend my reasons to exist in this country.' Sam and his family won that court case, but they were not granted indefinite leave to remain: they will have to go through the same process every couple of years for the next decade, and they do not know if, eventually, they will be granted permission to stay for good — to make their home here for ever. We will be lucky if they do.

What the world needs, Sam argues, is a peaceful revolution: a change to the system. But he thinks adults don't really believe that change can come like that. 'They don't believe in the idea of a revolution, they believe in gradual change. And I respect that, and I know that there's a lot of truth and pragmatism within that frame of thought, but I feel like it shackles you. It pulls you down.' Look at Greta Thunberg, he tells me: she is asking for really radical change, necessary change — and it is adults that are stopping that from happening. For Sam, children can dream and believe anything is possible and see injustices that need to be rectified, now. But when they turn into adults, they become complacent and complicit in keeping things as they are and they want to let the process take its course. 'Tsk,' he says, 'I respect that, and I know that those are true statements, but it's a force that cuts me. There's a whole other realm of possibilities for how things could work.'

He seems to me so liberated in his vision for how the world could be, but not when it comes to adulthood. Being grown up, for Sam, means something boring. Taxes, heaviness, the realm of the feasible — and definitely no cartoons. Why, I ask him, doesn't he make adulthood part of his revolution? After all, being a grown-up can mean whatever he makes it, however he chooses to live his adult life. He replies, 'That's a lovely question. Why don't I?'

I feel I know instinctively that there is another side to adulthood that Sam does not see right now — I cannot currently see it in any detail either, I just know it's there, like when the moon is obscured by a tall building, but you can still sense its glow. Growing up as a process, yes — but as a process that is itself radical and liberating. A personal revolution for each of us. I cannot yet say exactly what it looks like, but I wonder if some of the young people I have met so far can help us to sketch an uncertain outline. Although each individual's revolution is so very different from the last, perhaps there are also some themes that overlap. Victoria, it seems, is engaged in an ongoing process of articulating her own identity, within her family and outside of it, on social media and off it; although leaving home brought with it a shocking kind of freedom she wasn't too sure she wanted at first, I wonder whether these experiences might all be part of the individual revolution each of us has to go through in order to become a separate person. For Sam, growing up so far has meant leaving but not letting go of his friends and family in Nigeria; it has meant standing up in court to defend his right and the right of his loved ones to remain in this country; and it has involved burying his mother and forbidding himself from crying. His independence has come at such a price; he has locked himself in a prison where he cannot cry, and now he cannot find the key. It strikes me that for him, the most radical revolution of all would be to find his way back to doing what all of us do, instinctively, with the first breath we take in this world. And for Boru … well, for Boru it feels too early to say. When I think of Boru, I feel a gut-clenching mix of worry and fear and hope and trust. I want to believe he will find his own revolution — his own way to freeing himself from drugs, to forgiving himself, to making a good life — but I cannot be certain.

There is a paradox here, and it's an intriguing one I think. There is something radical about growing up, something on the fringes of experience and feeling, something violent, extreme, and so intense it resists being put into words — but at the same time it is incredibly normal and natural, like breathing. It reminds me of what Freud wrote about the aspiration for his talking cure when psychoanalysis was in the early stages of its development, about the benefits of 'transforming your neurotic misery into ordinary unhappiness'.[23] Growing up often doesn't feel like fireworks or bungee jumping or dancing like nobody's watching, although it might do sometimes — it can just feel … okay. I understand this in a deeper way after my conversation with Tochi. As he walks into my flat, smiling broadly and generously, he seems totally at ease with himself, and I immediately breathe out in his company — it is as if he changes the atmosphere through his own calm and centred presence. At 22, he is waiting to start his first job in a few months' time, having taken a year out after university to explore and think about what he wants to do. When I ask him if he is an adult, he laughs and says, 'Legally!' In some ways, he thinks he is — 'Look, I have a beard now, okay' — but in other ways, he is very much not: 'I'm still living in my childhood home. At home, you can't be an adult. I remember five years ago, my mum getting told off by my grandad. At home, you will always be the child.' He remembers when he turned 18 feeling, 'Oh yeah, I'm a grown-up now, I can do whatever.' And now, 'I look back at how I behaved at 18, 19, 20, and I'm like, what a childish thing to do.' What to make of these earlier, not-so-adult selves, he is not sure. Although Tochi has felt himself growing up as the years have passed, he does not think he has followed a straightforwardly linear path; for him, development to and through adulthood is 'like a pinball machine', as he bounces from experience to experience, reflecting on those experiences, trying to learn how to respond differently next time, sometimes maturing, sometimes not.

I ask him about the biggest grow-ups in his life and he describes what seems to me to be a process of letting go. He told his parents he was gay when he was 14, and he describes their response as 'not great'. It wasn't that he was mistreated, he says, but at the moment when he spoke the truth about who he was, he met with 'an expression of disapproval, and that can be traumatic in itself'. He was hurt and upset for a long time, wishing they had reacted differently. As the years passed, he began to feel stuck in this position of having been wronged, weighed down by this justified sense of grievance. He says, 'Quite recently, I think there was a grow-up that happened, where I realised that adults are like grown-up children,' — it is not clear to me exactly what he means by this, but I wonder if it has something to do with adults not having all the answers, still being in formation, not always getting it right. 'I can feel sad about it, I am within my rights to feel sad about it, but I have reached a point where I don't feel I have to continue to be sad about this for ever. I've chosen to step out of the situation, to view it in a different way, which is to accept the flaws in my parents.' For all those years it seems to me he carried something of their reaction in him; he held on to their sense of disapproval and felt weighed down by his own disapproval of them. Now he has untangled himself from what his parents said and separated his view of himself from theirs. 'Now I think, well, I didn't do anything wrong. What you said was wrong. It's not on me, and therefore, I can move about my day.' He smiles.

A radical liberation, a quiet revolution, a man just moving about his day. This grow-up has freed Tochi from the shackles of judgement coming from outside him and inside him, and as he sits on my sofa eating a cinnamon bun, he comes across as simply, straightforwardly, okay in himself. I find I feel calmer just being in the company of a man so at ease, so free and comfortable with who he is. And what followed that letting go, what became possible with that peaceful revolution was a renewed capacity to experience the joy of being alive — the joy of being Tochi. We turn to the subject of privilege and its different forms, and he shares his dissatisfaction in the shape these conversations often take in our society; how so often they preclude the chance to talk about 'Black joy', about the excitement of being 'a queer person of colour', the pride of 'being a part of Black British gay history'. 'I enjoy being Black and being identified and associated with so much interesting culture and life and people,' he says. After we say goodbye and he closes my front door behind him, I think to myself, that must have been a really good grow-up. This is what seems to link the smaller grow-ups with the bigger grow-ups which make up the even bigger revolutions in Boru, Victoria, Sam, and Tochi: this sense of freedom.

Barbara Natterson-Horowitz, a cardiologist and evolutionary biologist at Harvard University and the University of California, Los Angeles, puts some flesh on the bones of this more optimistic understanding of adulthood. A common definition of an adult animal is one who has reached the age at which it can reproduce — but Natterson-Horowitz found something quite different in her research. She and her co-author Kathryn Bowers spent five years studying the transition to adulthood in wild animals around the world, and their conclusion is, 'The ability to reproduce is not synonymous with adulthood. This is true not only in humans, but across the tree of life. For many species in the wild, puberty — the physiological process of becoming reproductively mature — is just the beginning. These young animals lack adult skills in many areas; they may lack courtship skills because they haven't learnt mating dances, or they may not have social skills to acquire status within their group.' She found, just like Lord Scarman, Sarah-Jayne Blakemore, Ariel Nathanson, and those who went before them, that the boundaries between adulthood and what comes before it are much fuzzier than we might often assume. This discovery led the researchers to develop a new definition of adulthood for the animal kingdom, based not on an animal's biological capacity to reproduce, but on the mastery of four key competencies: staying safe, navigating social hierarchies, sexual communication, and leaving the nest to care for oneself. 'Safety. Status. Sex. Self-reliance.'

They found evidence that adolescence, this in-between period of being almost adult but not quite, of having an adult body but lacking experience, of being not a girl, not yet a woman, this 'weird limbo' of a life stage, does not belong to our species alone. It is universal, 'running like an unbroken ribbon from crustaceans to fish, amphibians, reptiles, birds, and non-human mammals'. They called it 'wildhood' — and this became the title of their book.[24] And not only that: they found that the coming-and-going quality of late adolescence — the to-and-fro of Tochi and Victoria between university and home — is not uniquely human, either. It was previously widely believed that there was a fateful day when newly adult penguins would 'dive into the icy waters of the Atlantic and off they go,' she explains. But it turns out that this is not always the case: in a number of penguin species, researchers have identified 'extended parental care'. If there is not enough food, or if the young penguins' hunting skills are not sufficiently developed, they return to their parents, who continue to feed them. 'They literally have left home, but they've come back, because they can't yet make it on their own,' says Natterson-Horowitz, noting that this parental strategy is used by both people and penguins alike. It is as if the words of the

Children Act echo across the animal kingdom, that we must continue to support the young, to the extent that their welfare requires it.

Discovering that adolescence exists in other species has provoked a shift for Natterson-Horowitz in her understanding of this life stage in humans, too. 'Adolescence can be painful and hard, but it turns out if it is going to transform a juvenile into a young adult, it has to be hard. Human adolescents and their families should take some comfort in knowing that the trials and tumult of this phase of life are necessary, and they are not alone.' She adds that trying to protect adolescents from these normal difficulties and pains may be unwise, as 'studies of wild birds, fish, and mammals show us that animals protected from these arduous experiences may be poorly equipped to handle independence'. To grow up is to struggle — another element to add to the definition we are building.

Discovering all this has left Natterson-Horowitz with 'an expanded perspective on the transition to adulthood'. One of the biggest questions that she had as she began this research into adulthood was, 'Why become an adult?' In the wild, animals must become capable adults in order to survive, but in modern life that isn't the case for us, so what is the upside? Writing her book has led her to an answer: 'adulthood is about mastery and competence, it is about realising potential and finding personal agency. We may be too close to our human selves to recognise this, but looking across species, it becomes very clear.' She shows me a video on her book's website of adolescent Laysan albatrosses as they watch and attempt to mimic the elaborate, magnificent courtship dance of their elders.[25] I watch the young white birds practise and spot them getting the timing wrong, I notice when they hesitate, so uncertain, and I smile as they fumble their attempts at the intricate beak-snapping version of an Inuit kiss, catching their beaks on each other's. Natterson-Horowitz explains it takes up to four years of practice to master these movements. I watch another video, this time of adult Laysan albatrosses. I am astounded as they all, in perfect time, bend their legs, beak to the ground, and straighten swiftly up, beaks to the sky. The beaky Inuit kisses that follow are so fast and so precise that they begin to blur in front of my eyes. I understand what Natterson-Horowitz means when she tells me how, through this work, she has recognised something that isn't always appreciated within 'our youth obsessed culture': 'the magnificence of being a grown-up'. She has seen it while watching the mastery of an adult who can hunt and feed and protect and create and lead. This, she says, is 'the species-spanning majesty of adulthood'.

The species-spanning majesty of adulthood. I love her impassioned description, and I find myself totally caught up in this intoxicating image. Perhaps a little too caught up. I know I have a tendency to idealise adulthood — and that is a dangerous path for me. I think as a teenager, I was so caught up in the idea of being a perfectly competent, masterful adult that I didn't allow myself the struggles that, as Natterson-Horowitz suggests, make up a vital part of adolescence.

At the time, I saw my friends who were struggling and I tried to help them, and I wondered why I seemed to be getting a relatively smooth ride through the teenage years. I thought I was lucky — but I have just started to realise how much I have missed. Perhaps I had already locked myself in the adult department, already playing the role of responsible grown-up; maybe this is part of the reason I do not feel like an adult now — I did not allow myself to be a child, to be an adolescent, the one who needed help. I felt I already had to know the answers, too eager to reach what I thought was the finish line. I was so desperate to get things right, I denied myself the important experience of being real — of just being me.

The 'weird limbo' life stage of this chapter is about being a beginner adult — it is about having the capacity to accept the paradox that you both are an adult and are not an adult at the same time; being able to tolerate the fact that you are both and neither and in between. Because when we cannot tolerate the messiness of that, we might force ourselves to grow up too quickly, and then we miss out on the crucial steps towards adulthood which involve *not* being an adult. And I totally get the urge to skip that part. Being a beginner can be exciting, but it can also be awful, truly awful. The sense of unrootedness, precariousness, of not knowing anything, of being judged — by others but worst of all by oneself — the total lack of self-belief. It's awful! I know it well. When I first began training to be a therapist, it was a lot like being thrust back into adolescence. The fear, the inexperience, the not feeling good enough. While tidying up recently, I found a quote I copied down I don't know when. It was a line from a paper on psychoanalysis: 'The beginning therapist is mostly at sea.'[26] So simple and so true. At first, I approached my training in exactly the same way as I approached my adolescence — as if I was already supposed to be the grown-up. I didn't ask the questions I thought were stupid, because I thought I should already know the answers, like a child who thinks she needs to be the parent. It took a lot of analysis for me to see what I was doing, and for me to start asking those questions, and thinking about why I hadn't been able to ask them before. But I did start asking them. What I am learning again and again from my analysis, and from my training, and from Natterson-Horowitz, is that new beginnings are messy because they have to be. The point about adolescence, the point about being at the start of something, is not to get it right, but to have experiences and to grow from them.

For Boru, the struggle to grow up has meant becoming an addict and then fighting that addiction, falling in love and then breaking up, losing his mind and then finding it again. Despite going through all this, he says, 'I don't feel like my life has begun.' And in a way, he is right; he is just about touching the edges of adult life. This is why Nathanson loves working with young people at this life stage. 'From my experience in therapy, this is the most meaningful part of life, because you can turn a lot of corners and change a lot. It is a moment in which you are suddenly out there in the world in a different way. You've gained some sort of perspective from moving to this twilight zone, this in-between place, and a lot of good things can happen at that time,' he says. Early adolescence is too young and too stormy; in mid-adolescence things are starting to get a bit easier, but in late adolescence, into the early 20s, 'That's the point in which this adult can be in the driving seat for the first time, looking around, noticing, reflecting. It's a great time for change.' Because that is the thing about adulthood, Nathanson says: 'You only know where you are at a certain point ... and then it changes.'

On New Year's Eve, about a year after Boru came to my flat, and a few days after I write the last sentence of the last chapter of this book, he sends me a message on WhatsApp: 'I always think back to our conversations and how they helped me.' As I read on, tears blur my vision. He writes that he has had a good year. That he got clean. That he has started cycling again — has started to love it again — and has a new job as a cycling instructor. He writes, 'It's weird to really think of the future with as much giddiness as I do now.' I feel extraordinarily moved by his words, and grateful to know this brave young man. I also feel hopeful, because he seems to have found that capacity in himself, which I want to believe lies latent in all of us, including in me, although it can feel so out of reach at times: the potential to keep growing up.

Chapter Two

Contents insurance

'Blackbird'
Song by Lennon-McCartney

A baby is crying. He is sitting in his bouncer and kicking his legs; he starts off softly, a quiet moan. In the time his mother takes to put down her sandwich and walk over, the sound has already grown into a full-throated wail, desperate and demanding, as if he fears he will feel like this for ever, trapped and lost. His mother lifts him from the bouncer and holds him to her, bobbing him on soft knees, speaking gently and calmly, telling him it is okay, that she is here. As he continues wailing, she asks him what is wrong, wondering aloud if it could be his nappy; she sniffs, but he is clean. He cries louder. She wonders if he might be too cold; she feels the back of his neck but he is baby-warm. At the touch of her fingers on his skin, he starts to calm, and he purses his lips, forming a silent 'O'. She asks if he wants a feed, unhooking her bra and exposing her nipple, which he takes in his mouth, hungrily.

Do you have contents insurance?

I think you can tell a lot about a person by their answer to this question — a 'yes' wins 673 adult points. I had never given it much thought until the issue was forced upon me recently. I was sitting in a local café, chatting with a friend, when I glanced down at my bag and saw empty floor. The bag, which had been there, was no longer there. I thought there must be some mistake; I took deep breaths and walked around the café, looking under the tables; I asked the staff; I looked in the loos just in case. After a few minutes, I understood that I was unlikely to see my bag again. I'd lost my laptop, my notebooks, my phone, my wallet, my keys. It felt like I'd lost everything.

Of course I had not lost everything: I had lost some possessions, most of which were replaceable, and I was fortunate enough to be able to afford to replace them. But I gave myself such a hard time. I felt sick that I had not just kept the bag on my lap, I pummelled myself for being so careless. My friends were quick to console me: it could happen to anyone, they said; it wasn't my fault, they said. But what they said next was less comforting. 'Your contents insurance might cover it,' my brother-in-law suggested, three years younger but decades more adult than I am. 'You never know, you might have some luck with your contents insurance,' reassured another friend. 'Check with your contents insurer … You do have contents insurance, don't you?' asked my dad, ever hopeful, but, I think, already knowing the answer. Each time, I replied, 'Yes, I'll check,' and each time it was a lie. I do not have contents insurance.

This stage of life I am calling 'Contents Insurance' is when we are supposed to start ticking all the boxes off the adulthood checklist.[1] We are supposed grow into the adult-shaped suit that felt so big and baggy on us in late adolescence, and to become properly established, fully fledged, confident, and competent grown-ups. We are expected to become expert at, to use a word I really do not like and will not be writing again, 'adulting'. Less, as Shakespeare's Old Shepherd describes the 'age between ten and three-and-twenty' in *The Winter's Tale*, 'fighting, stealing, wronging the ancientry, getting wenches with child';[2] more getting promoted, never running out of milk, sorting out your pension. The grow-ups we are expected to work through in this period are to do with what Freud thought of as the cornerstones of our humanness: love and work. These grow-ups and their timing will be different depending on culture and class: in conservative (with a small c) Britain, they might involve on the love side, finding a partner, forming a stable relationship, making a home together, and planning to start a family; and on the work side, establishing yourself in a career and working your way up the ladder. Perhaps for some, these expectations feel very old-fashioned now: heteronormativity is increasingly challenged, and the working world has changed so much that a 'job for life' feels like a historical artefact. And of course many people defy these expectations and eschew these grow-ups, whether it's because this is not the kind of life they want for themselves or because circumstances make them impossible to achieve. But I don't think that all the talk of polyamory and freelance portfolio careers means these grow-ups have disappeared from our minds — I think these more traditional expectations still hold power over us, whether we adopt them without question, wrestle with them, or rebel against them. In any case, in this life stage, which maps approximately on to the early 20s and into the 30s for some, there is societal pressure to become completely responsible for ourselves — to get our shit sorted — to replace dependence on our parents with an unerring self-reliance, and to acquire contents insurance to protect the value of all our personal possessions in case of disaster, perhaps after soliciting numerous quotes and researching the matter on moneysavingexpert.com.

I have often heard people talk about buying white goods as a moment of facing their own sense of grown-upness (or lack thereof), the prosaic washing machine symbolising a kind of cleaning up of their adolescent act. But for me, contents insurance carries more meaning for this life stage than any other cliché of adulthood — I think because it is so boring. It requires doing research and admin and paying for something that you might never need, even though you might end up spending more on contents insurance than you ever claim on it, because that is the responsible thing to do. As a symbol it also carries that peculiar aspect of adulthood which is that it seems to feel so automatic and inevitable to some people, but so bewildering and unlikely to others (including me). It was only my dad, who knows me too well, who actually asked me if I had contents insurance when my bag was stolen; everyone else who mentioned it just presumed I did. But for me and the friends among whom I sought solace, knowing intuitively that they did not have contents insurance either, it is more complicated than that.

Where this metaphor falls down — and I'll admit it does not take long — is that once you've decided on an insurance policy, all you have to do is pay your money and the next moment you're insured, and if you keep paying your premium, you'll stay that way. Growing up is different. One of the most beautiful descriptions of growing up I have heard came from Adam — more from him later — who told me: 'It's the difference between a train arriving in a station or the sun rising. Everyone knows when the trains arrive, like an old steam engine with loads of noise and smoke, and it's exactly five thirty-two or whatever. And it's there. Growing up is not like that, right? Adulthood is probably more like the sun rising. You don't know exactly when it happened, but you're aware of when it's happening. It gets brighter.'

This understanding is shared by Jeffrey Jensen Arnett, Professor in the Department of Psychology at Clark University in Worcester, Massachusetts, who made psychology history just over 20 years ago by proposing a new life stage, which he called Emerging Adulthood.[3] Although we speak online, I can immediately sense his confident, easy nature; from his warm smile to his considered, thoughtful manner, he seems like a man who is comfortable just where he is. He is 62 years old and says, 'I feel like I've been an adult for a long time. But what initially prompted me to study this question myself was that I felt I hadn't reached adulthood.' There is hope for me yet.

Arnett had always imagined he would be an adult by 30. But at that age, he was still struggling with Freud's cornerstones of humanness: he had yet to find a partner and to secure a stable job in academia. It was not until his mid-30s that he got that job and met the woman who is now his wife of 25 years; it was only after they bought a house together and started thinking about having children that he began, finally, to feel a little more grown up. 'All those things went into feeling adult for me. And as often happens in the social sciences, I thought, well, this is how I've experienced it — I wonder how other people have experienced it?' And so he began to research. He tells me — and it feels a little too close to the bone — that he began by studying people in their 30s, reasoning that he was in his 30s, and didn't feel he had reached adulthood, but 'I soon discovered they already thought they'd reached adulthood and had felt adult for a while, so that's why I began studying the 20s.' Ouch.

He eventually defined emerging adulthood as taking place for most people between ages 18 and 29. At the beginning of this period, very few people feel adult, but by the end of it, by the time they hit their late 20s, almost everybody he asked would reply yes, they did feel like an adult, and then they would usually mention responsibility. 'That's the first word that comes up above all: responsibility,' he says. Responsibility links what he calls 'the big three' — the core elements that constitute adulthood, according to the vast majority of his interviewees: first, the capability to take care of themselves; second, being able to make their own decisions; and third, financial independence.

Over the 30 years that he has been asking people this question, I wonder, has he noticed changes in the responses? His answer surprises me: 'No.' The results have been consistent, from the early 1990s through to today. 'It's interesting because obviously societies change, there are economic ups and downs — but the responses to that question haven't changed,' he says. In different parts of the world however, researchers have found different results: Arnett's question has spawned studies in India, South America, China, and elsewhere, which reveal something about how our understanding of adulthood is not universal, but shifts according to culture. One of Arnett's students, Juan Zhong, went to China to interview young women who had migrated at around age 20 from rural villages to the city, where they live in dormitories and work six days a week in a factory. She asked them about what it means to be a grown-up, and their responses were not the same as those of Arnett's interviewees; there were subtle but important differences, Arnett explains: 'It's really eye-opening, a contrast to anything that's been found in the West.' These young women had in mind a slightly different 'big three' criteria for adulthood, orientated more around taking responsibility for others rather than for oneself: first, learning to care for parents; second, settling into a long-term career; and third, becoming capable of caring for children.[4] On learning this I am struck afresh by how I am still struggling to pin down the meaning of this word 'adulthood', how it seems to change from culture to culture, from person to person.

A significant step in Arnett's personal transition to adulthood was when he realised, he tells me, 'that I had found this thing, this great big question, "When do you feel like you've reached adulthood?", that nobody else had really asked. And obviously, that is a fascinating question. So I thought, okay, this is how I'm going to make my name, and I did.' In reality, it was not so straightforward: Arnett had to work through an internal struggle before he could put Emerging Adulthood on the map, and this was the biggest grow-up of his career. Researchers and clinicians have discussed life stages since the birth of the science of psychology around the late 19th century, and these concepts were based on writings that were thousands of years old. This left Arnett questioning himself. 'Nobody had invented a life stage before, nobody had declared a new one. I was still young at the time, in my 30s. Who did I think I was?' But he finally decided that it had to be done. In 2000, he published a paper called 'Emerging adulthood: a theory of development from the late teens through the twenties', which has been cited over 18,000 times and counting. That is a big deal — he pretty much went viral, developmental-psychologically speaking. That is not to say that his ideas have been accepted by everyone: some argue that emerging adulthood is not universal and therefore cannot constitute a life stage; others that it is limited to people who are privileged and that the concept means little to those from poorer backgrounds, a charge which Arnett entertainingly dismisses. He describes it as 'the claim — and I do underline claim — that it only applies to the elite, the advantaged, the middle and upper-middle classes, that it leaves out the poor and those who don't have the advantage of a university education. And to be honest, it's a load of crap.' He says he took great care to interview mostly people who were not college-educated and who came from a mix of social classes and ethnic backgrounds, so as to construct a theory that represented a broad range of experiences.

As I listen to Arnett's story, an image comes to my mind of an arctic explorer battling alone through a snowstorm, the only smudge of colour in a bleak white landscape. Then I see him take a flag on a long pole, and stick it triumphantly into the ground, claiming his territory, conquering adulthood and its study. When I reflect on this image of adulthood as a mountain to summit, in which I might one day hope to stick my flag, the idea doesn't sit quite right with me — it all sounds very phallic, doesn't it? Though I suppose as a student of Freud, I would say that. I wonder if my discomfort comes from the part of me that knows I am currently, at best, only halfway up the mountain. I feel very much like an Emerging Adult. Based on hundreds of interviews with 18- to 29-year-olds, Arnett has identified five characteristics of this new life stage: identity exploration; focussing on the self (which, he emphasises, is self-discovery rather than selfishness); a sense of 'in-betweenness'; an optimistic feeling of possibility; and instability (in relationships, accommodation, working life, and more). Almost all of these apply to me: the only sense in which I could be described as fully emerged is in the stability of my marriage and accommodation — but I am still experiencing a certain degree of instability in my working life, what with embarking on training in psychodynamic psychotherapy in my 30s, and, well, starting to write a book.

I wonder what it means, that I still feel like an Emerging Adult when, by Arnett's timeline, I was supposed to have Emerged several years ago. There is a very particular kind of anxiety that comes with feeling like you are lagging behind everyone else. It makes me think of a *Time* magazine cover from 2005, which I came across in my research, featuring an adult man sitting in a child-sized sandpit alongside the cover line, 'They Just Won't Grow Up'. I feel for that man in the sandpit, I really do. I feel like shouting into the void, 'They Just Won't Fuck Off'. Arnett's theory is a welcome tonic to this kind of judgement. Instead of blaming young people for not growing up, he seems to be suggesting that society needs to adjust its expectations; that we should not condemn young people for not being adults, but give them time to emerge. This is something I am learning for myself through being a patient in psychoanalysis and also through my psychotherapy training; you just can't rush growing up. No matter how hard you try, you cannot force yourself to mature any faster — in fact, trying to will often get in the way and slow things down. I just wish Arnett could have opened that age window a little wider, past 29, so that I could breathe too. It is starting to feel quite airless here, like the walls are closing in. I am only in the second chapter of adult life, but it feels like I have already run out of time. It is becoming difficult to think.

I had to look further back into our past to open that window, to give myself the air to breathe and the space to think again. In Steven Mintz's book *The Prime of Life: a history of modern adulthood,*[5] I read that 'Adulthood is one stage of life that lacks a history. We know a great deal about childhood, adolescence and old age in the past, but adulthood remains a historical black hole.' In fact, his was one of only two books about the history of adulthood I could find in the British Library catalogue, both about America, in contrast with the dozens of books focussing on adolescence and childhood. Perhaps that is why, as Mintz writes, we all carry this 'myth that the transition to adulthood was more seamless and smoother in the past, as well as the notion that the adult life course was more stable and predictable than it has become'. Faced with a black hole of an unknown history, we cover it up with a blank canvas on which we paint an idealised version of our past — and that only makes us feel more inadequate and stressed out that we don't seem to be keeping up with the 19th-century Joneses. Of the period Arnett calls Emerging Adulthood, Mintz writes, 'The perception of the twenties as an unsettled, anxious, and uncertain period of life has a long history. Every generation at least since the early 18th century has had to contend with insecurity and self-doubt in the process of seeking rewarding work or a romantic partner.' This was one of many comforting lines from his book that I enthusiastically noted down, mostly because it made me feel better about myself, rather than for strict research purposes. I also copied down: 'Vacillation, doubt, uncertainty, and lack of direction have long characterized early adulthood,' and — my favourite — 'the bridge years between adolescence and functioning adulthood, often romanticized as a period of exploration and self-discovery, are, for many, a period of uncertainty, ambiguity, and flailing about'. Flailing about! Rarely have I felt so seen. I recall a sense of consolation at Natterson-Horowitz's understanding that the struggle from adolescence to adulthood is fought across species; I think I am now experiencing something like that again in learning how that struggle has been fought across centuries.

But in certain ways, Mintz suggests, the conditions in which young people must find their way into adulthood today have become more treacherous. What is distinctive to this generation of emerging adults is the financial debt that many young people now carry alongside the near-universal psychological doubts and the ultra-competitive job economy in which they must fight off the timeless emotional insecurity. This line from his book reads like a dark joke: 'The post-World War II economic boom allowed young men, even those without a high school diploma, to obtain a job sufficient to support a family by their early twenties.' He explains that the traditional image of the grown-up we share in our collective mind came together in the 19th century and culminated in the 1950s, that one characterised by women in pinnies holding babies and men in suits holding briefcases, possibly containing their contents insurance policies. In this image, adulthood represents a plateau, and it is described by words like 'serious', 'stolid', and 'settled down'. This began to change in the 1960s, when the economy shifted away from manufacturing, and jobs with middle-class salaries demanded post-secondary education; at the same time, it became more socially acceptable for young people to live together before marriage. Together these two phenomena opened up time and space for exploration in the domains of work and love. People began to see their 20s as the age of independence, which has led in our lifetimes to 'more diverse and individualistic conceptions of adulthood' as ideas around gender roles, sexuality, relationships, work, and home life have become more flexible and fluid. This might be part of what makes the question of adulthood so anxiety-inducing, Mintz suggests — unlike the generation who came of age in the 50s, we don't have a fixed image in our collective mind of what it has to look like, hence my own struggle to define it. 'Many of the stresses of contemporary adulthood grow out of the lack of a clear consensus in the definition of adulthood today. It is much harder to be an adult who determines her or his own path than to follow a culturally prescribed life course.' These radical social shifts have given us more freedom in many ways, but they have also taken away our script. We have to improvise. We have to try to get to know ourselves as individuals and discover what we want, rather than relying on what society assumes we want. We have to be brave.

One thing that has changed — and one of the insights from Mintz's book which fascinated me most — is that during the 17th century, age just wasn't that much of a thing: 'Age was an imprecise category, and key life experiences were not tied to distinct ages.' Young men would marry after they had achieved economic independence, which usually meant waiting to receive their inheritance following their father's death. Our obsession with age solidified over the course of the 19th century, and can be measured, he suggests, in the appearance in the early 1870s of mass-produced birthday cards. Birthday cards!

Our shelves would have been emptier, but I wonder if all of us not-quite-adults might have been less neurotic had we lived in the 17th century; today we seem to think about growing up only in terms of milestones achieved by a particular age. In 2019, the Office for National Statistics brought out a special report showing how, as a nation, we are reaching the traditional landmarks of adulthood later and later, with young people in the UK staying in education, buying their first home, and becoming parents at an older age on average than the generations before them.[6] Over the decade prior to 2019, the average age at which people left full-time education increased by two years to 19. The most common living arrangement for 18- to 34-year-olds in 2017 was in the home they grew up in with their parents; two decades earlier, the most common arrangement was in a couple with at least one child. In America and Australia too, people are hitting these markers far later than in previous generations. It is easy to see how rising house prices, declining salaries (relative to inflation and living costs), job insecurity, and a rocky economy has contributed to this financial infantilisation.

'Putting pine nuts on your salad doesn't make you a grown-up,' Fleabag's sister tells her scornfully in the TV show of the same name, about a woman in her 30s working out how to live.[7] The thing about statistics, then as now, is that they are always about jobs and houses and marriages and babies. They show us the Instagrammable clichés of what it means to be a grown-up: the 'some personal news' tweet, the engagement selfie with the rock on full display, the ultrasound scan shared with hundreds of friends and followers. Of course, these kind of external markers of progress through life often require, and bring with them, a certain internal maturity. As Tochi described, it is hard to grow up into an adult when you are living at home with your parents for whom you may always be a child; having your own space, earning an income that enables you to live independently — these are all important external conditions that facilitate development and growth. But they do not constitute growth itself. It is not that hard to look grown-up on the outside and be anything but on the inside. I should know. This is the kind of performative adulthood, like pine nuts on your salad, that is not necessarily matched by something real and solid growing underneath.

There must be more to being grown-up, and to not growing up, than these statistics can convey, mustn't there? In fact I wonder if our focus on these measurable, quantifiable, concrete delayed landmarks — the moving out, the mortgages, the marriages — gives us an easy way to define adulthood that is also a way of not thinking about a deeper sense of not-grown-upness. One which is much more uncomfortable, unsettling, disturbing. I once had a vision of myself as a wizened, old tortoise, stretching its neck vulnerably out of its thick, heavy, dark brown shell, and underneath that shell, there was just darkness and some wisps of smoke. What if that is all adulthood is — just a shell, a carapace, covering up nothing but emptiness and smoke?

When I was a child, I loved reading Jacqueline Wilson's books. She is a phenomenon: she has written more than 100 books, which have been translated into 34 languages, with over 40 million copies sold worldwide. She writes about children dealing with very grown-up problems who are surrounded by adults struggling to cope; mental health difficulties, homelessness, violence, and the social care system are all common themes. But I do not think that that is the most significant characteristic of her work, or what compels the hundreds of young readers to send her letters each week. Rather, it is something to do with how she writes children's minds. It does not feel like you are reading what an adult thinks a child feels: she seems to inhabit each child's psychological skin. I am excited and nervous as I dial her phone number. Who better to ask, I think, about what it means to be a grown-up?

She does not agree. 'I don't think I'm the right person to give a view on this,' Wilson says. She spends her days thinking about children, being interested in children, and is not remotely interested in acting like an adult: 'The adult thing, the so-called adult thing … I mean, from the way you are speaking it's as if things are slanted, and when you achieve adulthood, that is somehow the pinnacle, whereas I think that's when you start to pretend. You pretend that the most trivial things are important and join the world of showing off about holidays and kitchen units and stuff like that, which doesn't particularly interest me at all.' Her perspective reminds me of Sam's, and this sense they both convey that adults lack something important that children have. For her, so-called adult life is 'the boring nitty-gritty' of life admin — the paperwork of buying contents insurance. She accepts that we do change and develop as a result of our life experiences, but, more importantly, she says, 'at the same time I think there is a part of you that is the same whether you're 6 or 60 years old'. In what she says, I understand that for her, adulthood can only ever be pine nuts on your salad; for her, an adult self is like Winnicott's False Self, something pretend growing over something true. She disputes this idea that we do all grow up into adults: 'I think we all have a sort of idea of what an adult is. But I think if we could see inside even the most secure-seeming, ultra-mature-seeming person, I think they have just learned how to pretend to be an adult.' With experience, we learn to put on a kind of armour, to play the role of someone who is an adult. 'I think that's perhaps why I like writing about children most of all, because I think they haven't learned to pretend like that.' I listen to her, and I think again of that image of a tortoise shell, this adult-looking persona that I have built for myself. It looks solid and real, but it feels deceptive, like a simulacrum. But what is it covering up? Could there be a more real kind of adult hiding underneath?

I ask her what it is like to spend so much of her time writing the thoughts and feelings of children, as a woman in her early 70s. She tells me she can remember quite clearly what it is like to be a child, and so can easily relate to children. 'But I had an odd childhood. In a way, I was required to act like an adult, as a child.' Another person who found herself in the adult department far too early. She had an 'extremely difficult and controlling mother', and from the way she says this, I suspect it is an understatement. She began ticking off the so-called markers of adulthood when she was still an adolescent, leaving home and becoming completely financially independent at 17; marrying what she calls 'stupidly early' at 19; having her daughter at 'just 21'. She had so many adult responsibilities when she had not yet grown up, and she learnt how to act like an adult even though she didn't feel like one. She reflects, 'When you haven't had the most secure and loving childhood, perhaps that does mean that you're always a little bit obsessed with it.' Four months after our interview, Wilson comes out publicly as gay — although this was no secret to those who knew her, and she had been living with her partner for 18 years.[8]

What changes as children grow up, she argues, is that we learn skills, we get better at coping with life's difficulties. But what that really means is we find new ways of squashing down our anxieties and worries — and we don't realise we're doing it. 'People might not be aware of all this. I think a lot of people block things out in various ways by keeping busy, by watching television, by looking at Facebook and Twitter and all the rest of it, and they divert themselves from really, really thinking about what they are doing. I think it's much easier for people to cope with things when they are not thinking about what really concerns them,' she says. I know that what Wilson says is true. I know that I do this myself, when I waste my evenings on Twitter. And yet, I also feel that there is something missing here; that pretending to be grown-up while seeking to bury our true feelings under landslides of tweets and Instastories is one version of adulthood — but it cannot be the only one. What, I wonder, might a more real kind of adulthood look like?

I tell Jacqueline that I disagree with her, in that I think she is exactly the person that I needed to speak to. The kind of adulthood that she is describing, something false, like a cover-up — I too think that this is a kind of adulthood that many of us probably inhabit. But I also believe there is another kind of growing up, another kind of adult state of mind that doesn't mean papering over or trying to turn away from our child-like anxieties and fears. Something true. 'I'm still feeling my way towards it,' I say, 'but I know it has nothing to do with kitchen units.'

Adam is 34 years old. He works for a bank, and is in the process of buying a house with his wife: so far, so grown up. But as he sits cross-legged on my sofa, wearing jeans and a plaid shirt, clean-shaven, eating a chocolate Hobnob, he describes something I think many of us can relate to: that sense of growing out of adolescence with a feeling that 'no one told me what to do, no one explained to me how I was supposed to be able to manage this and that or the other, how I was supposed to do adulthood. You feel like a pretender in an adult's body.' His outside did not match up with his inside — and to some extent, it still doesn't: 'I feel like I'm not a real adult.' He doesn't think anyone he knows would say that about him, but that is how he feels. He can feel something changing; he is, gradually, becoming more grown up, more experienced, more mature. 'But it feels too slow. It feels like I'm behind the curve.' When I look at him nibbling on a Hobnob, I have a sense of something vulnerable and heartrendingly honest simmering close to the surface.

When Adam was studying for his GCSEs, he decided to apply to join a sixth form military college and become an Army officer. It was highly competitive and getting in would be tough: his teachers worked with him to improve his grades, and when he was accepted, he was elated. 'I went to a normal secondary school, and everyone else was just going to the normal sixth form college or into a trade, and a couple of bright sparks were off to private education. I guess it was the first time in my life where I stood out, and I was known as that kid going to this army school, and that was amazing,' he says. He got what he wanted, but it was not what he needed. At 16, he 'went from boyhood to being treated like an adult'. He had not been away from his parents before, except for the occasional camping weekend; he still felt like a boy, but now he was expected to be a particular kind of man. What he experienced was 'nothing overly dramatic', what he calls 'mild bullying', the kind that happens in the Army, 'unless you're the bully'. I get the sense he is plucking one anecdote out of many when he tells me about messing up a Bible reading in the morning service in the chapel: 'One of my commanding officers said — and you can imagine how these words stick in your head — "You're a failure and a let-down to yourself, to this school, and to the British Army."' As Adam repeats this condemnation, I see such sadness and desperation in his eyes, and it feels to me like he is hearing them as a boy, being punished and punishing himself, over and again. His identity at that college was fixed: he was a failure. 'I had a nickname: Ultimate Shitter. Shitter was a term for someone who was crap at everything, and I was the Ultimate Crap At Everything.' As he speaks, I understand that there was not one single traumatic event that marked him for life; this was a cumulative experience of being made to feel so inadequate, so out of place, such a disappointment. Once a week, students were allowed to make a phone call. 'I remember going into a room and calling my dad and just crying, saying I want to come home, I want to go away from here. Just talking about it now sends shivers down my spine.' I can feel the shivers too. There appeared to him to be no way out — until there was. He was pulled into the principal's office and told he was underperforming, that he had to improve if he wanted to stay. He did not. His father came to pick him up. 'It was a huge relief, driving away from the place. And then I came home and just vomited all night.'

I feel a lurch in my stomach at Adam's words, as if the vomiting up of that experience is not so distant. I wonder if Adam's mind and body were trying to get rid of the shame and failure, to get it all out, so he would not have to suffer any more — if something similar might be going on now as he tells me this story. Relief does not seem a violent enough word to express what it meant to him to leave that place, to leave that part of his life behind. But although he left that school never to return, the school has never really left him. He still finds it hard to pack a suitcase because of the experience of packing to go to Army college: 'This week, I'm going away, and it's going to be a great holiday. But I will feel nervous, anxious, and a little bit down as I pack a suitcase. It's like a hard-wired memory. Like a smell or a sound can take you back to a point in time — packing a suitcase takes me back to that.'

The memory of the trauma lives on, and not just when he's packing suitcases; it is bigger than that. 'There's still parts of the way I interact with the world that are from the fall-out of that experience. It was such a poignant moment in my childhood, and what happened in the years afterwards ... It's all connected,' he says. The message from his teacher and commanding officer has taken up residence in his mind. The shape it takes now is in the way he relates to himself, in his attitude of: 'I will not fail again. It is not allowed, it's out of the question. It cannot happen. But obviously it does — and so when it does, I cannot deal with it. I cannot process failure.' Adam's internal commanding officer, just like the real one, cannot tolerate the very human capacity in all of us to fail. That has led Adam to put himself under unrealistic and unbearable pressure, which has in turn made him less likely to seek help when he needs it, which has in turn made failure more likely, and more catastrophic.

The most recent example of this was just a couple of years ago, when he was promoted to a prestigious role at work. People used to joke that the job was cursed because his predecessors had all burnt out or been fired — but rather than being a big red flag for Adam, this just made him all the more determined to succeed. After he had been in the role for some months, his wife sat him down and told him, 'I want my husband back. I want you to come home. I want you to have a normal job. You have proved yourself. Leave now.' But Adam couldn't really hear her; the words from that commanding officer, shouted at him when he was 17, were drowning out her voice. 'No,' he told her, 'I must succeed. I must.'

He had been working on a big report all weekend and into the night. In the moment of handing it over, he felt a sharp pain in his stomach. Later that evening, the pain grew so bad he couldn't sleep at all — but still, the next morning, he got out of bed when his alarm rang, dressed, took the tube to work, nearly collapsed, got off at the stop by his office. The usual five-minute walk from the station took 20 as he clung to the walls of buildings to stay upright. He says, 'I was just so weak, physically falling apart — yet I was still dragging myself in to work.' A colleague saw how ill he was and sent him home, his first sick day in seven years. When he returned to the office a week later, he couldn't even focus long enough to read an email. 'I'd stare at my computer screen for 10 minutes and not know what I was supposed to be doing.' He had blurred vision, headaches, no motivation. He was empty. Finally, he realised he could not go on, and he was signed off work for two months. He tells me it felt very similar to leaving Army college, and I ask him about the difference between the two: 'One was an actual experience of being told I was a failure,' he says, 'the other was something I created inside myself.'

Recognising this has been one of the most important grow-ups of Adam's entire life, and it has led him to this important insight: 'I think one of the things about growing up is actually having the ability to look after yourself.' For him, adulthood is 'having the self-awareness that you're causing yourself problems'. It is being patient with himself, taking the time to notice if he's working too hard, and be careful. It's deciding to leave the office so that he doesn't overwork himself and burn out again. My own sense of what an adult is — of what contents insurance is — begins to come into sharper focus as he says again, 'It's about looking after yourself.' Over the last year, he's learnt more about what those words mean to him — how to spot the signs that he is slipping back, how to react differently when he gets stressed. There are moments in his job where he thinks he could go all in, pull an all-nighter, try to be the hero who can do everything. But he notices that instinct, and he stops himself. He tells himself: 'No. I'm not going to do that, I'm going to go home to my wife, and do other things.' This is what growing up means for him.

I reflect on how the words 'Look after yourself' can have different meanings, depending on the tone, on the emphasis. '*Look after* yourself' can be a kind appeal to a friend to take care of themselves — 'Look after *yourself*' can be an aggressive rejection, a refusal to take care of somebody else. I suspect the tone of what it means to look after oneself can change very quickly in Adam's mind too, as in my own. But while Adam is learning how to look after himself, he is not there yet; this is a process that is very much ongoing and he is reliving this grow-up again and again. Just under a year before our interview, he decided to run the London Marathon. Prior to that decision, the extent of his running regime was to go for a jog every year on Christmas morning, for between 5 and 20 minutes. And yet he was soon pressurising himself to run a sub-four-hour marathon. He 'trained like crazy', he says. 'It would be -5 degrees outside, and I'd go for a 10k on a Tuesday night at 10 pm, come back, have an ice bath.' Just hearing about it makes me feel cold. He knew something was going on: 'I'm not a runner, and I never will be. I'm never going to be Mo Farah, right? But I was like, I want to be the champion, I'm going to impress the hell out of everyone.' It still took him a couple of months to realise what he was doing — that he was repeating the same pattern, still running away from failure. At that point, he could put a stop to it: 'I saw it for what it is, and I was like, look after yourself. Enough is enough. Just getting across the line and enjoying your day is a great thing.' And, for a while, running seemed to become a way out of repeating that pattern for Adam. He started to see his training as an opportunity to get some headspace, and he'd use the time to work out problems, to listen to podcasts, or to run with his friend on Saturday mornings. 'It was great, it became an enriching part of my life, rather than something to hurt me.' Perhaps this was true at the time, or perhaps it was a story Adam liked to tell himself — or perhaps it was both. Either way, it didn't last long. He began to feel the stress mounting at work and at home, and the pattern began to repeat itself, again, despite himself: he signed up to run an organised half-marathon once a month, and his own half-marathons every Saturday morning. About a month before coming to my flat, he felt a bad pain in his leg and went to the physio, who told him he had a stress fracture from overtraining. 'I limped home and I thought, I've done it again.' That realisation was a grow-up, I think — perhaps not so different from the one I faced in my first session with my analyst, when I began to understand that the running I had thought of as 'me time' and managing my anxiety was actually time I spent running away from myself.

When he tells me this story, I have an image in my mind of a little boy Adam, dressed in a Superman costume, standing on a window ledge getting ready to jump because he believes he can fly. At times of stress, Adam seems to experience a total denial of his limits — as if he cannot know what he is feeling in his body and his mind, what he can cope with and what he cannot; it takes a physio to tell him he has broken a bone to stop him training. I think he is right, an essential part of growing up is about taking care of yourself, but before we can do that, we have to know ourselves, to know our boundaries and our vulnerabilities, to know basic things like when we are feeling stressed, when our body hurts. I share this Superman image with him and he tells me, 'To some degree, for me, synonymous with adulthood is manhood. I guess the question is, what is a man?' One answer that most of us encounter as we make our way through the world is what society tells us that a man should be — as Adam puts it, 'You subliminally absorb that it's someone who can play sport, who can fight, who doesn't cry, who just gets on with it.' He is working his way towards a different answer: 'Manhood, I suppose, is finding out where you are, as a man. Because society gives us a twisted, warped version of what manhood should be. Manhood is what you define it as. What are you like? What are you like? What are you like? This is such a big question, and I think it must be difficult for him to know what kind of man he is, because he still hears that commanding officer's voice so loud and strong. He is so terrified of failing that he doesn't really know what it means just to be himself.

I can relate. I have never been to a military college, but I certainly have my own version of his commanding officer in my head. His voice was so much a part of me for so long, it was like that insidious background music you don't even notice is incredibly annoying because you are so used to it. I didn't know he was there until I started psychoanalytic psychotherapy, when he made himself felt in the very first session.

From the start, I experienced my therapist not as an understanding, containing, non-judgemental figure, but as an extremely critical and brutal teacher telling me I was doing everything wrong and I was a terrible person. I thought to myself, 'I'm paying this woman to help me, and all she's doing is criticising me! How rude!' But with time — and it felt like a really, really long time — she helped me to realise that something else entirely was going on. She might respond to a story I told her with something along the lines of 'I think you felt very out of control' — and I would hear something along the lines of 'YOU CRAZY WOMAN WHY ARE YOU SO CONTROLLING YOU ARE SUPPOSED TO BE A PATIENT AND HERE YOU ARE JUST WANTING TO CONTROL EVERYONE AND EVERYTHING WHY CAN YOU NOT GIVE UP YOUR INFANTILE OMNIPOTENT WISHES WHY ARE YOU SO SLOW AT THIS THANK GOD MY OTHER PATIENTS ARE NOT THIS BASIC AND YOU THINK YOU CAN BE A THERAPIST ONE DAY? JESUS H CHRIST WILL YOU GIVE UP ALREADY.' I would feel so attacked and criticised, and I'd tell her about that feeling. We'd talk about it and I would come to realise, consciously, that she had not in fact been critical of me, that she was accurately describing my state of mind — but I would still feel criticised. Then perhaps later that day, or the next, her words would float through my head and I'd think, 'She's right, when that happened I did feel really out of control.' I'd realise the words I had heard as so vicious and cutting were actually true; she had understood something.

It took me a surprisingly long time — embarrassingly long, given that I was also training in psychotherapy and was learning all about this as I was having the treatment — to realise that it was not my therapist who was criticising me. I was turning everything she said into a criticism. Analysis was giving me the chance to hear how I was talking to myself.

It was like I was hearing her voice through a filter, so that in my mind she became a perverse hybrid of an abusive policeman, an abusive teacher, and an abusive parent. One of the most ingenious of Freud's ideas was, in 1923, to draw a map of our minds, and to locate this policeman-parent-teacher hybrid function within it: he called it the 'superego'.[9] The first time I read about this, I thought: Oh yes, I've definitely got one of those. He described it as a psychological agency, the part of the mind that observes itself. It is partly conscious and partly unconscious, and functions as a conscience, tending towards perfectionism. We can think of the superego as an internalised parental authority — but often, the internal parental voice bears very little resemblance to the parents' voices in reality, as Freud wrote: 'The superego seems to have made a one-sided choice and to have picked out only the parents' strictness and severity, their prohibiting and punitive function, whereas their loving care seems not to have been taken over and maintained.'[10] So even if your parents were loving and caring, you could still end up with a brutal superego. That was one of Freud's most important discoveries; you do not have to have experienced violent trauma in external reality to suffer psychological distress in your internal world — although it helps.[11] In people experiencing a bout of depression, or as Freud called it, melancholia, a person's superego 'becomes over-severe, abuses the poor ego, humiliates it and ill-treats it, threatens it with the direst punishments, reproaches it for actions in the remotest past which had been taken lightly at the time'. Ah, I know it well. It is like the opposite of contents insurance; instead of an internal voice that looks after us and protects our sense of self-worth in a crisis, this is an internal voice that degrades, punishes, and diminishes whatever we might value in ourselves for the slightest slip-up.

In some better-adjusted, less neurotic people, the superego is not such a harsh, punitive, and tyrannical internal figure. I have yet to meet these people, but apparently, the books tell me, they do exist. There is such a thing as a helpful, motivating, nurturing superego; it can have a benign function, allowing us to feel contained, keeping us safe. When I first read about this, I thought, I don't know what this means. But some months ago I went on a charity run, and I found myself jogging in front of a man and a little boy, who I presumed was his son. As we ran, the father kept up a continual, gentle patter, and I couldn't help myself but listen: 'You're doing really well, that's it, just keep putting one foot in front of the other. Now, we've got a hill coming up, it doesn't look too steep so I think we can manage it — but if it gets too much, we can always stop. I think we can give it a good go though, it doesn't look that much steeper than the hill we've just done, and you made it up that one without stopping, so let's give it a go.' I know it sounds strange, but as I listened to his words, I felt huge emotion welling within me. It was like I was listening to the kind of internal voice I wish for, but do not have. Of course I know nothing about that boy or his father or their relationship, but from what I heard, it seemed to me like something very important was taking place, as if this man was — whether consciously or unconsciously — trying to give his son a superego that is protective, rather than punitive.

I recently came across a brilliantly titled paper, 'The good, the bad and the superego',[12] in which the psychoanalyst Bob Hinshelwood traces the biography of a superego in healthy development, from infancy to adulthood. Following the ideas of the psychoanalyst Melanie Klein, he explains that in early life the superego is characterised by 'mutual self-hatred and punishment', and, after a lot of to-ing and fro-ing, if all goes well, the adult superego sees 'the emergence of a self-forgiveness'. He writes: 'We need to consider the superego as a process, it is a journey from deathly punishments to forgiving reparation.'This, I think, is what it means for our superego to grow up. Mine and Adam's superegos still tend to err on the side of maniacal punitive monster — but we're working on it. As Adam has become more aware of his fear of failure, he has begun to confide more in some of his colleagues, and created a new kind of working culture where they help each other rather than compete against each other. As my analysis has progressed, as my analyst has offered me the chance to hear the harshness of my internal voice, something has begun to shift. The tone of it has changed. I think it has, if not softened, at least begun to wax and wane; it's not that the Commanding Officer has gone away, but he isn't always shouting, and I have started to feel less anxious, some of the time. It may sound small, but it is a start, and it has had a big impact on my quality of life — feeling anxious every day is a horrible experience, and I am no longer suffering in quite the same way. Nevertheless, the self-forgiving superego Hinshelwood describes still feels a long way off at times, and I feel an ache of longing for a grown-up superego like this — for an internal sense of forgiveness when things go wrong, a kind of resilience and robustness in the face of setbacks or disasters. These are the tools that enable us to truly look after ourselves, like that man was looking after his son. This is the kind of contents insurance I am in the market for — I just wish moneysavingexpert.com could tell me where to find it.

This quest for contents insurance I am on is a story that has been told in different ways and by different people for hundreds of years. In his history of modern adulthood, Mintz writes about the 18th century rise of the bildungsroman, the novel that traces the story of coming of age. These books, he writes, explore the transition 'from innocence to wisdom, ingenuousness to experience, naivety to maturity', tracking 'a young person's process of soul-searching and self-discovery'.[13] He gives examples from Jane Austen's *Pride and Prejudice* to Balzac's

Comédie humaine, through to more modern examples by Toni Morrison and J. D. Salinger. I wonder if we aren't going through something of a bildungsroman renaissance today, from thrilling new voices and in different forms. I'm thinking of the novels of Sally Rooney, who so crushingly captures the sense of alienation of the not-quite-adult, and then in describing it so tenderly, turns that sense of isolation into a feeling of connection. Of Michaela Coel's *I May Destroy You*, whose writing and performance brought to life the violence and rage and self-destruction we try not to see in ourselves, that we try to cover up on social media. And of one of the most original and compelling fictional characters I have encountered, Queenie, from the novel of the same name, by Candice Carty-Williams.[14]

Queenie is a Jamaican British 25-year-old woman trying to make her way through the worlds of work and love. She has a lot to battle with, from losses in her past and present to growing up as a Black woman in a racist society. The book opens with a gynaecological exam, and as the novel progresses, we develop an even more intimate relationship with Queenie's inside world. When I read this book, I wanted to know more about her creator. I knew she had something important to say about growing up and hoped she could help me figure out what an adult actually is.

'I really don't know what an adult looks like,' Carty-Williams, age 30, tells me. She has a mortgage, a good credit rating, good friendships, a good job, and those things seem to her to be some of the markers of adulthood; 'but adulthood also seems to be about a sense of self, I think, and I don't have that. I still feel like I'm 15. I feel like I'm a 15-year-old doing adult things. So I am playing as an adult, but I'm not an adult yet,' she says, quickly adding, 'maybe'. She is just as confused about it all as I am. A friend recently asked her, wouldn't she rather be called a 'woman' than a 'girl'? 'And I was like, well, I don't know. I don't know at what point I'll feel like a woman. I still feel like I'm a girl, struggling, who's still not there quite yet.' This is something she thinks about often, what it means to be 'a functioning adult'. When she was younger, she thought that part of being an adult is about not being afraid to do things — but she seems to feel more afraid of things as she gets older, not less. 'I always think I should be better at being fearless or more confident. But then I think I also have to respect the person that I am, and I'll get there at some point, but I'm just really not there yet, you know?' Oh, I do know, I do know.

She conveys a clear understanding of why she thinks she feels this way. 'My parents have not given me a framework of being people who are together and self-sufficient in any way,' she says. She helps her mother financially, and recent conversations with her father, who was out of touch for years, have exclusively been about her giving him money or paying off his mortgage. A lot of being a grown-up for her is about money — and she knows why. 'I grew up poor. You know when you have your gas and electric on card and key respectively? The people who lived there before us had jimmied with the gas card so you never had to top it up. If we had had to pay, we would have been fucked. It's the old classic — we had to choose between food and electricity sometimes.' This is why she feels so afraid — she lives in fear that she will be thrust back into poverty, that the financially secure life she has built for herself will be taken from her. It is a particularly powerful fear: 'There is nothing quite like being anxious about money, as we know. It has its own unique feeling in the body and the brain.' And it spawns many others: 'I guess I'm scared that I can't help my mum. That is my biggest fear, because when we didn't have anything, she always made sure that me and my sister had enough.' In growing up, she has defined herself in opposition to her parents; everything she does is focussed on being able to rely entirely on herself. If there's anything that needs doing in her house — if a fuse needs changing, if her boiler breaks down — she can fix it. 'I taught myself to do that a long time ago. I don't like relying on people.' It is as if she has done all the research into contents insurance and has got the best deal on the right policy — but she feels she lacks the psychological kind. Because what looks like responsibility and self-reliance on the outside does not necessarily feel that way on the inside. As a child, she had a fear of being left behind: 'My dad wasn't really there, and my mum was in and out, and so I always had a fear of being abandoned.' About a year ago, she realised that this fear has never left her — she is still operating under the assumption that everyone is going to leave, and that, she feels, 'is a very childlike thing'. At times, 'it makes me feel like I'm eight years old and I'm wondering if my dad is coming at the weekend.'

I tell her about Arnett's theory of Emerging Adulthood, and she likes the idea that we grow into adults over this elongated period following adolescence — but she says, 'I think the suggestion that when we're 30, we are an adult — I can't find that for myself.' She is 30, but she feels 15; she is a full-grown woman, but she is also still a young girl, 'vulnerable and fearful'. She asks herself, 'What is adulthood, when that inner child is always going to be there?' But the question doesn't sit quite right with her, because from the time she was born, she was never the child: her nickname was Mother. As soon as she was old enough to talk, adults in the family would confide their secrets and their problems in her. She understood from this that she was strong, that she should look after people and listen to their problems and try to solve them; 'That I should basically be an adult from a really tiny age, which I think is a form of abuse, when you're telling a child that so-and-so had an affair and your co-worker did this and that person wants to do this to you.' We are familiar with thinking of child labour as a form of abuse, but she is talking about the emotional labour which many adults unconsciously expect the children in their care to perform, and which is equally disturbing.

When Carty-Williams was in her early 20s, she fell into a nervous and depressive episode, and this brought with it a new kind of understanding of what had happened to her growing up. 'For as long as I could remember, I've been trying to be an adult and look after everyone. I had never been allowed to be a child. And no child should ever have to go through that,' she says. How can you grow up when you have not been a child, I wonder. This is the danger of finding oneself in the adult department too early. 'I think there's a part of me that's like, fuck being an adult, because I've been trying to be an adult all my life, and it's hard, and I'm not ready, and I wasn't ready.' She is done trying to be strong. 'The strong Black woman is such a thing. It's a really horrible, oppressive thing. I think that Black women are often the carriers of other people's problems, because people understand that we are strong and that we must carry everything. And that really is a very cruel space to occupy, because we already have our own shit.'

What has helped her is her friends. The people she speaks to daily are her Black female friends, 'and I've never felt so valid or seen or understood in all my life,' she says. They all have different backgrounds — she is of Jamaican and Indian heritage, and they have Nigerian and Jamaican and Ugandan and Ghanaian and Trinidadian roots — and yet by many people in this country, they are seen as the same, and that means they have something important in common; 'I think we all get what it means to be navigating this world and this space as a Black woman.' When she was younger she had a lot of white friends, and when she tried to talk to them about her experiences, there was lots of 'oh, you're imagining that', 'don't take that so seriously', 'just lighten up'. But with the friends she has now, the response is very different: 'I understand that, I'm sorry that that happened to you, would you like to talk about it?' Or 'Let's talk about it when you've processed it a bit more.' She says this has transformed the way she feels about herself; it's the difference between feeling hurt by something and then being told you're overreacting, and feeling hurt by something and knowing that you are valid and seen and that you have space, that you're allowed to feel hurt. These relationships are what has nourished her, sustained her, helped her to develop. 'That has made me feel most myself, I guess — rather than most adult. Maybe being myself is the best I can do at this point on this journey to what is maybe going to be adulthood.' I wonder if, maybe, being herself and growing up are not so different.

One of the most powerful moments from our conversation comes when she says sadly, angrily, 'Why wasn't I just allowed to have parents who chatted to themselves about money problems or problems in the family. Let me be a kid, let me read books, let me go and hang out with my friends.' This is grief, real grief at being locked in the adult department way too early, and with no way out. She is very envious, she says of people who had 'what looks like a normal childhood. But I know that's not a real thing. I think a normal childhood is as fairy tale as *Cinderella*.'

I agree with Carty-Williams, that the notion of a 'normal childhood' is a fairy tale. But in studying the theories that different psychoanalysts have elaborated about how an infant's mind grows and develops, I have absorbed an image of what a nurturing, healthy, good enough childhood might look like. It is an image that begins to come to life when I speak to Gianna Williams, a child and adult psychoanalyst and Member of the British Psychoanalytical Society. I am particularly keen to speak with her, because for the past six years she has led infant observation seminars for trainee psychoanalysts. She has learned and taught about infants in Italy, France, Spain, Turkey, and Latin American countries, and so she knows something about what links the early life of babies in different parts of the world. When we meet in her comfortable and warm consulting room in Hampstead, north London, I sit down in the seat her patients would normally occupy and take in the atmosphere — there is something about the place that creates a feeling of quiet productivity, of a mind at work. Williams tells me, in a thoughtful, gentle, rhythmic voice, 'It has been very interesting to hear about infants in different cultures. But although certain aspects might be different because of the culture, I think there is something that I have found that is very central to infancy that doesn't depend on the culture: the feeling of being held.'

This feeling of being held is understood by psychoanalysts not simply as a physical experience. While the baby's body is held in the parent's arms, the baby's mind is held in the parent's mind, bringing a sense of comfort, of groundedness, of continuity. And when a parent is psychologically healthy and able, they will, through empathy and understanding, use their mind to help the infant to process some of the feelings and difficulties the child is not yet developed enough to make sense of. There is a beautiful name for this, which has filled me with a kind of warm fascination from the first time I heard it: reverie. The revolutionary psychoanalyst Wilfred Bion used the word reverie to describe, among other things, what I understand as a kind of loving conversation between a parent and their baby, that doesn't take place through words alone. Williams says: 'I think real reverie is the parent saying, "I wonder what the matter is? Could it be this? Could it be that?" And the infant perceives this attention, and this attempt to understand him.'

This is one of Bion's most compelling ideas: as Paolo Cesar Sandler writes in *The Language of Bion: a dictionary of concepts*, Bion took nine years to develop it, and 'the deepest and most secret mysteries of human life are explored within this theory'.[15] I have only a beginner's understanding of it, which I think will nevertheless be enough to get us somewhere.[16] His theory is based on the notion that when we are born, we are born into a terrifying state of newness. We are totally helpless, experiencing a maelstrom of never-before-felt sensations and emotions in our body and mind that seem to be bursting out of us, uncontrolled and uncontrollable; little wonder, then, that babies scream like they do. A loving parent, by holding the baby in their arms and in their mind, by trying to make sense of what their baby is experiencing and to symbolise it, to put it into words — by reverie — can become the container for these overwhelming feelings. It is like the parent is chewing the emotional cud, digesting the baby's feelings to feed them back in a more manageable form. If all goes well, the feelings then become less overwhelming, less terrifying, and the baby has the experience of feeling contained. Williams explains this is a process of trying to understand, not just hitting the nail on the head, but exploring through trial and error — could it be hunger? Could he want a cuddle? Could it be she is in pain and cannot tell me what is bothering her? 'I think "I wonder" is a very important part of reverie and the containment process. There is a feeling of containment in feeling that there is a real attempt to make sense of something, rather than a certainty,' she says. This is not necessarily something that happens out loud — it is a state of mind. It is this instinctive gift of attention, the ability to be with uncertainty and to bear not knowing, from the parents who are able to give it, that ultimately allows their baby to develop the capacity, eventually, to contain themselves. It allows the baby, then the child, then the adult, to develop their own thinking, feeling mind, to symbolise their emotions without being overwhelmed, to be self-contained. This is how we learn to look after ourselves. This containment is a kind of contents insurance — and it is fundamental to growing up.

When I'm with Roxy Legane, I think, 'This is a woman with contents insurance' — and I don't mean the moneysavingexpert kind. I ask her if she considers herself grown up, and she tells me, 'I'm not a child any more. I have a lot of adult responsibilities — but I still feel young.' She is 28 and runs an organisation she started called Kids of Colour, which provides a space for young people to explore their experiences of race and identity. When she is with young people, listening to them talk about what they're going through and the support they need, often she feels she can provide that support, and in those moments, she feels like a responsible adult. 'And then, on my days off … I can feel like a child again.' This sense of feeling like a child is quite nebulous, not so much expressed through activities like playing or running around, but something to do with how she feels in herself; 'just, my way of being can be more childlike', which I understand to mean more vulnerable, the one who needs support rather than the one giving it. For her, this life stage is characterised by a feeling of 'You've got to pull it together, because you can't blame it on being in your early 20s any more.' She is not referring to getting a job or a house or a partner, but to something more day-to-day. 'There are things now that I have to reflect on more, because I can't just keep making excuses for my behaviour.' For example, she has had problems with alcohol since her teens, and for the last decade she has thought she probably shouldn't drink, but it is only in the last year that she has stopped drinking. She explains, 'When you're early 20s and screwing things up, you can sweep it under the carpet and get away with stuff, not address it, allow yourself to continue to fall into that hole.' Now, at 28, she feels she can no longer afford to sweep things under the carpet. She is studying, working, engaged in different projects, and supporting different young people. 'I need to be okay. I can't continue down that path any more.' She is a woman with things to do.

When she thinks about adulthood, she says, 'boring things come to mind. Just responsibilities, the mundane everyday — the things you don't want to do.' Then she corrects herself: 'But actually, I know in my daily life that what being an adult brings is a freedom and choices that you didn't have when you were younger, growing independence, and growing confidence in yourself.' When she says this, I think, Aha! I knew it! I knew there was more to adulthood than kitchen units! I think that is a crucial grow-up at this life stage: to find, or at least begin the search for a definition of adult life that is more profound than kitchen units, more substantial than pine nuts on your salad, more bearable than a heavy, impenetrable tortoise shell. To find a way to exist in the adult world that has real meaning.

She is pretty happy being an adult at the moment. She hasn't always felt this way — and she does recognise she almost certainly won't always. She tells me it is an interesting moment for us to be having this conversation, because if we had spoken four years earlier, it would have been very different. 'I think I was just sadder, maybe.' She used to compare herself negatively to her peers — some of whom own houses and have big salaries and impressive job titles — and find herself wanting. But that internal conversation has shifted since she launched Kids of Colour in 2018. 'I've started to make a space for myself in an area of work that I am really interested in and enjoy, and that I can do.' She's meeting people she looks up to as role models, and her work and her activism have become such a central, core part of her life now that she doesn't really think about houses and salaries and job titles any more. Her loved ones have noticed, and they say things like 'she's really come into her own'. And that does seem to be what's happened. 'I've found this space that I feel happy in. I like what I do, I think I'm good at it, and I think it's important.'

I ask her about the challenges that young people of colour in particular face when it comes to growing up. She tells me that the biggest impact is on young people's confidence in themselves: 'If you've got young people who are suffering racism from every angle — and I think particularly young Black boys in this case — they're not starting from the same point as other people going into adulthood, because their confidence has often been diminished, along with their self-worth.' Then there is the huge impact of racism on their mental health, there is the trauma of being over-policed, of being told constantly that they're aggressive and threatening, of being seen as less able, and there is so little mental health support that focusses specifically on racism. Just as troubling is the fact that our education system does not reflect on race or on how these experiences might have a long-lasting impact on children in their development. She tells me that young people of colour experience constant knock-backs at school, and gives one example of many she could choose from. In a workshop she ran, a girl shared her experience of other students saying it was unfair that she was so fast at running; that it was because she was Black. 'And the result of that was that she had to run in a heat by herself at sports day. She was one of the only Black girls at this school in a particularly white area.' How othered this girl must have felt, when this wonderful talent she had trained so hard to hone was reduced in this way by the envy of others, used to bully her. Another young woman told of an experience she had while at school, within the last decade, in which a teacher made them play a shockingly racist board game. 'You won if you had the most slaves on your slave ship at the end of the game. It was a slavery boardgame he had made himself.' Just telling this story left this young woman shaken up.

And these experiences do not ease as young people leave education for the workplace. Those Legane meets are anxious about job interviews because they question whether they have to change their hair, the way they speak, the way they hold themselves. 'They're already struggling with being exposed to racism in the workplace, but feeling that they can't address it because they don't want to lose their jobs. So they're having to sacrifice their integrity on things and keep quiet, just because it's safer,' she says. And it is just at this time, when adult life is supposed to be taking off — when we are supposed to be taking out contents insurance both internal and external — that the young people Legane meets are able to begin to deal with trauma of racism from their childhood. There is no space in our society to explore and talk about the deep impact of racism, she explains, so young people of colour find themselves carrying the weight of these experiences into their adult life — it is only in early adulthood as they begin to develop the emotional language to articulate their feelings, that they can begin to work through their suffering. The early 20s, she says, can often be a healing period, 'which can be hard and really exhausting — and also really valuable'. She is keen that I understand that racism does not define the young people she works with; there is much more to them than these difficult experiences. 'So much of their joy and happiness can come from being a young person of colour, from their identities, cultures, and faiths. It's also beautiful to see young people celebrating who they are, and I think as they grow up and their confidence grows, that celebration can grow too.'

As a mixed-race woman with a white British mother and a Black father from Mauritius, Legane's experiences of racism have a particular texture. She is racialised differently from both her parents in our society, and often people don't know what to make of her. She is viewed as other, but, she says, 'It's actually quite difficult to articulate, because you're never sure what's happening to you. I've been invited into white spaces because of my privilege and proximity to whiteness — but in those spaces, people might be quite racist in front of you because they view you with a white lens — but then, at the same time, also see you as a person of colour.' She gives an example from her school days of a white girl saying to her, 'Oh, you're actually really nice; I thought you were gonna be a lot more ghetto.' That statement feels so twisted, I can only imagine what it might have been like to hear it as a teenager — to be so aggressively othered in your group of friends, and to have that presented as a compliment. 'You're welcomed into white spaces as a mixed-race person, so you naively think things are fine, and then things like that come up,' she explains. 'If you're racialised, you're viewed as the other. You never know what you're going to face,' she says, adding, 'I definitely wished I was white as a child.'

She does not feel like that any more. Part of growing up for Legane has been developing an appreciation for her identity, for what she looks like, for her work and what she can bring to it. But that has not meant erasing the little girl who struggled. When she hears particularly upsetting stories at work, she'll go home and, 'sometimes just cry, and not really want to talk about it, not want to address it'. I find myself thinking about what she says next long after our interview ends: 'I guess you could say those are childlike responses — but actually, I still think they're a part of me working out how to deal with these things. I'm trying to make sure that I am flexible with how I allow myself to respond to everything. I'm trying to allow myself a varied number of adult ways of responding, and to know that it's okay sometimes just to shut off. It might come across to people as quite juvenile, but actually it's a coping strategy as an adult.'

I am quite stunned when I hear this — I think it might be one of the most grown-up things I have ever heard. What a generous, kind way of responding to yourself, to your less grown-up parts; to be in a state of internal reverie; to truly look after yourself, all the different parts of yourself. That is what I call contents insurance.

This is helping me to see that growing up can mean something real. An adult does not have to be someone who is obsessed with kitchen units, but can be someone who knows who she is and understands herself, her reactions and her responses. I do not mean to put Legane on a plinth for us to worship as some kind of perfect, godlike adult, and I am not saying, this is what a grown-up is. But I am beginning to feel something solidifying in my mind, as if in the grey clouds of confusion that surround me, I can just about make out the outline of something which may lead me towards a deeper understanding of what it means to grow up.

'We are like trees,' Williams tells me. Through her work observing babies and analysing patients including children, adolescents, and adults, she has developed a profound understanding of what it means to grow up, and she shares with me a beautiful image that captures how she thinks about it. If you look at the cross section of a tree trunk, she says, you will see the rings that mark the history of that tree: at its core you find the smallest ring from its earliest days, with rings getting bigger and bigger as the tree has grown upwards and outwards, through to the newest ring covered up by the bark on the outside. We still contain a baby part, a child part, an adolescent part — they never go away, they are always there, under the bark, under our skin. She tells me how, as a therapist, 'All my experience with children is very, very useful in my work with adult patients. And I think we're always finding the infant, the young child, the adolescent in the patient. Like the circles in a tree, they're all there.' Boru, Victoria, Samuel, Adam, Carty-Williams, Legane, me — we are all working out how to take care of ourselves, the different rings inside us, to insure our valuable contents. Growing up at this life stage means developing the capacity to do this — to tolerate and attend to and take care of the smallest rings inside us when we are in distress, to wonder what might be wrong without leaping to conclusions or solutions, to hold on to ourselves. To find a more meaningful sense of adulthood, one that isn't quite so warped by being thrust into the adult department before we were ready. I still don't have contents insurance, but as I type these words, I think, what a novel idea, and I realise something for the first time: what I have inside me, even if it is just wisps of smoke right now, it has value, and it is worth insuring. Perhaps this is what psychoanalysis means to me; perhaps psychoanalysis is like a very, very, very expensive kind of contents insurance. My childlike feelings are not something to be dismissed, to be beaten down, to be policed and sent to prison; they can be contained, thought about, understood. This is central to the definition we are building of what it means to grow up, and it is central to this life stage, when we are no longer right at the beginning of adult life, but still early in the process of finding out who we are. Meeting these people, writing about these ideas, having psychoanalysis, has opened a window. I can feel movement, like a breeze is blowing through my mind, rustling whatever's there, blowing the dust away. I can feel something changing inside me.

Chapter Three
The ghosts in the nursery

'Ghostbusters'
Song by Ray Parker, Jr.

A baby is hungry. She cries urgently, and her father recognises the call; heeding the need for food and comfort, he brings her the bottle. But unlike the last feed, when she speedily took the teat in her mouth and sucked with satisfaction, this time she spits it out angrily. It is like the bottle has gone from something good to something bad. She cries panicked, hiccoughing cries.

Her father persists. He talks to her in a soothing voice, he sings to her, and she begins to calm. He gently presses the teat into her mouth and she spits it out again, but with less venom. He tries again, and she takes the teat into her mouth. There is a short pause, and he holds his breath. He feels the pull of his daughter's suckle, and the rhythmic rise and fall of the bottle in his hand, of her chest in his arms. He breathes out. The bottle has become something good once more.

As I begin to work on this chapter, I am afraid. I'm scared of what I will feel, of what longings and truths I will come to know through its writing. The nursery and all it houses — pregnancy, parenthood, growing up — has always felt so far away for me. Starting a family has only ever been something I could speak about in the future conditional, something I might want one day, someday, but not yet. In all these years, that psychological reality has not changed — but so much else around it has. The biological reality now is that I can no longer afford to think in terms of one day, someday, not yet; I have entered my mid-30s, and in the economy of fertility, the currency is time and I am spending beyond my means. The social reality now is that most of my friends have had children, or are trying to. I am surrounded by motherhood or its potential, engulfed and at times suffocated by the motherhood of other women. Yet more suffocating is my own indecision, my own oscillation between wanting and not wanting; one day, I think, yes, I do want to have and love a child, to raise that child, and to be its mother, to be a family. The next day, I think, no, I am not ready, I am not grown up enough, I do not want to make the necessary sacrifices. As I ricochet between certainties, I find myself less sure of everything, especially myself.

'Ghosts in the nursery'[1] is the name of a famous psychoanalytic paper, the one that made me realise I couldn't not study the ideas of psychoanalysis. I read it and then I made my husband read it, and then I made my mother read it, and they both understood something about why I felt I needed to be a therapist. It is such an evocative phrase, the ghosts in the nursery, and it means different things to me at different moments. For this chapter, the ghosts in the nursery are the unresolved traumas and conflicts, the early experiences and necessarily forgotten emotions that cannot be known about, our deep-seated fears and doubts that are too powerful to be felt. Helplessness, need, terror. They simmer away in our unconscious most of the time, but at significant moments — moments of change and upheaval, moments where we face the most major grow-ups of our lives, when the heat is turned up — they bubble up to and over the surface. There are many of these significant moments that make the temperature rise in our inner world: starting school, leaving home, finding a partner, breaking up, becoming a grandparent, retiring, facing one's own death. But perhaps the most demanding of all of these grow-ups is becoming a parent. If we do this, we have to face that we are moving up a generation, taking on the role of our parents or carers, becoming for another what the first and most significant others in our lives were for us. It involves enormous loss which often goes unmourned, perhaps because of the excitement of a new baby, perhaps because parents feel guilty for feeling it; this is the loss that comes with growing up, the loss that accompanies change and development. In the nursery, at least, we become the adults in the room. We are the grown-ups. Or we are supposed to be anyway.

But it is not just those who have children, or who can have children, who come to face the nursery's ghosts at this life stage — my ghosts are raging, even though I have no nursery, and don't know if I ever will. Those who do not become parents also have to face demanding grow-ups. This life stage is when relationship and reproductive possibilities become most urgent, whether or not they are fulfilled; it's when we are meant to be our most productive at work; and it's also when I have become most aware that I am supposed to be a grown-up by now. When I see that it has been referred to in the psychology literature as 'the rush hour of life',[2] I give a hollow laugh of recognition; no wonder I am feeling stressed, stuck, and angry at everyone. It is the period described as 'Established adulthood: a new conception of ages 30 to 45'[3] by Associate Professor of Psychology at Emmanuel College, Boston, Massachusettes, Clare Mehta and colleagues. The precise timing of each individual's passage through this phase will depend on biological, social, and cultural factors, of course — upon the expectations we and those around us have of ourselves. And while many people do cement relationships and have children earlier in life than this, Mehta and her colleagues report that in developed countries, 'work and family life transitions that historically took place when people first reached their twenties are now typically taking place when people reach their thirties'.[4] Between 2000 and 2014, the proportion of first births to women aged over 30 rose in developed countries, declining among younger women.[5] I wonder how this will play out in the decades to come; whether more of us might not become parents at all, if families might grow smaller.[6] In 2019, Australia hit its lowest birth rate since records began in 1935.[7] For some it may be a choice, for others it is a question of biological, social, or financial infertility, as people cannot conceive, cannot find a partner they want to have a child with, or cannot afford to start a family. These shifts are shaping our choices and our expectations, and even fertile people who do not begin or end their families in their 30s and early 40s, or who choose not to have children, nevertheless move through this period of life in the biological reality that their fertility is declining — both women and men — whether they know it or not. Whether you want to have a child or you don't, at this time of life, it is near impossible to avoid the question.

While adulthood may not necessarily involve becoming a parent, many people who have children tell me that becoming a parent is what made them into an adult. This is a very seductive idea. 'Wait until you have kids,' they tell me, more than a little presumptuously, 'then you'll feel like a grown-up.' It is almost enough to convince me to give it a try — almost, but not quite. I have the feeling that although the parenthood = adulthood equation seems ubiquitous, it doesn't always add up.

Tina Miller, Professor of Sociology at Oxford Brookes University, tells me that for many of the dozens of parents she has interviewed, a positive pregnancy test made people feel 'I've got to grow up now'. She conducted several fascinating studies in the late 1990s, early 2000s, and late 2010s, asking first-time parents about their experiences. She found that the transition to parenthood is often taken as a marker of adulthood, and having to be a grown-up is seen as a key aspect of being a parent. 'There's a real sense of having reached a new stage and having to be different in some way,' she says. In our society, 'Being a mother, being a father — they're such taken-for-granted dimensions of adulthood. It's part of the expected adult life trajectory.' And if you decide not to become a mother or a father — but particularly if you decide not to become a mother, she emphasises, because we so assume that of adult women — you're often having to explain why. But it wasn't only becoming a parent that led Miller to feel like she had made it to adulthood; even after having her children, she always asked herself what she would do when she grew up. It was only a few years ago when she became a professor, that she suddenly thought: 'Oh, I think this probably *is* what I do, and that must mean I'm grown up. I'm an adult.' She is in her early 50s.

As the author of three books, *Making Sense of Motherhood*, *Making Sense of Fatherhood*, and *Making Sense of Parenthood*,[8] she has learnt something about the growing up that can unfold — or not — in the making of a parent. A word that came up over and over again in our interview — as it did for Arnett and his interviews with emerging adults and as it did in my interview with Sam — was responsibility. Miller says, 'The big thing about being a mother or father is that there are responsibilities that have to be taken on. I can't think of any other way of describing it; a baby does have to be fed, does have to be dressed and occasionally taken out of the house — at a fairly basic level. And I think everyone is overwhelmed by those responsibilities.' On top of that, as we heard in the last chapter, there are also the even more demanding emotional responsibilities, to do with containing a baby's anxieties and distress, as well as one's own. Fulfilling the practical responsibilities Miller describes signals a form of adult practice, but it is not that straightforward: 'Within that, you sort of feel like you've lost yourself.' Many of the mothers she spoke to described the experience of going out with their baby and everyone else seeing them as a mother when they don't feel like one. They'd speak of sitting on the bus with a crying baby, feeling the eyes of the other passengers on them, the weight of expectation that they should know what to do. 'Being out and about with a new baby, you can feel so vulnerable because you can't perform this in a way that you think adult motherhood should be performed.' Society expects mothers to be adult women, and they may look like a grown-up parent on the outside, with a child to show for it and everything — but on the inside, many feel anything but; they might feel scared and helpless, less like an adult and more like a baby. Clearly the equation cannot be as simple as 'responsibilities = parenthood = adulthood' — at least, not for everyone. If it were, all those ghosts haunting all those nurseries would be out of a job.

When I arrive at Rose's home in Bristol, her 21-month-old has just done a wee on the floor. Her partner is cleaning it up — he waves to me from the other side of the kitchen — and Rose grabs a cloth to clean a second patch. Her child comes to watch her, and as Rose works on the stain, she tells her, 'See, that's where it was, now we've cleared it up. Do you want to see the mark where it was? Can you see it?' She is 37-weeks pregnant, and I can see the effort it takes for her to stand up. Her partner and child go out for a walk, and Rose and I settle in the front room, Rose trying to get comfortable on a beanbag, me on the sofa. She is striking, with arresting blue eyes, her hair long on one side, cropped short on the other. I wonder about these different sides, the multiplicity of selves housed within her. Not long after we sit down, she is telling me about the birth of her sister when she was 18 months old, about her mother, about her grandmother, and I can feel the ghosts from her nursery coming to join us. It doesn't feel like they are haunting us — more like sitting with us for a cup of tea, inspecting the books on the bookshelves, nodding along as Rose tells their stories, which are now hers too.

She tells me a little about what she was like as a child, how she liked to organise the button box and the clothes pegs. She remembers being at a coffee morning with her mum and falling over, cracking open her lip, and 'being scooped up and looked after'. She says, 'I remember giant tulips in the garden. I remember going into the freezer in the shed just outside the back door, nibbling away at my ice lolly and then putting it back because I wasn't allowed to be doing that. I remember talcum powder footprints round the fireplace at Christmas.' She talks about being at school and discovering her sexuality — 'So I'm 13, and

I'm a girl, and I fancy women really badly. And men.' — and about the bisexual erasure she has experienced as a bisexual woman who is also married to the father of her child. 'I look very traditional from the outside. I don't look bisexual. But I think sexuality is so many things.'

When I ask if she is now, at 33, a grown-up, she tells me, 'On paper, yeah. I've got a mortgage, I'm married, I've got a child and one on the way.' Underneath that paper, though, there is a more nuanced story, and as she has grown up, her understanding of what it means to grow up has changed. When she was younger, she had 'this massive need to live happily ever after — which is about becoming grown up'. She really wanted to get married, to have a house, to have children — to have what her parents had. Back then, for her, these were the markers of success, of being an adult. She would always talk about wanting children, but she sees now that she didn't, not truly. 'I only wanted them so I can live happily ever after. It was never a real kind of wanting.' This is such an insightful thing to say, and I can recognise it in myself too. When I type up our interview, I realise that I had been thinking what a great ending it would be for this book if I were pregnant as I wrote the last chapter. Now I can see this was a fantasy of a happily-ever-after, successful-adult ending; not a real kind of wanting. As Rose's words take up residence in my mind, their meaning echoes and bounces around, and I sense they will be very important for me in understanding what it means to grow up at this life stage.

Rose has found that the journey towards adulthood, whatever that looks like, is not so linear as she had imagined when she was younger — in fact, she felt the most grown-up she has ever felt just before her first pregnancy. She says, 'I'd got to a really nice point in my life. I was being an adult. I was making adult decisions. The adult me was much more present, was the biggest part of me.' But as her body changed and her belly grew, that grown-up feeling disappeared. She felt shocked that she didn't feel confident or in control, not at all 'like this Mother Earth figure, which I think maybe everyone expected of me, and I expected of myself, as part of this living happily ever after'. The physical symptoms, which she describes as one massive hangover with nausea that lasted 18 weeks, were not as disturbing as what she experienced psychologically. She felt fragmented, as if she were falling apart, like she was struggling to hold all the different parts of her mind together. 'I needed to be held like a child, like a baby. I was desperate for my mum to really hold me, and dealing with the fact that she couldn't in the way that I needed her to.' Her voice breaks and her eyes shine, and as she starts to cry, she seems at the same time very vulnerable and very strong. I pass her some tissues. 'I knew this was going to be emotional. I'm all right crying,' she says, and I sense that it is not to make me feel more comfortable, but because she knows it to be true. 'It was really this craving, this needing, and not being able to say enough how much I needed from either of my parents.' Having felt so adult before, once pregnant she felt more like a baby; desperate to be held, but without the words to communicate her needs.

Although this was very disturbing for Rose, I wonder if after she recovered, having been in this infant-like state might have helped her to empathise with her baby and the terrifying experience of being a newborn. I wonder if going through such distress, helplessness, and fear might have helped her to understand her baby's state of mind, and in turn support her baby to grow through it. The idea of parents getting down to their children's level can be seen very clearly in baby talk — what researchers call 'parentese'. You know what I'm talking about; the instinctive way most of us change our voices and our vocabulary when we talk to children, speaking more slowly and simply, expanding our vowels, and lowering the pitch of our voices. The social psychologist Niarán Ramírez-Esparza, Associate Professor of Psychological Science at the University of Connecticut, Storrs, tells me about some fascinating studies she conducted with language researchers, to explore the impact that parentese has on language development in children.[9] As part of one study, 26 families with one-year-old children were given a light-weight digital voice recorder and a special vest with a pocket for it on the front, where the device could sit unnoticed against the child's chest. Each family made recordings of about 32 hours which Ramírez-Esparza and her team then divided up into regular time intervals, using software to identify who was talking when and to code different behaviours. The researchers were particularly interested in who was talking — an adult or an infant — and if the adult was using regular speech or parentese speech. They did follow-up studies to see how these children's language skills had developed, and the results were striking. They found a positive correlation between the adults' use of parentese and the infants' speech development: in families who used the most parentese in a one-on-one context, the infant had 433 words at two years old, while those who had heard less parentese had 169 words — and this correlation remains significant up to 33 months of age. Ramírez-Esparza tells me that this was the first time anyone had investigated parentese speech in family homes rather than in a lab, and she was surprised by just how clear the results were. The trend remained significant even when researchers controlled for the influence of socio-economic background. Isn't it amazing, I ask her, that we instinctively speak to children in a way that facilitates their language development? 'Yes, absolutely,' she replies, 'It's so impressive how people just naturally do this. They're not thinking about it, but when they approach a baby, they speak slower, they speak with this clarity, and in simple ways, being very empathetic.' It's as if we find a part in ourselves that can relate to what a baby needs. We think we have to be adults to be a good parent — and of course we do in some ways — but it seems to me a significant part of being a parent is also about being able to get in touch with the baby part of ourselves, to give that part a voice, and speak from there.

In the process of getting to know the baby part of herself, Rose has also met some of the ghosts in her nursery — they come from generations back. She alludes to family secrets and hidden traumas that still cannot be spoken, not among her relatives nor to me. She talks of the complicated emotional relationship between her great-grandmother and her grandmother, between her grandmother and her mother, and how she feels this has played out, more subtly, in the relationship between her mother and herself. 'As I brought my first child into the world, I was reliving my experiences of being brought into the world, but also reliving my mum's and my granny's. The story never ended. There's always a story with a little person who just tried really hard and was also vulnerable and had really difficult things to deal with.' Her great-grandmother was the eldest of her siblings, her grandmother was the eldest of hers, her mother was the eldest of hers, and so is Rose — and in a few weeks' time, her first child will become the older sibling too. As the eldest, Rose has inherited the wedding rings of the three generations of women before her. Rose knows these rings have meaning, but she is not quite sure what it is. She does know what it isn't, though: 'It's not this romantic fairy tale of these wonderful women in my life, these magnificent powerful women; they're just real people who were really vulnerable, had a load of crap to deal with, and just came out sort of in the middle ground, as good as they could be, and sometimes not good enough.' As I listen to Rose's stories, I can hear a different story underneath — a ghost story with a twist. It is like she is telling me, there are ghosts in this nursery, of course there are, but they are sitting here with us and that's okay. They used to be scary, but they're all right now, and she is in charge, not them; to paraphrase the song from the opening of this chapter, she is not afraid of any ghosts.

Rose's second pregnancy has been a very different experience. She thinks it is because she has learnt from the first time and now does not feel so at sea. 'This time, I don't feel like I've become a baby,' she says. She has told both her mother and father that she values and wants their emotional support, saying to them, 'I really need you. I really want you to know that.' Instead of feeling like a helpless infant who does not know what she wants nor how to communicate that, she feels like an adult asking for adult things. 'Like an adult asking other adults to parent me, hoping they can meet my needs, and also knowing that they may not be able to, that this is part of the story, and that I can tolerate that and survive.' It sounds very grown up to me.

But now Rose finds herself tangled up with another ghost. Her earliest experience of what happens when you have a baby was her younger sister coming along. She says, 'I think that was really traumatic for me — I was 18 months old, my dad was away a lot, and my sister cried a lot, and she needed to be held, she needed to be held very tightly.' Rose's mother tells her that she was a very content child, always happy, never causing problems — but Rose believes that this was a reaction to her sister's birth, that she felt she had to be a good girl. Now, she worries that her child, who at 18 months is about to become an older sibling, will face the same experience — which she imagines may have also been faced by her mother, grandmother, and great-grandmother, all firstborns. 'There are so many circles retelling the same story,' she tells me, and as I reflect on those words, I think it is a wonderful way of describing the ghosts in the nursery — the circles telling the same story, like the rings she has inherited. But she also seems to be saying that because of the understanding she has developed of herself and her feelings, she doesn't have to retell the same story; she can write a different one, by listening in a different way. She is getting ready to hold her first child more tightly again. 'I am thinking about how she will react to the new baby. If she seems fine, I'm not going to take that as her being fine, she might just be coping in a particular way. Of course, she might just be a complete arsehole, and that's another way of coping, isn't it? I think with both situations, she just needs to be held a bit more. I don't want her to be the big girl.' A new story is being written.

The writing of a new story is central to the 'Ghosts in the nursery' paper. The authors tell us, 'The largest number of men and women who have known suffering find renewal and the healing of childhood pain in the experience of bringing a child into the world. In the simplest terms — we have heard it often from parents — the parent says, "I want something better for my child than I have had." And he brings something better to his child.'[10] This is also Hemal's story.

Hemal is one of the most likeable people I have ever spoken to — and I've never even met him in person. I book my train tickets to visit him at home in Bolton, but we decide against it because there are stories on the news about a mysterious virus which has caused chaos in China, and there are some concerns it could become a pandemic, although I'm not quite sure what that really means. In any case, it seems wise not to travel for the moment. So Hemal and I have our interview by phone. I can hear him smiling, and I imagine a broad, open grin. His laugh, which erupts often into the conversation, is easy and warming. He is 43 years old, he and his wife have been married for 13 years, and they have two boys, aged 12 and 10.

There is something in his demeanour that is a cross between childlike and adult, and I think he articulates this when he tells me how the other day his wife walked into his office at home while he was on the phone to a colleague, and told him afterwards that he seemed like a totally different person. 'I think she means I was an adult — the way I communicated, the way I interpreted, the way I elaborated everything — it felt like I'm an adult. But I've got my childish parts, I've got my friends who I have a laugh and a joke with, the same with my children and my wife. I think at certain parts of the day, you really do feel like an adult; at others, you just feel like yourself. The person you've always been. That child.' His words remind me of Jacqueline Wilson's — that underneath everything, there's a child who hasn't changed. Hemal thinks that this capacity to grow down to connect with his children is important — it makes me think of a different form of parentese when he tells me that every day, without fail, he talks to his boys in a silly voice, jokingly play fights, chases them around the house, and gets chased by them. In some respects, he thinks that's what makes them all so close — that he can switch from being a serious hard-working adult to flicking the boys' ears. 'They've got to realise that you can connect with them — or maybe they don't realise it exactly but they have to see that.' If you're an adult all the time, he says, the connection is nowhere near as strong.

Hemal's boys are having a very different childhood from the one he had. By the time he had reached his younger son's age, his mother had died of a brain tumour; by the time he was his older son's age, his older brother had died of a heart attack. These terrible losses, at 7 and 11, shaped his upbringing and the adult he has become: a man who rarely shows his emotions. 'Something inside me was like, okay, you have to get on with it. I mean, I didn't sit down and slap myself in the face and say, "Right, Hemal, get on with it" — it wasn't a conscious thing, it just happened.' After experiencing such horrific trauma, he thinks he might have felt that he needed to cut off his emotions, because it seemed like there was just too much pain to bear. 'I think I became numb,' he says. 'Only when I sit with you, or I'm sitting with friends or family, and I reflect on it, can I talk about it and tell you what happened to me. Back then I couldn't say what had happened to me.' He describes that feeling, when he was young, as being in a trance, just getting on with things to occupy his time and his mind, getting on with his life.

His father, who died in 2018, worked night shifts in a cotton factory in Bolton, the first and only job he had after coming here from India, via Kenya, in the early 70s. In an uncritical way, understanding of the generational differences between them, Hemal explains that his father gave what was needed materially, but their relationship was not a close one — not like the one he now has with his boys. But Hemal grew up surrounded by lots of cousins, and he warmly describes 'the Indian family environment, where everybody's like a brother or a sister, and you're very, very close'. Some time after the deaths of his mother and brother, Hemal and his father moved into social housing, and Hemal moved into the adult department, taking on more and more responsibility: 'From 11 upwards, I grew up fast. From 15 onwards, I was a fully fledged adult, because I had to be.' As a teenager, he always had a job, whether it was a paper round or at the local DIY store; he made sure he did the best he could in school — and that meant doing well; he was always cooking, cleaning, putting a wash on; he organised the direct debits; he ran the house. 'All the things a mum would normally show you how to do — nobody showed me any of that, I just had to do it.'

It was at college, when he met the woman who would become his wife, that he was first able to begin to put these losses into words. 'Only then could I open up about it. When someone significant comes along in your life, you find it easier to talk,' he says. This opening up was a kind of growing up; he became a bit more of himself. 'When I talked about it for the first time in my life, I felt like it was off my chest a bit more. I must have been holding it in for all those years. It became real.' He realised for the first time just how much those losses had affected him. And although he is still not very emotional most of the time, when there is a death, it is like he goes back in time to being 7 years old. 'It takes me back to that point of losing my mum. That's what comes back, in the bottom of my stomach, that's what I feel. It brings me back to that moment, the first one.'

What has changed is his sense of loneliness. 'When I got married, I was hugely proud, and I think it was a big relief as well. I thought, I'm not going to be lonely any more,' he says. He met his wife at 16, and when they married at 30, he felt that he was always going to have someone. 'And I do, it's true.' Now he has a structure around himself that he has built, a network of friends and his wife's family, other parents they've met through the boy's schools; that's what has helped him to cope. My heart swells and my eyes sting when I think of all the connections and relationships Hemal has made for himself, and I find myself wishing his mother could have seen the good man he has grown into, the good life he has built with his wife, for them both and for his boys.

When Hemal's mother and brother died, father and son grieved separately. His father never spoke about either of them, or of his feelings of loss. He had what Hemal describes as a very traditional, old-fashioned view of parenting; he saw himself as the provider. This is not Hemal's view of fatherhood — this is a ghost he has laid to rest. 'I'm extremely close to my children, and I think there are things we do in life now that I missed out on a child, that I feel I'm somehow gaining back,' he says. He never had anyone to come and watch him play cricket or football; 'I'd just take myself to where I needed to go, I didn't have anyone on the sidelines to cheer me on.' But this morning, he went straight from his younger son's match to the older one's. 'I love doing all of that, I just love it. I want to be there to see them and encourage them, because I didn't have that.' He feels his sons have given him a second chance at a happy childhood, through theirs, whether it's holidays in Spain, going to the cinema, or going to see their favourite team play. But he still has questions: 'Nobody taught me how to teach my children, how to pass on those adult lessons. Just yesterday I was thinking, one of them is going to start shaving soon. Who's going to teach him? No one taught me to shave, but I'm going to have to do that.'

I wonder if this shift that took place in the fathering of Hemal to the fathering by Hemal might reflect shifts in fatherhood more generally in society; if, in a way, the relationship between fathers and their children might have evolved from distance to proximity, might have been through a kind of growing up of its own. But historian of fatherhood Laura King, Associate Professor in Modern British History at University of Leeds and author of *Family Men: fatherhood and masculinity in Britain, 1914–1960*[11], warns me, it's not that simple. She has offered to speak to me even though she is on maternity leave with her first child, and when I ask her if she feels like an adult now, she tells me she thought she'd feel a lot more grown up than she does. 'It's that classic idea that we compare our insides to other people's outsides; we look at people and think, well, they're so grown up, they've got it all sorted.' She thinks there is a risk of making exactly these assumptions with people throughout history as well. 'It's harder to know their internal way of thinking; harder to get a sense of their subjectivity — their idea of what they're like as a person.' She settles on an answer that is familiar to us by now: 'I must be a grown-up because I'm sat here in a grown-up house where I live with my husband and a baby — but I don't always feel like one.'

I ask her about the history of fatherhood, and she tells me there are two: one that takes place in the cultural discussion of a society, in the ideals of what it means to be a good father; and the other that takes place in people's homes, in the minutiae of what fathers are actually doing. And they are quite different.

Within the cultural discussion, a lot of shifts can be observed over the centuries, but not always in the same direction. Back in the 18th century, the emphasis was on the importance of men and fathers being 'sensible', in the sense of the word meaning feeling; being open to emotion and being tender with their children. By the 19th century, though, there's an idea that fathers should be more distant — that the emotional side of parenting is the mother's role and that men are there to discipline their children and help educate them, to be the breadwinner. 'So it's not a case of a linear pattern of fathers in the past being more strict, being less involved with their children's lives, and becoming progressively more so,' she says. In the 20th century, the emphasis changes again, and the focus moves to men changing nappies and being more involved in children's care — but this public, cultural conversation is not necessarily reflected in the private sphere: in people's homes, the trends are far less marked. 'Whatever period you look at, you can always find men who were involved in their children's lives, who were happy to take on different roles that might be seen as feminine, who were very caring and loving and tender with their children.' At the same time, 'Sadly you'll also find men who are violent or abusive, or just distant and uninterested.'

Over the last 30 years, she explains, there has been a lot of discussion in our society around how men have become much more involved in their children's lives than they used to be, 'and that's true, in that there are men who are taking on different roles, and trying to share equally with their partners'. But we should be wary of extrapolating these individual stories into society-wide trends, she cautions. Research that analyses how many minutes men care for children and how many minutes women care for children shows that 'change happens so, so slowly'. I can hear the irony in her voice when she tells me that at different points in history, 'we hear this narrative of oh, fathers have suddenly got involved in their children's lives — it pops up again and again'. She has seen the cultural discussion leading the headlines in the 50s, then again in the 70s, then again in the 90s. She wonders if this might have something to do with the fact that 'If everyone thinks, oh this is great, men are helping out more by changing a nappy — well, it lets some of them off the hook a bit.'

Where there has been a shift both in the cultural discussion and in people's homes is in the role fatherhood plays in adult masculinity; in what it means to be a man. Being a good father — not just fathering a child physically, but emotionally, too — has become a more significant part of how men think about what it means to be an adult. Before World War II, King says, everyone knew that 'real men don't push prams — particularly real working-class macho men; that was too associated with an effeminised version of masculinity'. By the 40s and 50s, the reluctance of fathers to be seen in public with their children had started to drop away, and the place of fatherhood in adult masculine identity had shifted: 'You see a real rise in men feeling, "I'm proud to be seen with my children." Being a good dad becomes a key marker of being a good man, rather than being in opposition to it.' This can be seen in the rise of celebrity dads, which is not such a recent phenomenon. We might think of David Beckham as the iconic celebrity dad showing off his kids, and that this all started in the 90s; but King has unearthed examples of footballers and film stars from the 40s and 50s 'brazenly showing off their fatherhood as a proud part of their masculinity'. She found tabloid features with pictures of Burt Lancaster, all muscles with his top off on one page, and fully dressed with his kids on Sunday on the next; and another feature with a photograph of the footballer Neil Dougall, who played for Plymouth Argyle, staged to show him in a changing room after a match, giving his baby a bottle, his toddler sitting watching.

One quote from her book really struck me — it's from Ferdynand Zweig, the 20th-century Polish sociologist, and it reads: 'The father is there to assist and help, to give guidance; but he is no more the master with the big stick.'[12] In the period from World War I to the 50s, there was a cultural shift around discipline, away from its more punitive form, King explains; 'Away from "Just wait till your father comes home", with the father as a bogey man who will give his child a beating or a stern telling off.' By the 40s and 50s, there's a feeling that fathers shouldn't be just a strict disciplinarian, but more of a guide, helping children to develop in different ways. This can be seen in the outlawing of some forms of corporal punishment in this period, and the move away from it in schools as well as in some families after extensive campaigning (although, shockingly, corporal punishment was not made illegal in English state schools until 1986, and in private schools until 1998).[13] This struck me as very similar to the growing up of the superego, and how the healthy adult superego treats the ego; not as a punitive disciplinarian, but as a helpful, motivating, guiding force for good. What is important about this, I think, is that the development of the superego and of laws against corporal punishment only takes place when a problem is acknowledged and faced, and when we feel compassion for the child inside us and the children around us.

The more I think about Rose's and Hemal's growing up and down and up again, the more I think the traditional shapes we have to represent the life course are no good at all. We tend to think of life as taking a linear trajectory, like a triangle shape on a graph where the vertical axis measures growth, the horizontal, time. So the infant is helpless, but as time passes, the child, teenager, and young adult becomes stronger and more knowledgeable, developing in physical and mental ability. Then at a certain point, we hit our peak and turn the corner at the top of the triangle — 'over the hill' as those cringe birthday cards say — and we begin our gradual decline in our bodies and our minds until we meet, as Shakespeare describes it in his Seven Ages of Man, our 'second childishness and mere oblivion, Sans teeth, sans eyes, sans taste, sans everything'.[14] This has not been my experience. My mind seems to grow up and down and left and right and back and forth, depending on what grow-ups I face and if I feel I can meet them, and how I am feeling about myself and others at any particular time. It has been the same for my training, and it has been the same, so far, in writing this book. It is not a linear route, but a path that bounces around, like the pinball machine that Tochi described in chapter one; if one were to trace my progress, the sketch would look less like a triangle, more like Mr Messy.

These images bring to my mind one of my favourite psychoanalytic theories: Melanie Klein's theory of the paranoid-schizoid and depressive positions, which the psychoanalyst Priscilla Roth called the 'two elemental structures of emotional life', considered 'perhaps her greatest gift to psychoanalysis'.[15] This is a theory not of a logical progression through developmental achievements, but an always temporary to-ing and fro-ing between two contrasting states of mind. It took me a while to get my head around this, but as I read paper after paper, sitting on my sofa with a cup of coffee, or at my desk with my head in my hands, trying to make sense of things, or in the classroom with my peers and tutor discussing the ins and outs of Klein's ideas, I gradually came to see how true this is to my own experience.

What was most exciting for me, learning about all this, was reading how Klein came up with this theory based on her observations of babies and their mothers, and analysing young children. By spending time, watching and listening and trying to understand, she developed the idea that newborns cannot hold both good and bad together in their minds; with a mind at such an early stage of development, an infant can only conceive of black or white, not grey. (You can probably think of many adults who are the same — and in fact, this is the point she was making.) This black-or-white view of the world starts with the mother, who is either experienced by the baby as feeding or not feeding, 'the gratifying (good) breast', or 'the frustrating (bad) breast'[16] — and she used the same language for bottle-feeding parents, too. It may sound strange and dehumanising to describe a mother simply as a breast, but Klein believed that babies cannot conceive of mothers as a whole person at this point. I wonder if perhaps some mothers have an awareness of this when they talk about feeling like a milk machine. This state of mind, which can only tolerate the idea of 'or', never 'and', she called the paranoid-schizoid position — schizoid as in schism, because its defining process is one of splitting things into all good or all bad. Anyone who has ever held a baby who is perfectly happy one moment and then screaming with rage the next, has seen this state of mind in action. This splitting, through a complex process, helps the infant to get rid of their anxieties and to feel safe — this is something that babies need to do in order to survive, to hold their minds together. That's the thing about seeing things in black and white; it can feel safer than seeing others in all their complexity, than accepting that people can be both good and bad.

As the infant grows and the mind develops, there also develops a capacity to withstand ambivalence and experience mixed feelings towards their carers. Gradually the baby comes to understand that the mother who feeds is not a different person from the mother who doesn't feed, but the same person who sometimes feeds and sometimes doesn't. Rather than splitting people into good or bad, the baby's experience of the world becomes more integrated — people can be both good and bad. Life becomes more complex and nuanced. This is a development to be celebrated — though it is, perhaps surprisingly, called the depressive position. Depressive, because although it is healthier and more realistic to see the good and bad in everyone, it is also far more painful, as we have to mourn the loss of our idealised gods, as well as of the unrealistic monsters it felt so safe to hate. We have to see that we too are good and bad, that we have both good and bad in us, and with that comes a sense of guilt. Klein saw that once we are able to occupy the depressive position, we don't just stay there; it can only be temporary. For the rest of our lives, we move between these two positions. Whenever my husband or I get particularly annoyed by someone and can't see anything good about them, we tell each other, 'You're getting a bit paranoid-schizoid, aren't you.' Perhaps that is our way of trying to take the sting out of it — because to be caught in this PS frame of mind is a horrible experience, whether it takes the form of a long-running grievance, or a wave of rage and fury, or a self-attacking loop of internal dialogue. I really wish I could grow out of it for good, and just live in the depressive position once and for all.

It's complicated, but as the psychoanalyst Peter Fonagy tells me, 'What I think psychoanalysis gives — or gives me — is a licence not to make things simple, but to be able to say, actually, it is complicated. If what you've arrived at is a simple solution, it's wrong.' Psychoanalysis changed Fonagy's life, back when he was a suicidal 16-year-old patient at the Anna Freud National Centre for Children and Families; when we meet 50 years later, he is its chief executive, and his CV is 82 pages long. He tells me how he came to this country as an adolescent refugee. 'I was quite unhappy, depressed, and suicidal, not in good mental health. I failed exams — by birth I'm Hungarian, and if I tell you that I didn't do very well in Hungarian A level, then you can see this was a fairly profound educational challenge.' Someone in his street knew about the Anna Freud Centre, and he was able to get treatment. 'I climbed out of it, but I was very lucky.' He talks me through how the analyst Wilfred Bion, who was psychoanalysed by Melanie Klein and who developed her thinking in quite brilliant ways, deepened our understanding of her theory of positions and why we oscillate between them. 'It's really all about arriving at increasing and decreasing and increasing and decreasing levels of complexity,' he explains, and he makes up the following story, 'plagiarising' Bion, which I am now retelling, plagiarising Fonagy.

Imagine you work in an office with a man named Frank. He is your nemesis, and you secretly hope to destroy him at all costs. At least, you do when you're in the paranoid-schizoid position.

In the depressive position, when a more mature understanding of the complexity of humanity can be tolerated, you can see Frank — who, in your childish way, you conceived of as your mortal enemy — does have some positive features. He is generous with getting the drinks in, he has a friendly partner, and they seem like nice parents, and when you met their daughter, you quite liked her. You reflect that his trying to undermine you at work might have partly come about because that was the position you were putting him in as your nemesis, because of this rivalry you created between the two of you. You might begin to think, it really shouldn't be like that, you should work together, collaborate. You had been bad-mouthing him, but now you start to think, perhaps it is time to revise your view. And so you try and have a more mature perspective, and you try to work with this man.

Fonagy picks up the story: 'And then the fucker is a complete git. As soon as you try to work with him, he tries to screw you. Your being more mature is met with complete immaturity and utter, devastating destructiveness from him. So you go back to, "He's a shit, I knew he was a shit, and what the fuck was I thinking about his good sides — it's a complete waste of time."' And you're back in the paranoid-schizoid position. Until next time.

This vivid dramatisation of Bion's thinking shows in an all-too relatable way how, Fonagy says, 'We move from immature modes of conceptualising the world, to more mature modes of conceptualising the world — only to be overcome by the challenges that the more mature modes of conceptualising the world present us with, so that we get thrown back into immature modes of conceptualising the world.' In infancy, achieving the depressive position is a fundamental grow-up, but we can't stay there for ever. Throughout our lives, we can only stay in a grown-up, depressive state of mind for so long, before we are thrust back into the more naive, paranoid-schizoid way of seeing things. So what does it really mean to grow up? In a life course viewed through this lens, 'progression is illusory', according to Fonagy, and he recalls the famous and famously confusing lithograph prints by the Dutch graphic artist M. C. Escher, depicting staircases that seem to go on forever, but don't lead anywhere. 'Progression is an Escher staircase; it always seems to be going up, but actually the going up is defined by the direction that the person depicted on the staircase is facing — because they could just as easily be facing downwards.' This is a pessimistic view, I think, but nonetheless realistic, according to Fonagy: 'The complexity of the human condition is such that you will never be without the need to address things in an immature, childlike way in order to be able to make it a liveable world.' I do find hope, though, in what Bion found in his clinical work with very psychologically unwell patients: that it is in the moments of shifting between these two positions that something creative can evolve. It seems to me that growing up must involve accepting these different states of mind, and understanding — as Rose and Hemal seem to intuitively recognise — that we can never leave these more immature states of mind behind for good.

The image of Escher's staircase stays with me, as I ricochet between not just depressive and paranoid-schizoid positions, but also between thinking adulthood is something real, something I am stumbling towards, and wondering if it is just a pretence — an illusion, nothing but a carapace, or a stairway to nowhere that circles back on itself. I wonder if I need to become a parent to grow up, or if I cannot become a parent until I have grown up; I do not know whether I am walking down the stairs or up them.

When I speak to Amy Blackstone, Professor of Sociology at The University of Maine, Orono, I feel like I am in conversation with someone who knows exactly where she is. We meet by Skype — she in Maine; me at home in London, and she tells me, yes, she does think of herself as grown up, as an adult. 'But it's interesting to reflect on when I think that happened for me. And honestly, I think it was about feeling secure in myself, sort of feeling comfortable in my own skin — and I don't think that happened until after 40.' She is 47 now. 'So it wasn't a magical thing when I turned 18, and it wasn't a result of finishing college, or getting my first job, or anything like that. I think it really was feeling solid in my own sense of self that made me feel like an adult.' Feeling solid in one's own sense of self — this is the meaning of adulthood I have been looking for. Now we're getting somewhere.

The questions of whether she is an adult, and of what adulthood is anyway, are ones she has been thinking about for many years, and her answers form the core of her personal and professional life. 'It has something to do with my own personal journey coming to accept my choice not to be a parent,' she says. Throughout her early adulthood, she did not feel inclined towards becoming a mother, but she felt pretty sure that one day she would wake up and, 'magically, this maternal instinct or biological clock or whatever would tick on, and suddenly I'd feel drawn to it'. So throughout her 20s, if people asked when she and her partner were going to have kids, she would say, 'I'm too young, not yet.' She entered her 30s, expecting that soon she would feel that overwhelming urge to procreate, but still nothing. In her mid-30s, she was at a turning point in her career, on the brink of consideration for tenure at her university, when three friends in quick succession told her that they were pregnant, and happily so, 'that they wanted to be mothers'. The beginnings of a decision began, gradually, to form in Blackstone's mind: 'I started to realise that I had never had this biological clock thing, and this maternal instinct that I had thought would kick in for me still hadn't kicked in, that I didn't want to be a mother. But I honestly thought that something might be wrong with me. I worried, am I a real woman, and am I a real adult, if I don't want to be a mother?'

To try to make sense of her own experience, a true sociologist, she turned to the research. She found a lot of work from the 70s and 80s on women choosing not to have children, but that had waned; in 2008, the year she got tenure, she decided to change that, and the more she studied, the more she felt she was reaching a conclusion that felt right to her. 'I don't think there was an instant that I decided not to be a mother; it was a period of many years, coming to accept the fact that I like my life as it is, and that it's okay to opt out of parenthood.'

She felt driven to make her choice more visible, to open up a conversation about the fact that parenthood is, in fact, a choice. 'Part of what I felt was lacking in public understanding about adulthood and parenthood was that the reality is you can opt in, or you can opt out,' she says. She has interviewed dozens of men and women about their decision not to have children, and written a book, *Childfree by Choice: the movement redefining family and creating a new age of independence.*[17] She recalls one woman and one man who both spoke about how unless they had children, their parents would not see them as having achieved full adulthood. 'They both lived on their own, the man owned his own home, they both had careers. But without children, they were seen as incomplete. And … I struggle with that one.' While understanding that raising a child does bring with it a whole new level of responsibility, and that being a good parent does require making adult decisions, she doesn't think that this is the only experience that teaches a person responsibility or how to care for others. What's more, she thinks it is extremely unfortunate that parenthood has been framed in this way: 'I think it's unfortunate because I don't know that everybody is cut out to be a parent — so why on earth would we be pushing people to do this?' She also thinks we need people who are contributing to the world, and to children's lives, in ways outside of parenthood. 'So I'm just speechless when I think about how parenthood has been constructed as the singular experience that instantly makes a person an adult.'

It sounds from Blackstone's research that deciding not to have a child can be a grow-up in itself. Many people she talked to took years to come to their decision, and spoke of the level of reflection, planning, and thinking that was required to come to a choice that felt right for them. Blackstone believes this thinking is on a different level from what many parents experience and describe, because for most people, parenthood is the assumed norm. 'I don't mean to imply that parents don't think about their choice — I know some think about it very deeply — but I think there is more opportunity for parents to think less deeply about their choice, than there is for non-parents,' she explains. At least one woman said in her interview that she felt her choice not to become a parent was more thoughtful, more carefully considered than any of the people she knew who'd chosen to become parents. Listening to this freed something up in my mind. It's not that I was pushed one way or the other to any decision of my own, but perhaps I began to understand that this to-ing and fro-ing was part of a significant and valuable process. I had not previously considered that choosing not to have children could be a formative experience in itself, an adult decision that requires a number of grow-ups: of not simply following the crowd, of working out what you really want instead of what your parents or your in-laws want or what your friends are doing, of really asking yourself, who are you? What are you capable of? What do you want from your life?

Deciding not to have children sounds like it was liberating for many of the people she interviewed, and for Blackstone herself, but, I reflect, there must be some loss that comes with this decision. What were the losses for her? She tells me she's glad I asked, because she feels it is something that is overlooked in these discussions, and while she knew that she didn't want to be a mother, she also recognised that there were experiences she would have to give up. Of course, the flipside is also true — if you become a parent, you necessarily forego certain experiences that you might have had if you had not had children. But acknowledging these losses was also an important part of the process, and it took her several years to accept that she would not have the same experiences as her friends or family or other women, and that she could live with that. Then she sounds embarrassed: 'Honestly one of the — this sounds so strange — but the one experience that I felt saddest about missing out on was what it would feel like to be pregnant and give birth. Which is funny, because so many of the child-free women I've spoken with have said that they're overjoyed they don't have to have that experience. But what it does to your body and how it feels is really fascinating to me.'

I also find it fascinating; the incredible miracle that is a baby growing inside a mother — not just growing inside the mother's belly, but inside the mother's mind as well. I wanted to find out more about the changes the brain goes through during pregnancy and birth, so I wrote to neuroscientist Elseline Hoekzema, Director of the Pregnancy and the Brain Lab at Amsterdam University Medical Center, who has researched the neurological changes in pregnant women. She replied, 'During this study, I actually became a mother myself, so it was very interesting also from a personal level to see these results. I've analysed many datasets on many topics in my career, but I've never seen changes that are so robust and strong. I can't imagine any other topic that would fascinate me as much, both as a scientist and a mother.' I ask her my favourite question: are you an adult, and when did that happen? 'I have the impression that becoming a mother has really completed my journey into adulthood. If I look back on myself before having children, it feels like I'm looking at a different more immature person in many ways. But perhaps I'll look back upon my current self in another 20 years and have the same feeling. Who knows, perhaps growing up never stops.'

When she began studying women's brains in pregnancy, very little was known about what goes on; although researchers had known for some time that pregnancy and motherhood change the brain in non-human animals, the topic was virtually unexplored in humans. She and her colleagues set out to investigate this through a brain scan study of women who wanted to become pregnant, through their trajectory into motherhood, so that every mother's brain could be compared to her pre-pregnancy brain. They also had control groups of people who did not become pregnant during the study.

What Hoekzema and her team found was absolutely extraordinary.[18] 'The changes were so strong and consistent that a computer algorithm could automatically identify all the women in our sample who had been pregnant based only on the changes in their brains, which is truly exceptional!' she writes. The data showed that pregnancy results in very strong, long-lasting changes in brain anatomy; researchers found pronounced changes in the grey matter structure of various regions of a woman's brain. In further analyses, Hoekzema examined the overlap of these regions with the different networks of the brain, and showed that these changes were strongest in regions playing a role in what she calls 'theory of mind'. Theory of mind is linked to a capacity to understand someone else's psychological state, their emotions and thoughts — it reminds me of Bion's notion of reverie. Hoekzema explains, 'It's an ability that plays an important role in parenting of course, as it's really vital for a mother to be able to read the signals of her infant and figure out what her child needs.' It's as if the pregnant woman's brain is growing her capacity for reverie.

To test this theory, Hoekzema did further analyses to test whether or not these changes might be involved in preparing a woman for motherhood.[19] One way of investigating this was by examining the responses of a mother's brain when she looked at pictures of her baby. The data showed that the regions of the brain that showed the strongest response to the photographs corresponded to the same regions which had undergone the strongest structural changes during pregnancy. 'It seems that these structural changes somehow help prepare a woman's brain to optimally respond to cues of her infant and thus to help prepare her for her new role as a mother,' she explains. And these changes persist for at least two years after giving birth.

I ask if this could be seen as a kind of growing up of a woman's brain, and Hoekzema replies, 'I think the brain changes of pregnancy can be looked at as a form of brain maturation, or at least a form of specialisation, that will be beneficial in the next phase of life.' The shifts can be compared to those that take place during adolescence, which are steered by increases in some of the same hormones that are surging in pregnancy. Direct comparisons show that the brain changes in girls going through adolescence and those of women going through pregnancy are extremely similar. But this is not the only route to this preparation for motherhood, she points out: 'This of course doesn't mean that someone who does not go through pregnancy is not fit to mother; think of fathers or adoptive parents for instance.' Animal studies have shown that there are various other routes to triggering this maternal behaviour, either by means of exposure to hormones or by a prolonged exposure to the young, which can also induce brain changes and maternal behaviours.

Her answers seem important. I think I was under the impression that I had to be ready, to be an adult, before I became a mother; perhaps that's part of why this question of how to be an adult has grown so urgent for me at this particular life stage. Hoekzema's research seems to show that pregnancy itself is a process of preparation, of growth, not just physically but neurologically. This readiness is something you can only come to through the experience itself. You don't become a parent just by conceiving a child — you grow into it.

And then comes Covid-19. Life as everyone knows it is upended. Asking questions about adulthood, about becoming a parent, about what the future might look like seems futile; a deadly virus is sweeping through the nation, we could kill our parents just by hugging them. The Prime Minister tells us we must all stay at home; for how long, nobody knows. Children are not in school; businesses are folding; domestic abuse is spiralling. My situation is much more stable than many, and yet, for weeks, I find I cannot write, and I am spending more time in the day than is socially acceptable in bed. It feels a lot like depression. I pull myself together for my patients, for my studies, all now happening remotely, but that is all I can manage. After I don't know how long, I begin to find for myself some space and light; some clarity.

I return to this chapter. I reread my interviews with Rose and Hemal, with Fonagy, Blackstone, and Hoekzema. I read what I have written and I see how much pressure I have been putting on myself to make a decision about parenthood, to be a mother Rose or a child-free Amy. I see how I have been trying to nudge myself into the certainty that I want to be a mother, in the same way I've been trying to nudge myself into becoming an adult. I come to realise that the least adult aspect of my whole situation is not the fact that I don't feel grown up enough to have children, but the fact that I think I need children to make me an adult. I come to learn in my analysis how I am turning to others, including my interviewees, to tell me what will make me a grown-up, rather than being able to experience a growing-up process within myself. I see how I have been trying so hard to get everything right.

These thoughts circulate through my mind, and a conclusion of a kind begins to dawn. The biggest grow-up for me right now is to stop bouncing between decisions and instead to accept my not knowing, to give myself time to work out what I feel and what I want, to realise that the balance between wanting and not wanting is not in my control. This is where I find some breathing space; in the understanding that this is not something I can rush. I am struggling to face this uncertainty — the uncertainty all around us, now more obviously than ever before in my lifetime — and to bear it.

I had so hoped that I would be pregnant by the time I finished this book, that this would be the happy ending I could write, in life as in prose. But now I don't know what my happy ending looks like. This is the crucial grow-up for this life stage, I think, essential to finding a way through the ghosts in your nursery — at least, it is for me: to work out what you want from life, and to disentangle this from what everybody else wants you to want, from what you think you should want, from what your family, culture, society teaches you to want. What brings me rare moments of peace, what occasionally settles my anxious mind, is the understanding, always fleeting, so hard to hold on to, that my ending is going to have to be one that I find for myself in the living and in the writing. Not one that fits with the story that I, or anyone else, expects me to tell.

Chapter Four
La selva oscura

'I Wish I Knew How it Would Feel to be Free'
Sung by Nina Simone,
written by Billy Taylor and Dick Dallas

Nel mezzo del cammin di nostra vita
Mi ritrovai per una selva oscura
Ché la diritta via era smarrita

In the middle of my life
I found myself in a dark wood,
Lost

Dante Alighieri, *Inferno*, Canto 1. My (very loose) translation[1]

A baby is trying to roll over. He lies on his tummy, one hand pressing into his playmat, lifting up his shoulder and his chest. He pushes harder, but he is not yet strong enough to lift and twist his body, and he opens his mouth with a small moan which quickly becomes a frustrated cry. He pushes harder still, straining the little muscles in his arm and neck, and as his arm gives way he gives an enraged, desperate shriek and drops back down wailing, humiliated. His grandmother comes to him, strokes his head and tells him, 'Don't worry love, you'll get there.' He moans softly as she gently lifts his shoulders and helps him to turn over, placing him on his back, jangling the toys hanging from above him.

The first time I gave any thought to middle age was during my first job in journalism, at the women's magazine where I worked in my mid-20s. The magazine was aimed largely at women in their 40s and 50s, and it was my job to find people from this demographic who had compelling stories to tell, and interview them about their experiences. I loved hearing about their lives. Some of them were well-known public figures — I was lucky enough to listen to Doreen Lawrence talk about how she was trying to make her life meaningful after the racist murder of her son, Stephen. Others were so-called 'ordinary' women, like Pamela Wharton, who finally fulfilled her childhood ambition to become a policewoman at age 42, or Kerry Elford who took up climbing at 50 and found a new passion, or Ros Freeborn, who went to art school in her late 40s and is now an artist. I became fascinated by the life stage that my interviewees were experiencing, which academics tend to call midlife,[2] and which the rest of us call middle age. Now I find myself reflecting on all these life trajectories and wondering, what made it possible for these women to grow into themselves at this particular time of life?

It was while working at this magazine that I first became consciously aware of the ubiquitous stereotype of the 'middle-aged woman'— boring, staid, frumpy. I'd never really thought about it, but I suppose I must have taken it as true before I got to know anyone who would disprove it. I soon started to find it misogynistic, ageist, and enraging. The women I interviewed were not boring, their lives were not boring. They were none of these things. They were vital, in both senses of the word, not just because they seemed to hold their families and our society together, but also because they were going through the most astonishing period of growth and development. Many were living through extraordinary flux, and described feeling emotions more intensely than ever before in their lives, facing losses that I knew I had not yet loved enough to comprehend. Sometimes these losses were unimaginable and tragic, the 'I just never thought it would happen to me' kinds of losses. But often they were the ordinary, inevitable losses that many of us might expect to face at some point, but that are nevertheless crushing: your child leaving home, leaving you with a partner you haven't lived alone with for two decades; being made redundant after pouring your whole identity into your job; your body changing, the menopause, your hair going grey. Surely these must be among some of the most demanding and painful grow-ups we ever have to face? Many of the women I interviewed spoke of losing their sense of identity, losing sight of themselves, and having to find themselves anew in order to grow up and out the other side. There's a reason why Dante Alighieri's *Inferno* begins with the narrator lost, '*Nel mezzo del cammin di nostra vita*', in the middle of our path through life, in '*una selva oscura*', a dark wood.[3]

Let us try to get a sense of the shape and feel of this dark wood, to trace its edges. What do we mean by midlife, exactly? You may be unsurprised to learn that there is no simple answer to this question. Sociologist Bethany Morgan Brett wrote her PhD thesis[4] on this question and she tells me, 'I spent seven years defining midlife, and … I don't think there's any clear-cut definition. If you ask people to define it for themselves, they will usually define themselves out of the category; they'll say it's 10 years ahead of them.' And if you turn to the academic literature, she explains, well, then it depends on when the author was writing. Elliott Jaques, who popularised the phrase 'midlife crisis', wrote in his 1965 paper that middle age started at 35 years old;[5] as she says this a nervous giggle darts out of me, midlife suddenly feeling uncomfortably close. 'Exactly!' she responds, 'But then the life expectancy was 70, so 35 was halfway through the life course.' Morgan Brett eventually decided on a window that opens around 40 and closes around 60. This window will open and close for different individuals depending on their experiences, their health, and their life situation, of course. But dig into the life-course literature, and you'll see that the frame of this window is very much still under debate. After all, not many of us can expect to live to 120.

While its boundaries may be fuzzy, the other characteristics of midlife are clearer. In her writing and research, Morgan Brett takes a psychosocial approach, which means she thinks about 'That interface between the psyche and the social world, how they can't be pulled apart because they're intertwined with one another. Because you can't understand the social without the psyche and you can't understand the psyche without the social.' I am struck by the clarity of her direct way of speaking and her ability to take something that feels messy and complicated and explain it without simplifying it. She must make a good lecturer, I think to myself, and it seems so unjust when she tells me she has just lost her job because of the pandemic. Some two years later, when we are next in contact and I have finished writing this book, she tells me that she has now left academia, and is working as a child and adolescent counsellor. I can't explain exactly why, but I feel very moved. It feels right. It feels like something has grown out of loss.

She has found through her research that in midlife, people tend to face issues that fall into three categories: first, their body ageing and their health; second, what they've achieved and what they would still like to achieve; and third, intergenerational relationships and staying connected with children and with parents when both are growing older, when children might need less care while parents might need more.[6] All of this leads to people experiencing many different emotions at once, leading to a conflict between an increased sense of responsibility, maturity, and wisdom on the one hand, and on the other, increased vulnerability, anger, grief, and anxiety. That's why she calls it a 'concatenation of events', because 'everything colliding at once can cause a bit of an explosion for some people'. Hardly boring, frumpy, or staid.

When I ask Morgan Brett, who is 41, if she is an adult, she tells me decisively, 'Yes.' She was 28 when she grew up: a close relative was murdered by their partner, and they had eight children. She was at the university that day, and no one had been able to get hold of her. When she went to her in-laws' house after work that evening, she saw the children and said, 'Oh hello, kids, where's your mum and dad?' That is when she found out what had happened, and that night they fostered three of them. 'So I became a parent at 7 pm on the 21st of February 2007.' That was the biggest grow-up of her life, and it made her into an adult. 'You are dealing with some really grown-up things. You're not just floundering along in your life, being a young person; you're going to social services meetings, dealing with the police, being a witness in a court case, becoming a parent. I think that makes you grow up very, very quickly.'

Now in her early 40s, Morgan Brett is just entering the stage of life she has spent so many years studying. She tells me that midlifers constitute an under-researched, neglected part of the population in the psychosocial field — and in many other fields too;[7] a demographic that doesn't really get acknowledged. I think it is interesting that she came to this topic before reaching midlife herself, and I wonder if there is some meaning here. Maybe part of the reason why there has historically been so little research might be to do with the fact that most researchers are in midlife themselves. Morgan Brett wonders with me, 'Maybe they don't want to acknowledge their own category.' Perhaps it is harder to study a group in which you see yourself, than to study other people — and maybe that is why I found writing the last two chapters so challenging. To study your own group means owning your own vulnerabilities and fragilities, instead of seeing them all in, for example, old people — they are the ones in decline, we are in the prime of life; or in teenagers — they are the ones with all the feelings and upheaval; we are perfectly stable. Nothing to see here.

When I ask Jon Simons if he is an adult, he replies, 'Has anybody answered that question by saying yes?' He is 46 and a professor of cognitive neuroscience at the University of Cambridge. He tells me, 'Obviously I am an adult if you define it literally. But do I feel like an adult? Most of the time not. I reckon most people think, "Maybe sometime in the future, and who knows when that future will come, I'll feel more like an adult than I do now."' It is surprising for me to hear this; Simons is my cousin — my eldest cousin, the firstborn of us grandchildren, and so to me, he has always seemed extremely grown up, even when he was 15 and pretending to be a magician to entertain my toddler friends and me at my third birthday party. Perhaps especially then. I have always looked up to him, and I always enjoy being around him, his wife, and their two boys. It is both unsettling and liberating for me to hear this beacon of adulthood, who is after all a middle-aged man, speak of himself in this way. He continues: 'I still look at other people, peers, colleagues, and think, oh, they've got it together, they've got a plan, they're all grown up — perhaps one day in the future, I will be too, and until then I'll just carry on winging it and hope nobody notices.' He thinks that many of us suffer from this 'imposter syndrome' most of the time, 'and those who look as though they don't are probably just more adept at hiding it than the rest of us'. I ask if he has felt any closer to adulthood as he has aged, and his answer is a yes and a no: as he has grown older, he's dealt with more situations, and through these experiences he has learnt to cope with things better — but, at the same time, the older he has grown, the more the situations he has had to deal with have involved greater responsibility, making decisions that affect not only him but also the people who rely on him: 'The stakes are higher.' It seems to me an unfortunate truth that the more you grow up, the more grown-up you are required to be. Feeling adult seems to move out of reach the closer he edges towards it — like our grandfather dangling his keys.

Conveniently, my cousin is a cognitive neuroscientist with a particular interest in midlife brains. I finally ask him the question that has been on my mind for many years, but which it has always felt too late to ask: what is a cognitive neuroscientist? He tells me, 'It's somebody who is interested in understanding the brain mechanisms that underlie cognitive skills and behaviour': he investigates how the different parts of the brain might interact to enable us to perform tasks like remembering things, using language, solving a problem. He and his team study healthy volunteers, scanning their brains to understand which parts light up when they're doing certain tasks, and they also study people with damage to different areas of the brain to try to understand how damage affects performance of those tasks. They sift through all this data, hunting for 'common effects and meaningful differences', and try to build up a theory about how different areas of the brain might work together to help us live our lives.

When I ask him for his own definition of midlife, first he talks to me about young adulthood, from the early 20s until the 40s; then he talks to me about older adulthood, from the 60s upwards; 'In between those two, there is another period, from the 40s to the 60s, which most people tend to think of as middle age, or midlife.' I think of the women I interviewed in my first journalism job, how society always seemed to define them primarily, if not only, as a wife / mother / daughter, always in relation to their partner / child / parents. I find myself feeling very annoyed. Isn't there a problem in defining midlife only in opposition to the life stages on either side of it, as the bit in the middle? Can we not describe midlife on its own terms? It is only some months later that I think about why this might have annoyed me so much. I think it has something to do with my beginning to recognise, through my analysis, the impact of being defined, and of defining oneself, in relation to others, instead of on one's own terms.

Simons can see my point, but argues that this reflects the fact that until fairly recently, science — as we saw with sociology — has largely neglected middle age as an interesting period of life to study. While cognitive scientists have studied child development for a century or more, older age for decades, and adolescence for the last 20 years, middle age has only really been a topic for research for the last few years; this is an extremely recent development. Part of the reason for this is to do with the speed of change in our brains at different times in our lives: in child development and older adulthood, changes take effect over weeks and months. 'These are timeframes in which you can see change happen, and change in science is a meaningful currency; things have to change in order for us to measure differences and try to understand what factors mediate that change — that's what science is.' The assumption, until very recently, has been that not much changes during middle age; that it's 'just a period when nothing really happens, it's pretty boring, so it's not really worth studying. People have neglected it for the more sexy and exciting parts of life'. Not any more.

It was while studying the memory of older adults that Simons learnt that it's what goes on before a person hits old age that determines much of what happens to them when they do. The question he is trying to answer now is: 'Can we identify something that happens in the 40s or 50s that might predict what's going to happen in the 60s, 70s, and 80s?' He and his colleagues and students are trying to establish what it is that differentiates Person A, who hits 70 and experiences memory loss and becomes unable to carry out tasks and look after herself, from Person B, who hits 70 and doesn't show any signs of needing help or care, and whose memory is just fine. Is it something that might have happened in their 40s or 50s? And if it is, is that something they can pick up if they test people in their 40s and 50s? And if it is, can they then do something to help those people and prevent them from suffering so much cognitive decline? Far from being seen as boring, midlife is now understood to be a high-stakes drama: 'This is a really, really hot area of study at the moment.' The sad reality is that once someone is already suffering from cognitive decline, it is too late to change that trajectory. 'But it might not be too late if we can catch that person when they're middle-aged, and give them some support to stave off that decline for a while, to help them live as meaningful and fulfilling and rich a life as possible, for as long as possible.'

I ask Simons if his work, like some kind of magical cloak of visibility, might also help us to see people in midlife as they are, rather than only as vectors for understanding older age. He accepts my challenge: 'We're studying the midlife brain primarily because of what it means for older age, sure, but in order to do that, we've got to study middle age in and of itself, to try and understand it.' He and his team are trying to figure out what kinds of questions to ask to understand what middle age is all about. What's going on in the brain in midlife, what's going on in people's lives, in their abilities, in their interests? 'Maybe, if we properly understand middle age, we will find that it isn't just some melange, just "what's going on in the middle",' he says. Work by him and others in the field is beginning to show that the assumption that nothing changes in midlife is just that: an assumption. 'I think there is a growing realisation that it is actually a really interesting life stage in itself. There is important, meaningful change that happens in midlife.'

So I ask him his own question: what is going on in the midlife brain? 'This is something we're only really discovering now,' he says, and it is a discovery that is hard for me to hear. While Sarah-Jayne Blakemore told us how the brain can continue to grow and develop through adolescence and young adulthood into the 30s and even 40s — and that is true, in terms of the brain's structure — there is more to that story. Although the structure of the brain is still developing, its functioning may have already started to decline, much earlier than we might like to think. 'Brain function hopefully goes up during childhood and adolescence,' says Simons, 'but then I'm afraid once it reaches that peak, perhaps in early adulthood, it may not be long before it starts to go down. That's when things can start to deteriorate.' From early adulthood! And that's being generous! And by 'things' he means the functions of memory, decision-making, problem solving, planning skills, and the ability to take in information and use it flexibly, moving it around and adapting it to new scenarios. And by 'deteriorate' he means really, really deteriorate: 'You can measure that deterioration;

even in somebody's 40s it can be worse than it was in their early 20s.' Oof.

This can be seen most clearly in the frontal lobes — the seat of the executive functions, where we plan, solve problems, and think about situations. 'The frontal lobes are the region of the brain that starts to deteriorate quite early. You can measure that deterioration happening in the 40s and 50s particularly — in middle age,' says Simons. A Functional Magnetic Resonance Imaging scanner — that's fMRI — shows how a brain responds to a task, as opposed to regular MRI, which depicts its structure. If you put a 20-year-old in an fMRI scanner and ask them to perform a task, you will see areas of the brain light up that often include the frontal lobes; if you get a 40-year-old to do the same, they are likely to show reduced activity in those brain areas. It can be as stark as that. MRI scans also show changes to the brain structure itself, changes that are known to be characteristic of older age, such as brain atrophy, the shrinking of areas of the brain caused by neurones dying and synapses tangling. This can be seen in the frontal lobes in middle age too.

I ask him, trying to keep the panic from my voice, if it is even possible for us to continue growing up when we get to middle age, if our brains are already deteriorating. This is where brain plasticity, that we first heard about from Blakemore, is a real source of possibility and hope. Simons explains that our brains are constantly changing throughout our lives according to the experiences we have. 'It's adapting, finding new connections, getting rid of old connections that aren't very useful. This constant rewiring is going on all the time; it's going on in this conversation for both of us.' This can be thought of as a kind of growing up that goes on throughout life; it means that although our brains may be deteriorating in middle age, they can also, in tandem, continue developing. 'By middle age, we may be working within greater neural constraints than we were in young adulthood, but within those constraints, there's still a hell of a lot of room for brain plasticity to do its thing.' I breathe a little easier again.

One way experts like Simons think we might be able to keep our brains in good shape is to build up what is known as 'cognitive reserve'. He draws a mental image for me of a deep well, full of experiences and cognitive abilities that we can draw on later in life. Evidence suggests that cognitive reserve comes primarily from new, stimulating experiences — that means everything from having a rich and varied social life to learning a musical instrument or doing a range of different types of puzzles, like Sudoku and crosswords. It looks like this is key for keeping your brain as healthy as possible, and one of the most stimulating things the brain can do is to encounter a new situation, a new challenge, and work out how to deal with it. This is one of the most powerful ways we can build up our cognitive reserve and make ourselves more resilient to decline. 'If you allow yourself to become boring and staid, if you don't ever have new experiences, if you fall into a midlife rut doing the same old things, there is a likely association with greater vulnerability to cognitive decline,' he says.

It strikes me that being a therapist must be a good way to fill your well of cognitive reserve. Talk about new, stimulating, rich, and varied experiences. Although lockdown has involved no travel to foreign countries, no thrilling adventure sports or Instagrammable scenery, my experiences as a therapist in training over this time have shown me how alive one can feel just listening to another human being talk about their life and their deepest thoughts and feelings, trying to think about and understand them. Every session is an emotional and intimate and yet formal encounter, that involves both parties opening themselves up to something new, to the risk and the hope of change. The 'emotional storm' — what is created, Bion wrote, 'when two characters or personalities meet'[8] — is powerful, surprising, and unpredictable. Definitely not boring and staid. And although my interviewees are not my patients, there is also an intimacy and a formality to the conversations I am conducting for this book. In this chapter, as I prepare my questions for the interviews with Kemi, Alex, and Sara, which you are about to read,

I find myself more aware of how each one is an exhilarating dive into a new adventure, where I will discover the contours and the details of a stranger's life. Each time, I ask my first question, and I have no idea where we will end up, but I know what I need to do: I need to give these people the space to tell their stories from beginning to end — or rather, from beginning to middle. I need to let myself get lost in their lives, and see where we find ourselves. In their telling and my listening, something grows between us, and as the process takes its course, I begin to recognise the value of allowing yourself to get lost — in your life, in your quest for the meaning of adulthood, in your analysis, in the middle of whatever dark wood you happen to be in. This is an important part of the process of growing up, I think, and it is not something I have let myself do before.

Kemi and I speak on the phone, and as soon as she answers, I hear the warmth and liveliness of her voice, and I find myself coming more alive in the listening. There is a childlikeness to her laugh, which peppers her conversation naturally and generously, her own form of punctuation. The drive and determination that has shaped her life story is echoed in the way she tells it, from the spirit and verve of her narrative, down to the direct, no-nonsense shape of her sentences. I ask her if she is a grown-up and she admits that technically, yes, she is — she has to be, as she is 54 and creative director of her own social enterprise, The Sew London Project, as well as a wife, and a mother of two sons, aged 23 and 17. But when I ask her if she feels like a grown-up, I get a different answer: she laughs joyfully and says, 'No, no, no, no. No, I don't feel so. I only feel that I have to act grown up, because I've got a label: 54.' That label doesn't change how she feels in herself: 'I feel very, very young.' When it comes to what it means to be middle-aged, she thinks a great deal has changed over the course of just one generation. 'When I saw my parents in their 50s, they both behaved old, and that was one thing I said I don't want to do. I don't want to grow up old; I want to grow up youngish and still be vibrant and relevant and approachable.' She describes herself as playful and fun-loving, an adult without having aged, and she thinks her 20 years as a secondary school teacher helped to anchor her in a more youthful state of mind: 'I was quite fortunate that the kids like me, and they shared their secret lingo with me.' They taught her the meaning of words like peng and lit, and I feel bruised to have to look them up on Urban Dictionary after we speak.

Bang in the middle of midlife, at age 50, Kemi leapt into a grow-up that would transform her working life, realising the dream she'd had since childhood to launch her own fashion design business, now social enterprise, The Sew London Project. To understand what a remarkable movement towards self-realisation this was, and, why it could only happen at this particular chapter in her life, we need to go back to the beginning — to before the beginning.

Kemi's parents moved to London from Nigeria in the 1960s as a young couple studying accountancy and book-keeping. Kemi was born in the UK and then, like many children of West African parents who came here to work and study, she was fostered from birth in a private arrangement — in her case, by a white family who lived in Brighton. She and her siblings would see her parents every fortnight when they visited Brighton and they would spend the school holidays together in London; the rest of the time the children lived with their foster family and went to school in Brighton. 'I was very fortunate to have a fantastic foster family — I know not everyone fostered when I was will have the same story,' she says, and tells me about the endless love and affection she received from her foster parents, how she remembers being doted on by them. 'We were so loved up by them — it wasn't that we were spoilt, but we were treated as special.' In particular, her foster mother would comment on how gifted and creative they all were. 'She noticed those things in us when we were really young, and that gave us a strong foundation for who we are today.' From early childhood, she and her siblings knew they had talent, and they had ambitions to use their talents and find creative fulfilment through whatever work they would end up doing.

But while her foster mother told them that so long as they put the work in, there was nothing stopping them from doing whatever they wanted when they grew up, they received a very different message from others around them. 'This was a time when racism was still right in your face,' she says; when on her way to school she walked past people calling out the n-word, or 'coloured', or 'w*g', asking her, 'If you got cut, would your blood be red?' This was not just on the streets, but at school as well. 'Something that really stood out for me in England as a child was that the educational system at that time was not in support of Black children,' she tells me, and it seems to me like a gross understatement. She reports all this in a matter-of-fact way, but when she talks about her foster mother's response, I can hear the pride and love reverberating in her voice: 'She gave us such strength. She was a very tiny woman, she must have just been about 4 foot 11, and she was not having it. By the time she was through with most of the kids in my school, nobody dared mess with us ever again.' But not even their foster mother could protect them from the racism that threatened to limit their horizons and stifle their growth. Kemi shares a memory, very sharp in her mind, of when she and her mother went to speak to her teachers about her options for secondary school and her future career. 'I was told point blank, to my face, "Oh, you're going to end up in a factory, you're not clever enough any way."' Kemi remembers the grief and anger on her foster mother's face, how she fought for Kemi and her siblings and told that teacher that they were gifted and clever and had bright futures ahead of them. But she could not unsay the things that teacher had said, which were so distressing and shocking for Kemi to hear. 'I kept thinking, is this going to be the sum total of my life? But I'm gifted and talented, I can do things ... I know that was something that broke me, on that day, hearing that.' She recalls falling into a depressed stupor, and it is heartbreaking to think of her as a young child, her sense of self and hope and ambition so brutally and ignorantly flattened.

But that is not where Kemi's story ends. Those words hurt her, they traumatised her, but she was able somehow — perhaps, I wonder, thanks to the love and encouragement her family had already given her — to find the capacity to turn them into fuel that drove her to prove that teacher wrong. She used those words as 'stepping stones', and changed that moment into a grow-up. 'Fortunately for me, that experience eventually became a motivation to prove to everyone that I was going to become something. It helped me, in a way,' she says.

She shares another memory from her schooldays, this time from Nigeria, where her parents returned in the 1970s, taking Kemi and her siblings with them. She was sitting in the classroom and the teacher asked them all, 'What do you want to be when you grow up?' Kemi sat in silence, the words of her English schoolteacher circling round her mind. But they were soon drowned out, as her classmates called out their answers, their voices full of energy and excitement: 'I want to be a doctor!' 'I'm going to be a lawyer!' Kemi was stunned, and as she gazed at her new friends and listened to their ambitions, she thought, 'Oh my goodness. I don't have anything stopping me from becoming what I want to be. I'm not being put down by the system, and I can become something.' She realised that her teachers and her society were not fighting against her, not trying to constrain her growth, but supporting her, helping her, so now there was no limit to what she might make of her talent and her creativity, other than herself. 'I remember acutely hearing a little voice in my head say, "Kem, you've got no excuse. No reason for anyone to say you can't achieve this because you're Black. You are now in a classroom full of children of the same colour, and there is nothing holding you back at all." That really was a trigger for me.'

This was one of many grow-ups from that time in her life. Moving to Nigeria was a huge change, and it brought with it many smaller ones; not only did she have to mourn the loss of living with her foster family, but also process the shock of living in a different country and a different culture for the first time in her life, one that was, confusingly, both her own but also not what she was used to. As much as she understood her Nigerian heritage through the eyes of her biological parents, 'as much as we were in touch with our African roots, by nature you take on the culture of the family that brings you up from birth, and I was being brought up by a white British family', she says. Although everyone in Nigeria spoke English, Kemi and her siblings wanted to learn Yoruba as well, and to understand the customs, like not talking back when your elders are talking to you. 'These were things we learned very quickly! It was a huge leap for us. It was like starting again.'

I ask how she feels now, as an adult, about her childhood spent growing up in both England and in Nigeria. 'I love my African heritage and I love my English heritage, and I wear them proudly. It is quite amazing having lived in both — it's been the making of me,' she says. She treasures her memories with her adoptive family in Brighton and the happy childhood they gave her — and at the same time, she feels she was robbed of her education and her sense of what she could be when she grew up. If she had stayed in England for secondary school, she knows she would not have achieved what she has. 'What Nigeria gave me was a belief in myself that I could be something, that I could attain to something. And I did all the things that I was told here I would never do.'

At 25, Kemi returned to England, married, had her children, and established a career as an art teacher — she got on with so-called adult life. Although she enjoyed teaching, and especially getting to know her students, she had always wanted to work in fashion design; that was her dream, and she wrote a blog she called 'Teacher by day, fashion designer by night'. For the time being though, she had to put that dream on hold: her children were her priority, and she needed the stability and regular salary and holidays that came with teaching to pay towards the mortgage and maintain family life. But she was wary of getting too comfortable. She remembers sitting in the staffroom at school and listening to her colleagues chatting, overhearing one say, 'Oh, I'm too old to leave this place, I'm just going to stay here until I retire.' She sat there feeling winded, thinking of all the things she wanted to do, and she realised that if she stayed where it was comfortable and known, where there were few risks but also few opportunities to branch out into fashion design, that she too would reach a point where she felt it was too late to grow.

It was at the start of midlife, when she was in her mid-40s, that Kemi faced her next big grow-up. Her school was restructuring and wanted to reduce the fine art classes she taught and for her to teach numeracy and literacy too — an unappealing prospect for her. At the same time, her sons needed her less than they used to: her older son was doing his A levels, and her younger son was due to start secondary school. They told her something which I find very moving: 'Mum, we're not kids any more. We're fine. You've taught us how to cook, so even if you're not home, we can rustle something up — we might not cook the way you cook, but we can cook.' It seems to me they were letting her know that they recognised how much she had helped them to grow up, and now it was their turn to help her. This was a gift. 'There was that confidence, that comfort, of not needing to worry that they needed me but I'm not there. I feel I'm in the latter half of my life now, and with my children's blessing and permission, it's like I have free rein now to do the things that I want to do.'

It was a release. She remembered the promise she'd made to herself in the staffroom years earlier, and she finally felt the moment was right to take the leap out of the comfort and safety of what she knew, and into the terrifying but exciting unknown. It was being in midlife that made this change possible; midlife as a 'concatenation of events' in a good way, presenting Kemi with a new opportunity to develop and grow.

She left her job with the plan that she was finally going to start her own fashion company. But she didn't take this grow-up all in one leap: she took a job in further education and built up her savings and cleared every single debt she owed before going part time to give herself more space for her next move. It was almost as if she needed to deal with all the unfinished business from the first half of her life before she could set in motion the new business that would shape the second. Then, just before her 50th birthday, she did it: The Sew London Project was born, and Kemi devoted her days to designing outfits for clients and teaching sustainable responsibility through sewing.

This was a time full of grow-ups big and small. 'It was exciting, exhilarating, and also scary at times,' she says, describing how, at first, she would start to panic when no new clients came by for two weeks, and worry about how she would pay the rent on her studio. 'But I've always been someone who could hustle.' I can hear in the way she says this that alongside the worry, there was also confidence, eagerness, and entrepreneurial spirit. She'd go to her studio and make a kaftan and share it on Facebook — and a friend would comment that she'd love to buy one, and then another and another, and before long friends of friends were coming to her studio, asking to try things on. Old students of hers, now at university, offered help with social media, and trained her to use Instagram and Snapchat. 'When I made my decision, I did it with all my cylinders firing, and I told myself, even if this fails, you're going to get yourself back up and you're going to get back out there again. And that has been pretty much what I've done.'

Midlife has brought with it a re-evaluation of what it means to be an adult. She now thinks of adulthood as a 'living document', in that it can never be one static thing, it is always shifting, surprising, challenging. She finds herself still asking her mother to treat her like an adult, only for her mother to respond, 'In my eyes, you're still a child' — and then Kemi will have exactly the same conversation, the roles reversed, with her 23-year-old son. This young man, who she used to take to basketball and football, who is now so independent and who she knows in another five years might turn round to her and say, 'Mum, I'm getting married' — he and his younger brother have taught Kemi that the dynamics of adulthood, of parent and child in particular, are always in flux. 'So for me, adulthood is not stable, it's almost like a bellow fanning the flames, growing up, growing down, constantly changing, evolving as you get older.'

When we speak, it is her fifth year of being self-employed, and she's clearly proud of it. During the first lockdown, when the NHS has faced a shortage of protective clothing and equipment, she has made medical scrubs for her two local hospitals, including the one where she gave birth. Post-lockdown, The Sew London Project provides sewing and crafting training for children, young people, and ex-offenders. 'Am I making millions? No, not quite yet. But I'm a much happier person. I remember that staffroom as a place full of people who wanted to do things and never did because they said to themselves, oh, I'm too old for that now. And that was one thing I thought I never want to do,' she says. I can see the courage and resilience she showed as a child running through her character, defining the adult she is and shaping the second half of her life as much as the first. Although her foster parents died many years ago, recently their great-grandchildren found Kemi on Facebook and, to her delight, sent her lots of photos from her childhood that her foster family had kept over the years. It seems to me that, many years after her death, her foster mother remains a powerful source of self-belief and courage for Kemi, helping her to continue to grow up into herself and to withstand the crushing forces that have sought to reduce her to something less than she knows she can be. She links her striving now, in the middle of her life, to being told at school that she wasn't clever enough to achieve anything: 'If you tell some children you're not going to amount to anything, it might well break them. That doesn't mean that those things didn't hurt me, it doesn't mean that those things did not have an underlying effect. But there's always the bit of me that goes, I'm going to be somebody, these are the skills I have, and I'm not going to hide. And I'm enjoying that freedom.'

Sara and I meet over Zoom. Her face appears on my laptop and a few seconds later she begins to speak, and I notice myself feeling calmer as she does; there is something very stabilising about the gentle rhythm of her voice and her easy smile. It is like something relaxed and sun-kissed is radiating out of her, and I can feel her contentment even through the screen; it is refreshing and reinvigorating to meet someone who seems so at peace.

I ask her if she is a grown-up now, at age 53, and she replies, 'Yes, I am, yes … with hesitation.' She describes a trajectory that is far more 'Mr Messy' or pinball machine than a straight line to adulthood, with a lot of getting lost in the middle.

In some respects, she grew up very quickly. By the age of 10, she was 5 feet 5 inches tall, and she had already started her period, maturing physically much earlier than her classmates. While they were all small and young-looking, she says, 'there was me, an adult body in a child'. I am so taken with this way of describing herself — not a child in an adult's body, which might seem more intuitive, but an adult body in a child, as if this too-big outside had to squeeze itself into her child's way of being, leaving her feeling that she was bursting out of herself, too big, too different. As well as standing out physically, she had a foreign surname and an older father — he was Polish, and 45 when she was born — and she thinks all this contributed to why she was picked on a lot at school. 'But instead of recoiling in, I fought out and I decided I didn't care that I was different. I decided to be different. I sort of rolled with it.' She discovered punk rock at age 11, and it was like an awakening; she loved the music of Kate Bush and Debbie Harry, and they became her style icons, as she became 'this punk-rock little kid'. She grew into a 'very fierce teenager', with a reputation for being a rebel, and moved out of her parents' home at 18. But underneath this grown up and resolutely independent exterior, it sounds to me like there was a young person who was perhaps a bit worried, and wanted to feel more in control of things. She remembers her mother as very untidy, and young

Sara hated how messy the house always was. 'All I wanted when I was a kid was an automatic washing machine instead of the awful twin tub we had, and tidy cupboards and tidy drawers. I wanted to get my own house and be tidy.' And when she did move away, she desperately missed the solidity and the stability of her father's presence: 'Suddenly I was in a house with no one to lock the doors and turn the lights out; I'd never slept in a house on my own before without my dad there, keeping me safe, and I was really scared.'

Not long after moving out from her parents' home, she became a parent herself. 'I was a very young mother,' she says: she was pregnant at 19, and 20 when her son was born. But this was no leap into adulthood: 'It felt like we were just two kids together, raising each other. I was winging it, pretending to be a grown-up.' She couldn't find affordable childcare, so she worked lots of part-time jobs and took her son with her. She'd start the day with a cleaning job early in the morning, then do a shift working in a bookshop, then work a second cleaning job at night. This was a time more of survival than of growth: 'I had to fight for things — fight for respect, fight for dignity. Being a single mother in the 80s, when the government was saying single mothers were the scourge of society — that was quite hard, because suddenly everybody's pointing fingers. People were quite vocal with their disgust.' She describes people shouting at her in the streets, while she was just trying to get by, looking after her little boy after a break-up. 'I think that blunts the edges off you, makes you a bit tougher.'

When her son was old enough to walk back from school and look after himself on his own for an hour at home, Sara had time to ask herself an important question: 'What do I want to do?' Now her child was growing up and becoming more independent, she could think about which direction she wanted to grow in herself. She wanted a career, and wrote to all the big-name companies on the high street, from Marks & Spencer to Boots, asking if they had any openings. Managers at Boots were so impressed with her at the interview that they offered her an assisting role on the pharmacy counter. She was scared to take it as it would mean learning technical skills and sitting exams, but she went for it, and she got such a high mark in her first exam that she was surprised into the realisation that she might be able to do it. 'I looked at the women who worked in the dispensary and thought, they know so much, they are so experienced, I want to be them. I got really hungry for it.' She spent the next few years studying and working and taking exams, eventually qualifying as an accuracy checking technician. 'I worked so hard for it, I was so proud.' But although she was developing and growing up in her career and in her sense of herself and her confidence, she still didn't really feel like an adult, and that was partly to do with how she was treated by others. 'When I was in my 20s and 30s, people, especially older men, used to talk down to me,' she says. She would be talking to a customer, explaining their medication, and he would diminish everything she said and interrupt with an 'I'll just get that man over there to explain it to me.' So as well as not feeling grown up in herself, she was not assumed to be a grown-up by many of the people around her: 'People treated me like a child for a long, long time, and it wasn't until my late 30s that that really started change.'

That was when Sara moved back to her home town of Richmond, some 20 years after she'd left, to a house around the corner from where her parents lived. Her son had left home and her long-term relationship had come to an end, and she felt the time was right to go back. Not long after she moved, her mother's best friend introduced Sara to her neighbour, who would become Sara's husband. 'And when I came home, it was like my parents suddenly went, "Oh, we can be old now",' she says. Her father was in his 80s and his health was failing, and her mother was struggling to look after him. Sara began a new phase in her relationship with her parents — and in her experience of adulthood. She'd check in on them every morning before work, then sometimes pop in at lunchtime, and every evening after work too. She got to know them again, this time as something closer to a grown-up. She describes her father as a very mature, dogmatic, serious, and intelligent man. 'He worked very hard as a blacksmith, and I think he was probably frustrated that he couldn't use his intelligence as he should have done.' Her mother was 12 years younger, and 'very immature, quite playful — she loved Marilyn Monroe and glitz and glamour and frivolousness'. Sara loved spending time with them in their home, and I can hear how much she still misses them when she says, 'It was such a nice environment, chatting to my mum and dad.' Together, she and her husband looked after her parents, and she felt herself growing up in the caring. 'I'd always wondered, would I want to look after my parents in their old age? It all seemed quite fearsome. But actually, it was a privilege to do it. It wasn't a burden. I feel so lucky, because I had the last five years of their lives with them.'

Then, standing at the gates of midlife, just at the start of her 40s, Sara lost both her parents; first her father, and then two years later, her mother. While she could accept her father's death at age 84, she felt cheated by her mother's, who died a decade younger. 'We'd grown so close in those past few years, we had such a good friendship … I wasn't ready to lose her,' she says. Sara was broken by the loss, and it is painful to hear her describe the aftermath: 'This massive wall of grief smacks you, oh, it takes your feet away from you.' She talks of acting like a robot as she waded through the banal, administrative tasks that occupy the grieving, taking up the empty space the loss has left: 'You go and get the death certificate, you organise the funeral, you go through the funeral, you clear the house, you deal with her effects.' But lying underneath that banality, threatening to erupt at any moment, was the sheer agony of losing someone she could not bear to believe was gone. She was clearing out the shed one day and found some antique bottles that had belonged to her father: 'My first thought was to run into the house to tell Mum what I've found, and I was running up the path and then suddenly I realised, I can't tell her, she's dead. It's like this steel wall just pops up and you run into it, and it smacks you again.' The last words her mother said to her were, 'Don't cry, darling,' and for at least three years, those words were the last thing Sara heard in her mind before falling asleep. 'It was almost like she was going to put her arms around me. Every night, every night, I thought of her every night.'

Sara found herself struggling to keep going. Staffing changes at the community pharmacy where she worked meant she was working longer hours, more intensively, and with less support. She suffered what sounds like a slow-burning breakdown. 'My brain had fogged, I was so tired, and I was grinding my teeth so hard in my sleep I had to buy special mouth guards and have massages on my jaw,' she says. She lost all her energy, and every step she took was 'like walking through quicksand'. All she knew was exhaustion, and she went from being a confident person to feeling worthless. Seeing her now, so energised and radiant, I can only imagine that what she experienced was a total deadening of who she was.

She was lying awake in bed in the early hours one night, and she got up, crept out of the bedroom, and sat at the kitchen table with a pen and a piece of paper. She says, 'I just thought: "I can't do this any more, I need a safety net. I'm going to write out my resignation letter, keep it in my handbag, and if I have another really bad day, I'll just quit."' She wrote it out by hand and put it in an envelope, signing herself a cheque for freedom that she could not yet give herself permission to cash. The next morning, over breakfast, she told her husband what she had done. He told her: 'That day has come. I'm going to drive you to work and you're handing in your notice today. We will cope.' So that's what she did. When her husband said those words, 'we will cope', she says, 'It was like the biggest, warmest hug, like I was being enveloped in the softest wool fleece you can have, like everything was lifted away.'

What followed seem to me like the biggest grow-ups of Sara's life — and they came in middle age. These were bigger than coping with discrimination as a young single mother, bigger than qualifying as a pharmacy technician, bigger even than losing her mother; she had no paid job to go to, but in front of her lay the most important work she would ever do. She had to learn who she was now, and find a new way to live. For the second time in her life, she found herself facing the question, 'What do I want to do?' This time, the answer was a simple one: to go swimming. But it didn't seem simple at the time. With her husband's help she developed a plan, the first step of which was to walk to town, less than a mile away. Previously, this really was nothing to her — but now it took courage. 'I thought, I'm scared. I can't walk to town, what if I get halfway up the hill and I can't go any further? But I did it. And when I did, I thought, I've done it! I can't believe I've actually done it! It was a huge, huge thing.' And then she walked to the swimming pool. And then she had to actually enter the changing room and put on her swimming costume and get in the pool. All sorts of fears crossed her mind — she imagined everybody else would be super fit, that she would sink to the bottom of the pool and drown. 'But then I thought, well, what would my mother say? My mother would say, "You hold your head up high and you go and do it." And then I thought, well, what would the old me, what would the other Sara do? That Sara would stick two fingers up to the world and say, "This is me, I'm going in, move aside." And I did it.' She swam four lengths, then went back home and slept for the rest of the afternoon. With every visit, as she swam length after length after length, her strength and resilience grew, and she began to find something of herself. 'It was starting to make me feel me again.'

Over this time, at the same time as working through her grief for her mother, she also had to mourn her job. 'I'd put so much pride into my career, and I'd worked really, really hard, and to think I wasn't going to have that again — that took quite a long time,' she says. But after about 10 months, she saw a job advertised: two days a week at the local museum, working in the gift shop and admissions. It was different from her pharmacy work — very different — but she got a good feeling at the interview. She got the job, and after easing into two days a week, she was soon working three, and then four or sometimes five. As time has gone on, she's gained confidence, and I can tell by the way she speaks about it that she really enjoys her work and her team. Whether she's helping decide what to sell in the shop, arranging the displays, or transcribing letters from World War II for an exhibition, she finds it fulfilling in a new way. 'I feel I am using my skills, I feel worthwhile.'

It was when her son and daughter-in-law told her that she would soon become a grandmother that Sara felt the tectonic plates of family, generations and adulthood definitively shift. Until then, she had been visiting her mother's grave in a field beside the house three or four times a week, but something changed when she got that news, and gradually, her visits fell to just once a week. 'And now I feel I only need to go if I'm on a walk and it takes me through there. That felt quite healthy, when I let that go. I thought she'd be glad that I was letting go,' she says. It sounds to me that through the preceding period of growth and development, she had been able to mourn the loss of her mother, and to look forward to the next phase in her life. She describes the moment of becoming a grandmother as feeling like a grown-up for the first time; it felt momentous that her child had a child, and the surge of love she describes for her grandchild was such a joyful and new experience, I wonder if it was intrinsically developmental. 'Suddenly I felt elevated to a much more mature level, like I'd moved up,' she says. She remembers warmly how much her own mother enjoyed being a grandmother, how she inhabited this role in such a comfortable, loving way. 'All the grandchildren loved her, and her house was always full of people, and it was, "Where's Grandma? Grandma! Grandma!" We all called her Grandma, and she wore it very well. And now I'm called Grandma. If I could be a grandma like her, a grandma who's cosy and warm and hugs you — that's always at the back of my mind. She left me that blueprint for what I think is how to be a good grandma. She's like an echo in my ear.'

What a beautiful way to hold on to a loved one after they have died, to carry them forward in your own life; an echo in your ear.

I ask her what it means to her to grow up, and she tells me, it is 'becoming mature enough to understand who you are, who you are as a person. To do that, to grow up, I had to deal with life situations, deal with them on my own, find the solutions, and cope and manage.' When she was younger, she used to think, I can't cope with this! I don't know what to do, I need to ask somebody, get some advice! It reminds me of my lifting up the bin lid full of writhing maggots, and needing to call my mum. Now she knows she can find the solution in herself to any problems she encounters. 'When my mother died, I had to walk through fire and survive that loss, carry on and grow up out of that grief, and into the truest version of myself.' And she did.

Sometimes, she says, she still feels like she's 'totally winging it', but there are other times when the thought that she's an adult really hits her, and she thinks, 'I'm grown up now.' She tells me that about once a year, she flies to America alone to visit her grandchildren. 'I get on this huge plane and buckle up and I look at the menu tucked into the seat in front of me, and the air steward giving the safety demonstration, and I think, oh my, I'm on an aeroplane on my own! And I do feel so grown up.'

Alex and I speak by phone, but we have met in person before, when I interviewed him for a newspaper about losing his father to suicide as a teenager.[9] I remember thinking that he looked tough, like he could handle himself. I remember being surprised and moved when I heard his voice quiver as he spoke about his father dying and when he talked about his sons. I was shocked that it was first time he'd really spoken to anyone in depth about what happened to him; when I interview him for this book, one year later, it is only the second time. 'No, I don't feel like a grown-up. I do not,' he tells me. It is a clear answer — if a surprising one, from a 46-year-old happily married father of two, who definitely looks like an adult man. But as he continues speaking, and as long-buried emotions and thoughts are finally put into words and spoken, I come to understand something about why that might be.

He knows that to understand why he doesn't feel like an adult, he has to start with his childhood. 'If I look at my childhood, it was shit. I don't have many happy memories as a child. I can't remember being read books. I can't remember cuddles in bed. I can't remember anything like that,' he says. His parents divorced when he was five and his mother was not considered responsible enough to look after him and his younger brother; they lived with his father and stepmother. The careful way he says, 'My dad was a hard man,' I get a sense of the fear and threat that coloured his upbringing. 'He was physically imposing. All the other dads were terrified of him at the football matches I played in when I was a kid — he was the really shouty dad.' Alex's father was the assistant manager of the children's team, and on one occasion he kicked the ball so hard at Alex he broke his wrist — but refused to take his son to hospital until the boy could prove his wrist was broken. That night when Alex tried to lift his dinner plate, his wrist snapped. 'Oh, okay, I can see it's broken now, I'll take you to hospital,' was all his father said.

The abuse was continued by his cruel and bullying stepmother. 'She hated us. She hit us every day. We would get hit around the head, we would get belittled.' Knowing that Alex hated tomatoes, she would serve them for every meal she could, and lock him in the garage for not eating them. To this day he cannot bear the smell of them. When Alex was 12 years old, he fought violence with violence: she had hit his brother and he told her, 'If you hit him again, I'm going to hit you back.' She hit his brother again. 'I really, really hit her.' He worried about how furious his father would be, but when he picked them up after football training, all he said was, 'Oh, she's not there any more.' Alex remembers, 'We thought he'd killed her for a minute, but she wasn't dead, she was alive.' Although he and his younger brother had each other for support, in some ways this left Alex feeling like he had to be more responsible, like out of the two of them he was the one in the adult department. 'I say that I feel young, but in a lot of ways, I've felt old for a long time. I always felt I had a lot of weight on my shoulders from being the older brother, protecting him from things that happened when we were kids; I think having this conversation is crystallizing this.'

I picture in my mind a household pulsating with aggression, where power was the underlying conversation topic and the threat of violence the only means of communication, the language passed down from adult to child. Alex did not learn to put feelings into words, but to put feelings into fighting. When he was bullied at school, he says, he couldn't talk about it, he just fought back. 'I learnt to shut off my emotions.' His wife complains that he doesn't show his feelings; he can understand her complaint, but he doesn't know how to be any different, because when he was a boy, he didn't have any space or any opportunity where he could feel them, talk about them, explore them, share them. But that doesn't mean he doesn't have them. 'I do have a very emotional side. There is a deep reservoir, deep down inside me. I stored a lot of emotions there when I was a little boy and locked them away, and I think sometimes they try to bubble to the surface. They're there, but he struggles to verbalise them: 'An artist can visualise a picture in his head and then translate it, paint it, but when I try to draw a picture, it looks like a 5-year-old's done it; that's how I feel with my emotions. In my head, I know how I feel about things, but to actually explain it feels difficult. Because then I start feeling emotional. As a man, as a boy, I was always taught not to show my emotions, and so I think I still have this conflict in me, that I'm worried about letting the emotions out.' He has told his wife his greatest fear is that one day something will make him start crying about everything that has happened to him, and he doesn't know if he'd be able to stop for days. I find myself wondering if that might be exactly what he needs.

As Alex hit his mid-teens, his father's drinking spiralled. He'd be drunk and asleep at his desk in his office, some embarrassed clients trying to wake him up; he'd be drunk at Alex's sixth form college parents' evening; 'He'd be drunk everywhere.' One afternoon his father disappeared from the house and Alex had no idea where he'd gone, and neither did any of the many friends or family he called. Alex found him that night unconscious on the ground at the end of the garden, and had to drag him to the house and call an ambulance. The next morning Alex went to visit him in hospital before going to his Saturday job at McDonald's, and his father was already on his way out: he told Alex to fuck off, and pushed him out of the way. 'That's how it was.' Alex's father made a suicide attempt later that year, and an ex-girlfriend of his dad's pinned Alex against the wall saying, 'If you don't do something, your dad's gonna die, you've got to do something.' He tells me, 'I tried to get him to the doctors, I tried to say, look, you've got a problem. But his view was, "I pay the bills, it's my house, I do what I want, who are you to tell me what to do?"' It sounds to me like Alex is defending himself against an accusation coming only from himself. I picture him as a helpless adolescent, caught in the no-man's-land between son and carer, responsible child and responsible adult, carrying the guilt and the pain of his deeply troubled father.

His father killed himself on 29 October 1991. A few days earlier, Alex had returned home after his Saturday shift at 6.30 pm to find his father asleep in the corner of the kitchen, 'all the washing up still there from the night before'. Alex tried to wake him up and, 'He went for me. He kneed me in the balls, tried to headbutt me. I managed to get out of that but he was a big guy, and the next thing I know we're trading punches.' His brother came running down the stairs, steamed into his father, and Alex walked out. It was the first and only time they had really fought each other like that. 'The emotion broke, I was outside the front of the house, crying, feeling pretty crap about crying, just angry.' He stayed overnight at a friend's. The next day, his father apologised, but Alex told him he wasn't interested, that 'last night was it'. His father said he was sorry, that Alex didn't have to worry, that he would support him through university. 'And I turned around and said, "How are you

going to fucking do that, Dad, you can't even kill yourself properly.'"
Alex slammed the door and walked out.

Alex went to stay with friends in Wolverhampton for the weekend.
He remembers it was a beautiful sunny day, and he was sitting in one
of their university rooms, having a cup of tea, when his friend walked
into the room, 'absolutely pale as a ghost'. He said, 'It's your dad, he's
dead.' Alex remembers getting the train back from Wolverhampton, his
grandad meeting him at Euston Station, the long walk up the platform.
The next morning, his grandad drove him home, and he remembers
getting out of the car and seeing all the neighbours' curtains twitch.

It was two months before Alex's 18th birthday. On the brink between
boyhood and manhood, this catastrophic and complicated loss left Alex
far older. 'If you lose someone at an early age like that, I think in some
ways it accelerates your growing up; I think I faced one of the worst
things you can probably face in your life, so in that way, it makes you
feel old and experienced,' he says. The kinds of questions on his friends'
minds were about what to study at university, who fancied who, which
bands to follow, and which rugby team would win the next match. But
when he was 17, Alex was at the vicar's house to plan his father's funeral
when he was asked, 'So, Alex, do you want to be buried in the same
spot? You need to tell us now because we need to know how deep to dig
the grave.'

At the same time as feeling too adult for his age, he says, 'The flipside
of it was the anger and the emotional fall-out almost made me hang on
to a crazy drink-and-drug-fuelled adolescence. It was all just part of the
trying to forget, I think.' At 19, he had a number-one, skinhead haircut,
a big gold earring, and gold chains. He left university in his early 20s
and saw his friends' excitement over how their lives were just about to
begin, 'but I didn't feel like that; I felt exhausted by life'. In rugby, he
always played tighthead prop, the most aggressive, physical position; he
was angry at the world and at what had happened to him, and he fought
a lot — that was where he got his enjoyment. 'When you're confident in

your strength and you've got a chip on your shoulder from things that have happened to you, perceived injustices, you're on a hair trigger, ready to respond to the slightest provocation.' He says that he wasn't a bad guy, he never picked on people who didn't want to fight him because there were plenty who did. He had guns waved at him, knives waved at him; he fought with belts and sticks. He recognises that a lot of people who did what he did might have ended up in prison, or stabbed, or shot. He was lucky, he says.

Although it could have turned out very differently, looking back, Alex now sees this time as having real value: 'I came out the other side, and now I feel I got something out of it that helped me. I had such an intense 20s that it got everything out of my system. I'm not proud of some of the things I did and said, but equally I think it was a kind of validation, a kind of growing up and working all this anger out.' At the time though, he just felt stuck. Stuck in this adolescent life, unable to grow out of it. If he wanted his 30s to be different from his 20s, he needed a grow-up that would shake everything up. 'I think I recognised in myself, I needed to get away. I was in a rut, I was partying too late and spending all day in bed. I had to put myself somewhere completely new, I had to try to change things, and there's nothing like moving to the other side of the world to get a fresh perspective.'

At 29, Alex left Sussex, the city he'd lived in since birth, and moved to the other side of the world, and his partner joined him six months later. In the 10 years that had followed his father's suicide, every time he saw a friend, he would hear a reminder of what had happened to him in their tone of voice and see it in their eyes. 'By moving to Australia, where no one knew me from Adam, I wasn't defined by my mates thinking, "Oh look, this is Evs, he's a top bloke but he's had a bit of a shit time, keep an eye on him, he's a bit of a loose cannon,"' he says. Instead, the narrative in his head ran, 'Hello, I'm Alex, and I can be whoever I want to be.' I am struck by how different this is from the alternative Nathanson spoke of, the bullshit artist inside us who says, 'I can be whoever you want me to be.' This was Alex defining himself, refusing to be defined by others, and it led to a very important shift in emphasis: 'Thinking about it, that was the first time I didn't define myself by what I'd lost, but I began to define myself by what I had.'

And what he had was a life that he and his partner had chosen and built for themselves in Bondi, 'probably the coolest suburb in the world', where he had the distance, the physical and emotional distance from the people and buildings and triggers for memories, to be able to work out who he really was now. Moving to another country involved significant challenges of organisation, administration, and self-determination — setting up new bank accounts, finding jobs, having the right visas — and all these smaller grow-ups led to bigger ones. 'My extended adolescence tapered off — it didn't completely taper off, because there are a lot of fun places in Sydney ... but it gave me the chance to reflect on the kind of person I wanted to be. I got into boot camps and the outdoor life, I started swimming again. And the fact that we got married out there, we had our first child out there, made it a really special time.'

There is a long pause, and when he begins speaking again, I notice the pitch of Alex's voice has changed. He sounds choked and nasal. I find tears leaking out of my eyes as his voice cracks. 'I had the first hour with him,' he says. After their baby was born, Alex held his new son in his arms. 'It was 8.30 on a lovely autumn morning, we were looking out at a beautiful sky,' he says. The midwives told him that skin to skin contact with a baby helps bonding, so he took his shirt off, and felt his newborn's soft skin against his chest and arms. 'So I'm standing there with my son, and I just held him and I made all these promises to him. I was never going to let him down. I wasn't going to kill myself. In that moment, I realised I had the power to change my family's story, that it wasn't a case of repeating the past; it was a case of, this is my boy. And I'm in charge of the script here. And it is going to be okay.' In that first hour, a new father holding his new son, Alex saw new possibilities opening up before them. 'Reflecting on my life and his, what his life was going to be, it felt like a culmination of half a life's work, that I'd finally got to that point. It was powerful. I bonded with him so tightly. For me, fatherhood is everything. It's the most important, most grounding thing.' He faced down the ghosts in his nursery, and they backed off. This was the biggest grow-up of his life.

After nearly a decade in Australia, Alex and his family moved back to the UK, to Sussex, where he was born. He was happy to be back — he loves the Downs, the beach, the football team. But as his 40th birthday and midlife proper approached, he had to face another important grow-up, and this one was painful. He found himself caught up in a toxic web of comparisons. 'I was getting really stressed about some friends achieving more than me, being high up in their companies or setting their own businesses up themselves. I think one of the dangers, especially with LinkedIn, is you think everyone in the world is doing better than you.' It was as true for Alex at midlife as it was for Victoria in adolescence. This is the brutal self-harm of what the psychotherapist Windy Dryden has called 'comparisonitis'. Social media makes it worse, but it didn't start there — this is plain old, nuts-and-bolts-of-being-human envy, which Aristotle defined in the 4th century BC as pain at the sight of another's good fortune, stirred by 'those who have what we ought to have'. Caught up in desperation to achieve what others had, Alex tried to strategise his way to the top, changing jobs quickly to get promotions and pay rises and climb the ladder — or rather, the Escher staircase that leads to nowhere. Because it didn't work. 'I thought that was what I needed to do to get on, but I was just making myself more and more unhappy.'

Then something happened that shook him off that Escher staircase of envy: a friend's marriage broke down, and much of what he had earned was lost in the divorce. It was a shock for Alex, and he saw his own life in a new light. He thought about his home, his marriage, his family. 'I looked around me and I thought, you know what, I've got all this.' For the first time, he understood the parable of the tortoise and the hare: if he kept going at his own pace, then he should end up with financial security and the mortgage paid off. If he stuck to his own path and looked after his marriage and his sons, he could end up with a comfortable life, which was worth more to him than the next big promotion. His definition of success and happiness changed, as the parable of the tortoise and the hare became a 'coping mechanism' for the jealousy and envy of what other people have, 'and that was very liberating', he says. 'I started enjoying my life for what it is, having a family, rather than basing everything on financial success or career status, and I stopped blindly comparing myself to people I went to school with.' This was another reckoning with the ghosts in his nursery, a realisation of his life's mission, to break out of the painful history of relationship breakdown, abuse, and addiction that defined the other men in his family. 'Now I see my role in life as creating a platform for my two sons not to suffer that. Not to see their parents throwing plates at each other, not to watch dads punching stepdads, not to hear arguments every night and kettles of water being thrown and glasses being smashed. I feel happy in myself that I'm going to give my boys the opportunity to be happier. My kids won't have what I had, and I would define that as a successful life.'

This seems to me like such an important grow-up, and thinking about Alex's understanding of it, and the understanding that has been building with every life stage I explore, has helped me to define more clearly what a grow-up really is. I think it is a working through of something difficult that leaves us feeling that we can move forward with more freedom than we did before, separating ourselves from those who went before us and those around us. We don't ever grow out of jealousy or envy of others, I think — but we can learn to accept it in ourselves, and find a way to be with it, a way to use it to find out what we really do want from our lives, and what is just a distraction. We can learn how to prevent it from destroying our appreciation for the good in our lives. This investigation is a grow-up that is perhaps most urgent in this life stage, but that comes into all the others too, I think — at least it has for me.

It strikes me anew that so much of Alex's experiences of growing up have been about finding his own definitions — of himself, of childhood, of adulthood, of fatherhood — and breaking free from those handed down from father to son. This is the process that I am going through too, in my own way, in my analysis and in this book; one that I am still trying to grapple with. There was something about being in midlife that made this more possible for Alex — specifically turning 44. His father was 44 when he died, and Alex worked out the exact date that he became older than his father had ever been. Until that moment, he says, 'he was always a shadow, standing over my life'. He has never forgotten a TV drama he watched when he was a teenager about a man who hunted down Nazis after the war. He remembers one scene depicting this character's recurring nightmare, in which he is seen covered in bandages and blood, carrying a dead Nazi on his back, symbolising the weight of everything he had to shoulder. 'That was what it felt like for so long with my dad; it felt like a weight, like a physical body on my shoulders.' When Alex turned 44 and a bit in June 2018, two years before we speak, 'It felt like I had been walking up the stairs with this body on my back, and suddenly I had reached the entrance and daylight, and I dropped the body. It felt like dropping the 16 stone that my dad weighed, like it dropped off my shoulders for the first time. That weight fell off me.'

And yet, despite what he has achieved, despite his content family life, despite finally freeing himself from the weight of his father — Alex does not feel like a grown-up. When he is stressed about work, he has moments and days where he reverts to feeling totally consumed with anger about his childhood. 'It's almost a weird place of comfort for me,' he says. He knows at times like this that his wife worries about him. He has told her — and he means it — that he is not going to kill himself, but that doesn't mean that he doesn't still struggle with grief, rage, sadness. 'As much as I know I'm coming out into the light now, and I definitely feel like I don't carry the baggage I did, I cannot uninvent those experiences. Much as I wish I could have a lobotomy and forget it all, I can't.' He has some memories that he cannot bear to go back to. Sometimes they appear as videos in his mind, flicking from one to the next, 'tsk tsk tsk'. He visualises putting them into a box, and then he puts that box into another box, and he locks that box and hides the key in another part of his mind. 'I read somewhere once that suicide is like a nuclear bomb, because not only is there the explosion and the immediate devastation, but the fall-out lasts for so long. It's one of the most difficult things to overcome. I think perhaps that's why I feel I've never really grown up. Because I've never come to a complete accommodation or peace about what happened to me as I approached adulthood.' He remains stuck at this grow-up, and at times he cannot stop the questions from haunting him: 'Could I have done more? Could I have done something to stop it?' Sometimes he closes his eyes and he is a scared 17-year-old again, his dad's ex-girlfriend shouting at him, 'If you don't do something, Alex, your dad's gonna die.'

But when he opens them, he is not that 17-year-old any more. Now he is the father of two boys, who are growing up in the same town he grew up in, but in a very different family. When he walks the same streets he walked as a teenager, he no longer feels trapped by his violent past. 'I like the guy I am now. I'm quite happy with myself, content with what I am,' he says, and I find there are tears in my eyes. He can see himself growing old in Sussex. 'Sometimes I think, well, I'm probably over halfway through now. And that feels weird.' Although part of him thinks he may have already passed the half-way point in his life, another part still doesn't feel like he has reached it yet, and he hopes that he has many more years than that to come. But he does feel conscious now that his time is getting shorter. 'I've been going for walks every day during lockdown and I find myself looking at older people sitting on the benches, and trying to get inside their heads a bit. I wonder, what does it feel like to know you're probably into your last decade?' I think of 17-year-old Alex, sitting in the vicar's living room, being asked if he wanted to be buried in the same grave as his father. 'I told him, "no thanks",' he says. 'That grave was dug for one.'

Kemi, Sara, Alex. These three individuals, with their very different stories, all found themselves near the middle of their path through life, lost in a dark wood, struggling for air. For Kemi, it was the suffocating feeling in that staffroom, that she too might simply stay there just because it was easier and more comfortable than taking a risk and pursuing the work she had always wanted to do. For Sara, the loss of her mother combined with the pressures and absence of support at work left her grinding her teeth so hard in her sleep she had to wear a mouth guard. For Alex, it was the weight of his father's suicide which sat unyielding on his shoulders, oppressive, stifling. And each of these individuals, for very different reasons, found in midlife the breathing space they needed to take a gasp of fresh air and drink it in. There is a risk of idealising these experiences, of hearing straightforward happy endings, but that would do them, and ourselves, a disservice; these people are not clichés, but complex and nuanced, and their stories are richer for it. Kemi is proud to run her own social enterprise, but there are still frustrations and sacrifices and difficulties, as there were when she was a teacher. Sara still misses her mum, still thinks of her most nights, still hears her words, 'don't cry, darling', though she visits her grave when she happens to pass by rather than feeling she needs to go every day. Alex has built a good life for himself despite suffering so much as a child — he has, mostly, banished the ghosts from his nursery — but he still struggles with the dark thoughts he has locked away, boxes in boxes in boxes, he still wishes he could bury that key and forget where he hid it. But I have the sense from speaking to them that for each of these people, while the approach of this life stage and its grow-ups left them holding their breath in fear, hitting midlife propelled them somehow to work through these fears and grow-ups, and that they are now breathing more freely than before.

What is it about midlife specifically that means it can be such a fertile period of growing up?[10] Oliver Robinson, Associate Professor of Psychology at the University of Greenwich, specialises in the life-course,[11] and he tells me he thinks the symbolism of feeling like you are halfway through life is significant. 'It's that sense of reaching a point where you are in a position to re-evaluate things, when the feeling that you might have more time behind you than you have ahead of you starts to shift the narrative tone.' It is that shift in tone that really gets to the heart of what midlife means for Robinson, and he draws on the work of psychoanalyst James Hollis[12] to describe the texture and flavour of feeling in the middle: 'You realise you have less time than you had before. You feel the strange tension of continued growth with very apparent decline. And you feel this sense of opposites, that you're both young and old simultaneously; it's very contradictory. And you start to think about death more, you get the sense of where you're going.' As he says this, I find myself thinking about Alex: I can see him in my mind's eye, taking in the older couples sitting on the benches on the seafront in Hove as he strolls past, trying to get into their heads, wondering what it is like for them to be so near the end. 'And, if it goes well,' Robinson continues, 'you start to lose these intense ambitions of young adulthood, this constant drive which makes it so difficult to enjoy the present moment, as well as this tendency to judge yourself and others very readily. It's an encounter with your unconscious to some degree; an encounter with a lot of illusions and delusions — and it's an opportunity to wake up to those.' The psychological shift to midlife, the real grow-up of this life stage, involves a letting go of our more narcissistic ideals, he seems to be saying, for something more grounded, more rooted in reality, more grown up — to find the tortoise inside us, rather than the hare. 'Because on the other side is this insanely simple solution, which is that where you are is all you ever are.' It's so obvious, and it can feel empty of meaning when you see it printed in a cursive font on a mug or as a caption on a photo of a beach on Instagram, but when you realise it for yourself, as I know Alex has, but as I haven't yet, it can change the way you live. Robinson continues: 'This is the realisation: that the next book, the next whatever, is never going to make you happy, bring you the reputation you crave — no! It's bollocks. It's never going to happen. Because in the end, you only ever are where you are. And then maybe, one day, you can sit down and think, I'm not going to compare myself with anyone any more, I'm just going to be here. It's all right here.' He adds, 'It took me 40-something years to be able to do that, and I'm still getting the hang of it.' Robinson is 43, and when I ask him if he feels like an adult, he does not hesitate: 'Yes.'

Not everyone reaches this level of grown-up Zen in midlife — for some, the insane ambitions, the narcissistic ideals, and the next new thing prove too tempting, whether that's buying a flash car, leaving your family for a partner half your age, or one of the various other clichés that have come to be known as a midlife crisis. This has been midlife's only sexy USP, one of the only things to put midlife on the map until Simons and others started their research. It is such a tired stereotype now, I find myself grimacing at the idea of writing about it, especially when so many of the people at this life stage whom I have interviewed have made huge changes in their lives, been through such significant and meaningful transformations that could never be reduced to a neat, midlife-crisis-shaped storyline. But when I read the paper 'Death and the midlife crisis',[13] in which Elliott Jaques first popularised the term, although I don't agree with everything he wrote, I find some of it quite persuasive, especially the lines he quotes from Dante, which I've also quoted at the start of this chapter. Jaques — a psychoanalyst — writes about a 36-year-old patient who says, 'Up until now, life has seemed an endless upward slope, with nothing but the distant horizon in view. Now suddenly I seem to have reached the crest of the hill, and there stretching ahead is the downward slope with the end of the road in sight — far

enough away it's true — but there is death observably present at the end.'
He later told an interviewer that this patient was, in fact, himself. This
is the traditional, triangle-shaped graph of the life-course, rather than
our Mr Messy, pinball-machine theory of development, and although
it does make for a compelling narrative, it still seems too linear to me
— but perhaps that is the critique of someone who has not yet reached
midlife (although I'm increasingly aware that I'm not far off it). Jaques
continues, in a passage that now reads like something from another era
— which, of course, it is: 'The individual has stopped growing up, and
has begun to grow old. A new set of external circumstances has to be
met. The first phase of adult life has been lived. Family and occupation
have become established (or ought to have become established unless
the individual's adjustment has gone seriously awry); parents have grown
old, and children are at the threshold of adulthood.' This is simply not
the case for many individuals these days, and it feels very old-fashioned
now. I think of Kemi, her occupation was established, but she completely
unestablished it and started again; I think of Sara, her family established
by 18; I think of Amy Blackstone, 47 and happy as Larry embracing
her child-free life. To consider any of these people as 'individuals whose
adjustment has gone seriously awry' seems misguided and judgemental
today.

But what Jaques writes next … this bit, I think, still makes a lot
of sense: 'Youth and childhood are past and gone, and demand to be
mourned. The achievement of mature and independent adulthood
presents itself as the main psychological task. The paradox is that of
entering the prime of life, the stage of fulfilment, but at the same time
the prime and fulfilment are dated. Death lies beyond.' This part rings
true. This, I think, is the defining aspect of being in midlife; this is how
we can define it as valuable on its own terms, rather than as 'the bit
in between'; it is the window in which a shift takes place, when the
inevitability of death heaves into view, not imminent, but no longer lost
in the distance. It acts like a filter, changing the way we experience time

— if we let it. This is one of the most important grow-ups of midlife.

For Sara, it was the death of her parents that changed her sense of herself and propelled her into what Jaques calls 'mature and independent adulthood'. Morgan Brett has found in her research into midlife that this is not unusual, nor is it straightforward: the loss of parents can be what she calls 'a pivotal moment of feeling grown up, of not feeling like somebody's child', but at the same time, feeling like 'a midlife orphan'. I think of Sara hearing her mother's voice every night, the wish to be wrapped in her arms. This ambivalence — feeling two things at the same time — is key to the midlife experience, says Morgan Brett, 'At one point someone might feel that they have a huge amount of responsibility on their shoulders, that they have become more grown up within their family because they are now the older generation; but they can easily flip into a psychological state of feeling separation and loss, of being orphaned, childlike.' This is the loss that leaves even the most mature adults feeling like an abandoned child, which child and adolescent psychotherapist Ariel Nathanson describes so beautifully: 'The moment of losing a parent is poignant. It's very painful. You can never lose a parent as an adult, because regardless of your age, what you feel in that moment is that you as a child have lost your parent.' But, he explains, if you are a healthy adult, you can look after that child, the adult part of you parenting the child inside: you can be two things at the same time. He continues, 'I remember it happening to me, and in those moments, you kind of feel both; you feel in an extremely distressing infantile state of mind, which is very frightening and sad, but at the same time you're able to come into contact with this other, more grown-up being, who holds things together.' The adult can take care of the child 'in a caring, benevolent way'. I find this such a moving depiction of what it means to feel grown up, to be able to look after oneself. He adds, 'If you think about bereavement as something that comes in waves of intensity, as an adult you become aware that there is a space between the waves. But if you are just a child with no adult state of mind, then you drown, because you feel it is going to go on for ever. If you're a child with an adult around you, the adult can hold their breath, knowing that after this wave, there will be some air.' I try to hold on to this, because it feels like a very important characteristic of adulthood, one to add to the definition we are building: an adult can hold their breath, knowing that after this wave, there will be some air.

Josh Cohen, the psychoanalyst and author of *How to Live. What to Do.*,[14] seems to me to be living his best (mid)life. He tells me on Zoom, 'I feel happier in myself than at any other stage of life.' I ask him if he is an adult and he replies, 'That's such a lovely question. I'm going to say yes. Which always seems like the riskiest possible answer.' His answer is yes because he is 'aware of and alive to the currents of childlikeness and childishness and of infancy' in him, and how easily and quickly he can revert to all those states. But he also thinks that in some ways, he was born to be an adult; his personal history and his character mean that he actually likes the conditions that define adult life. For him this means having a family and assuming the role of a parent, of the 'reliability and steadiness and benign predictability' that comes with that, the characteristics of his midlife which, he says, 'I think suit me.' He thinks it is 'something to do with that internal state of non-turbulence, of being not very easily stirred to extremities of mood. I think I've always had something of that. Adulthood, in some ways, has felt like a bit of a coming home for me'.

When I hear this, I think, 'Wow, that sounds pretty great.' Steadiness and predictability, non-turbulence, rare extremities of mood. I know little of what this man speaks. He will later call this experience 'a kind of coming into my own'. I understand the words he is saying, I agree it sounds like a meaningful way of thinking about what it means to grow up, but I feel like he is describing a state that is not currently possible for me. I seem to be experiencing more of a coming apart, especially in my analysis.

On Monday, Tuesday, Wednesday, and Thursday mornings, after I shower and have my breakfast; instead of going to my analyst's consulting room, I come back to my lockdown consulting room — my bedroom — and I lie on my back on the bed, and put my phone on 'do not disturb'. But while the volume of external disturbance is turned down low, the volume of internal disturbance is turned up to the maximum. I put in my earphones and I phone my analyst. She says 'Hello.' I say 'Hello.' And then there is silence. I say what comes to my mind, and my analyst responds, and somehow, over the course of this process, it feels like my mind is coming apart, like bits of my mind, that never really belonged to me but which I thought were mine, are falling off, and that I am left with nothing but gaps where bits of my own mind should be. I feel like I am a jellyfish, a wobbly-wibbly blob, unformed, baby-like, amorphous, helpless, unknowable. I feel like I do not know who I am, if I even am an 'am', if I have a mind to realise or to think at all. I come to see how much I have been clinging to friends, to parents, to teachers, to my husband, to my analyst to tell me who I am, to get them to tell me what I think and what I feel, because I simply do not know myself. These are the parts of my mind that are dropping off, I think — the parts that belong to others. But what is left behind? Just jellyfish and gaps, it seems to me. I lie on the bed and I experience this sensation of a mind that is full of holes where something important should be, something that enables me to be me. Something that is me. So far, no dice. I am lost. But if I have learnt anything from Kemi, Sara, and Alex, it is that getting lost is an important part of the process of growing up.

After each session, I sit on the balcony for a bit if it's sunny and look out at the trees, and then I begin working on my book, or I make a coffee, or I do some reading about psychoanalysis. That is, I try to put myself back together again and get on with my day, thinking thoughts and having feelings like everyone else, living this adult-seeming life. I google jellyfish and I discover that they do not have brains, hearts, or eyes, and that some fossils have been estimated to be more than 600 million years old, predating dinosaurs. This makes sense, I think. This is how I feel sometimes — like I have not really evolved. My friends and my family reassure me that they do experience me as someone with a brain to think, a heart to feel, and eyes to see; as an adult; as someone with a self, as someone who is neither unformed nor prehistoric. And I know that I have this experience of myself as well — not when I am in analysis, but when I am writing this book, when I am sitting in the room with a patient, when I am having a drink with friends. So which is the real me, the wobbly, unformed jellyfish or the adult? Well, reflecting on what Cohen tells me next, I think, it must be both.

'I think of childhood and adulthood as different psychic states rather than developmental stages,' he says — not unlike Klein's theory of the two positions. 'There's a horizontality about them; that is, it's not a hierarchy from one to the other. When I say, "I'm an adult", I mean that I feel like I occupy the psychic state of an adult. When you see me walking along, or in a photograph, you probably see an adult; somebody who occupies his age, who occupies a state of mind and a style of being that is at his age, someone who is comfortable in the skin of his age.' I ask Cohen to describe, from the perspective of a psychoanalyst, what an adult state of mind feels like to inhabit — just to torture myself a bit more — and he tells me, 'I would say it's one that is not overburdened by anxiety. It's a sense of not feeling particularly pressured to be anyone other than who I am, or to perform a self for anyone else. It's a kind of independence of mind and spirit that isn't overly burdened by the expectations of others.' This is something I so desperately want for myself, something that I crave with such longing, that it is quite hard for me to hear the words. And when I ask him my next question — what that process of growing up involves — his answer circles around my mind for months after, something I feel I have been hearing from my psychoanalyst in different words and trying to understand in different ways ever since I started therapy. He says, 'I think it involves a process of gradual separation; separation from the figures around you who are seeking consciously or unconsciously to shape who and how you are.' It means leaving behind the question of the internal marketing manager — 'Who do you want me to be?' And asking instead, 'Who am I?'

I do not know the answer to this question. I wonder if it got lost somewhere between what Cohen describes as 'the two poles of childhood': he explains that we forge an identity in our youth through on the one hand, play, imaginative life, self-exploration, and solitude; and on the other hand, through mimicry and imitation of, and compliance with, the adult world. No one can reach a healthy midlife without being initiated into both of those paths, he says — the child's inner world and the adult's social world — but one of the features of Western middle-class life is that the adult's world is privileged so much over the child's. 'The exploratory imaginative life of the child is corralled into the path of expectation and achievement and conformity to adult goals.' He describes the pressure-cooker atmosphere of a certain kind of middle-class parenting where you send your child to a tutor and you communicate to them from the age of about 4 that there are many steps, in which they are now being initiated, to becoming a neurosurgeon or a partner in a big law firm. 'I think that will produce a kind of a parody of a grown-up. It will produce a very good impersonation of somebody who knows what being a grown-up is in all the externals.' He tells me about visiting a nursery with his wife for their first child, and his impressions of the woman who ran it. 'The basic principle of all the creative endeavours was that she never praised the work; she never said, "Oh, what a wonderful picture, how beautiful, let's hang it on the wall."' He remembers very vividly her saying, 'The only questions that I ask are: is it finished? And are you happy with it?' For Cohen, this is fundamental. He understands that in asking these questions, the picture remained as something that belonged to the world of the child, rather than appropriated for the adult world as something to be judged, compared, found wanting. 'She gave the picture to the child.'

This story gives me an ache in my chest. I agree so hard with what he says next: 'The attitude of our educational system and child-rearing experience seems to run so much in the other direction that we send children the message all the time that their basic task in life is to please us.' I do not know when I last did a piece of work for myself — if I have ever done this as an adult. The propelling force behind everything I have written has been the drive to create work that pleases others. That has been fruitful in some ways — it has helped me to achieve some degree of professional success — but it has also taken me away from myself; it has meant that much of what I do is about the reactions of everyone else. Psychoanalysis is offering me a way to understand this, and, together with this book, I hope, a different way to write, and to be.

At least, I tell myself, I have another decade or so before I get to midlife proper, to find these missing parts of myself — I hope I can manage it by then, so that I can feel something like what Cohen has experienced, midlife as 'something like arrival at oneself'. He explains that many of us live most of the first half of our lives — up to 45, say — accumulating various milestones and achievements and defining ourselves in relation to external and internal aims and targets and desires. 'It can be very exciting, certainly very involving, and it can be turbulent, but it also means that you are always seeing yourself in relation to something that is ahead or not yet; it's not quite realised. You are referring your present self to a future self,' he says, and I realise with a sick feeling in my stomach I have just done exactly that. I have turned Cohen's words into a milestone to be achieved, into a target I desire to reach, into something my present self is hoping for my future self. But, he says, somewhere around middle age, somewhere in your 40s or your 50s, there might, hopefully, be a moment where we feel that we are done with all that accumulation, and that is what he calls being in midlife — 'In the sense that you are immersing yourself in the life that is there right in front of you.' You are in the middle of your life like you might be in the middle of reading, or in the middle of eating. You are right in the middle of living. I think of Alex realising he doesn't want to keep chasing after the next promotion and pay rise, how much he values his family life. Cohen continues, 'It allows you to enjoy what is in front of you. People often become interested in aspects of life that involve immediacy — it might be gardening, it might be walking in nature, it might be baking.' He calls this 'an embrace of middle age, rather than running away from it'. The draw of these activities is that they allow us to focus on what's there and available, on where we are. 'We aren't in this state of frenzied looking ahead of ourselves, which doesn't allow for much interest in the garden or the birdsong.' This is the key to a midlife well lived, this is the difference between being lifeless and staid versus being alive and at peace with oneself: 'It is something to do with a settledness that is not necessarily an ossification or becoming jaded. If middle-aged life is going reasonably well, it gives you a new sense of liveliness, because it's not the liveliness of somebody who is chasing exhaustingly after the next thing, but the person who is actually excited by what's in front of them.'

I think of Kemi and the fulfilment she is getting from being her own boss, using her skills, passing them on to others. I think of Sara, who really seemed to glow with the sunshine of the Dales, who found a way back to herself through walking, swimming, being a grandmother. I think of Alex, who has finally realised that he already has the thing that matters most to him, a family, so he can stop racing ahead as a hare and just enjoy being the tortoise. But, I wonder, am I in danger again of idealising midlife? That would be just as shallow, one-sided, and false as retelling their stories as midlife crises — Sara who burnt out, Kemi who left her stable career, Alex who lost himself in comparisons with everybody else. Cohen tells me there is an important difference between a crisis and a transition: 'A transition doesn't induce some destructive conflict with where you are; it doesn't mean that you have to lay waste to the life you have built for yourself. It can be a kind of movement from one place to another.' This is the nuance I must not lose when thinking about the pains and the pleasures of midlife and the difficulty, the wrench, that comes with any kind of change, especially with growing up. I am reminded of what the psychologist Oliver Robinson told me, right at the end of our interview: 'In my final two minutes, I'll say this: in psychology there is this rather simplistic assumption that satisfaction is always a positive outcome. It is, under certain circumstances — but so is dissatisfaction under certain circumstances.' Something he thinks that psychology and psychiatry get wrong is to constantly pathologise feeling bad; in other words, to take feeling sad, unhappy, or anxious as a symptom of an illness, something wrong that must be medicated away. That is not always the case, he says: 'Feeling bad is a driver for change in the way that nothing else can be. If you have strong negative emotions, if you feel yourself falling apart, then listen carefully to what you should and could change in your life.' Feeling unhappy, he is saying, is an extremely significant and valuable experience, and we need to learn how to understand what it means. 'At all points in the lifespan, learning how to attend to the negative feelings and movements within one's body and mind, and learning to make changes accordingly that move you through to the next stage rather than regressing back, is crucial.' Moving through or regressing back — we have to pick one, because we cannot stay the same. If we are happy, we will want to continue as we are, just carry on doing what we're doing in the hope that we can stay happy; 'That's the joy of happiness. That's also the stupidity of happiness.' Stupid because, of course, no matter how hard we try, time passes, and nothing stays the same.

Chewing all this over, I find my mind returning to the 'barrier of inertia' first described to me by Simons. The barrier of inertia is a term which refers to the feeling of lassitude and laziness which stops us from having the new experiences in midlife that could help shore up our cognitive reserves and protect us, to some degree, against decline in the future. He explains, 'When we're young, we're thirsting for new experiences. We're constantly going, oh yeah, I really want to go to Ibiza or experiment with drugs or take risks.' But as we get older, as we settle down, take on responsibilities and demanding jobs and dependents, 'There is an inertia to discovering and doing new things — much easier not to bother. Much easier to sit down in front of Netflix, to say, "Oh, I'll do it tomorrow.'" But if we can break that barrier once, if we can make the choice to do something new one evening instead of watching Netflix, he thinks it might gradually become easier and easier to make that choice again and again, evening after evening — and if we can wear that inertia down, we could end up doing new things more of the time, from meeting new people to learning another language or a musical instrument. And this could change not just our current life stage, but the next ones too: there is evidence to suggest that someone who can break through that barrier of inertia might also be someone who is less vulnerable to cognitive decline later in life. 'The field is too young to be able to say that's proven — but the evidence is pointing that way. That's the hope.' He is researching interventions that can support or motivate people to understand this, and to take the steps they need to force themselves to break through that barrier.

I wonder if there is another reason why people choose to watch Netflix rather than doing something new. I think people lose themselves in their screens night after night because they don't want to engage with the reality that is confronting them. And by people, I mean me. And by reality, I mean many things, from the everyday unhappiness we feel, to the brutal, immutable fact that time passes and that loss is inevitable. It seems to me that to choose to do something different, to turn away from our screens, we would have to engage with what that choice really means; the choice to come alive, to try and keep our brains and our minds alive while we can, because our time alive is limited. That, to me, is the truly troubling barrier of inertia; the wish to avoid reality by killing off our minds and our brains with screens rather than to engage with it, to really see it and feel it and try to understand it, and to mourn, and do the things that make us feel more alive, and that could keep us alive. That could help us to keep growing.

Reflecting on this, I realise I have been thinking about growing up all wrong. I have been wishing that I could finally become an adult and finish with all this growing-up business. Now I am beginning to see that that is a dangerous wish indeed. It's not a question of growing up by the time you get to midlife — all done, thank you very much, can I have a badge. It is a question of how to keep growing up, through midlife and beyond, for as long as you possibly can. Adulthood not as a finishing line but as a continual process of transformation, development, and self-understanding. That is the crucial grow-up of midlife.

I am finding all this growing up so, so difficult — even with all my privilege, my loving family, my loving partner. That is what has surprised me most of everything I've learnt so far about what it means to grow up — how difficult it is. I feel I understand Bion's quote in a new way — I get why, 'Of all the hateful possibilities, growth and maturation are feared and detested most frequently.'[15] The loss, the frustration, the wish to go faster than I can. At times, I feel like the baby at the start of this chapter, desperate to sit up but unable to do it by myself. I am so used to trying so hard to hold everything together, and I have a sense that maybe I just need to stop trying, to let myself fall, and let my analyst catch me. But it is not so easy for me to do that. I think it might take a very long time. For now, though, I am beginning to get a sense of the part of me that is so afraid of falling. I am beginning to feel the shape of the bits of me that don't really belong to me, but to other people's expectations of me, which have also become my own expectations of me. I am beginning to feel curious about what Cohen described as the 'currents of childlikeness and childishness and of infancy' that run through me. Perhaps I thought I had to magically get rid of those currents in order to be an adult, and to wave goodbye to the paranoid-schizoid position once and for all, never to return. It is so hard to let go of that wish. At least now I can see that I don't have to be the hare I have always thought I was. I do feel very lost right now, but I can also sense there is a meaning to this lostness, that getting lost is an important part of growing up. This is the challenge I am facing in psychoanalysis, and it is the challenge faced by every person who is struggling to grow up:

to find ourselves alone and lost in a dark wood and to try, as Kemi, Sara, and Alex did, to see the truth of that, and to really think about who and where we are. That is the only way through.

Chapter Five
Young-old rising

'Run That Body Down'
Song by Paul Simon

A baby is weaning. Sitting on the sofa in the grey winter light, her mother hears the rain start to fall as she unclips her nursing bra and offers her daughter her nipple, for what is now the only breastfeed of the day. But the baby does not snuggle up towards her, latching eagerly as she usually does. This time, for the first time, the baby sits up tall and decisively turns her head away. Her mother gives a small, barely audible gasp of surprise. 'You don't want to?' she says, half asking, half knowing the answer. 'Are you sure you don't want to?' But she can sense her daughter's resolve, and understands that a corner has been turned. We might wonder what internal shifts have driven the external movement in this child; does she feel sated, ready to grow up, and be more separate? Or is she desperate to be in control of the loss she senses approaching, scared by how dependent she still feels? Her mother gazes at the back of her head, and in that gaze is both relief and sadness, excitement at the freedom to come and pain at realising, too late, that her last feed was the final feed. She does up her bra, hugs her baby tightly, settles her in the playpen, and goes to fill the kettle.

If you have grown old, you have grown up. This is the assumption we make, most of the time without knowing we're making it; that advancing age correlates automatically with adulthood. It seems like one of those heavy, solid, never-to-be-questioned, true truths — like, a parent is not a baby, or adults have contents insurance, or pain is bad. But from everything I've learnt so far from my interviewees, and through my own experiences, it seems to me that of all the different ingredients that might, mixed together in the right quantities and cooked at the right temperature, produce something like a grown-up, age is far from the most important. The link between growing older and growing up is more complex than it appears to be, than we might like it to be. If we can hold on to that complexity, then I think we might get somewhere with this whole question of what it is to grow up into an adult.

It gets harder to hold on, though, as we begin to think about the last stages of life. It is far more comforting to assume that questions of growing up, of being an adult, of what is an adult anyway, must have already been answered by someone who draws a pension, or who has a free bus pass or a grandchild. But it is worth trying to bear some discomfort. Because if we reduce people in the last decades of life to a collection of pensions, free bus passes, and grandchildren, then we are starving them, and ourselves, of something significant, something vital. Something happens when we start talking about older people — perhaps even more than when we talk about the middle-aged and the young — where stereotypes and generalisations take over, where the assumption of personhood, the obvious truth that everyone has a unique mind, set of experiences, and inner world is lost. Something much flatter and greyer emerges, lacking depth and colour and truth, something that appeals to our basest drive to reduce other people to a set of foregone conclusions and rob them of their complexities and their life. That, as the historian of old age Pat Thane tells me, is 'the stupidity of assuming that past a certain age, everyone's much the same, that they have the same sort of experiences. But they don't. People are very diverse, and that's very important.' One of the most thrilling and terrifying things I have learnt through becoming a psychotherapist, and through having psychoanalysis, is that not only is every person completely different from everyone else, but also often completely different from the person they think themselves to be.

I wonder what continuing to grow up might look like when you become old; does it feel different from growing up when you are young? And what do I mean by 'old' anyway? As I type that I realise what a huge question it is — perhaps one of the biggest. Like 'What do I mean by woman?' or 'What do I mean by love?' or 'What do I mean by bad?' Is there an objective external reality, a number of years spent alive, that constitutes 'old'? Or is it something that a person feels, or doesn't feel, in themselves, regardless of age? Can it be both?

Researchers who study the life course[1] define old age as the stage that comes after middle age. For those of us who survive long enough to reach it, it is the bit in between the middle and the end, between midlife and death. Whether we are talking sociology or medicine, neuroscience or history, old age is said to begin somewhere around 60. I had always assumed that in previous centuries, when life expectancy was lower, that people must have hit old age much earlier in life. In fact, Thane explains, that is a common misconception based on a fundamental misunderstanding; historically, high infant and child mortality rates did lower average life expectancy, but those who survived past childhood had, she says, 'a good chance' of living into their late 50s or 60s. I was surprised to read that what we think of as old hasn't changed much in thousands of years. Thane, Visiting Professor of History at Birkbeck College, London, writes in her book, *The Long History of Old Age*, 'over many centuries and places there was remarkable continuity of how old age was defined', from ancient Greece to medieval Europe or 19th -century North America.[2] In the crusader kingdom of 13th-century Jerusalem, knights aged 60 or over were exempt from military service, as in medieval England where men and women were liable for compulsory work under the labour laws until age 60, and the upper age for jury service was 70. Not so different from today, where in the UK, US, and

Australia, people receive their state pension somewhere between 60 and 70, and those aged over 70 have the right to be excused from jury service. And when does old age end? For once, we have a very clear answer to that question: with death. That means that for some, old age covers a longer period of life than any other, far longer than infancy, childhood, adolescence, emerging adulthood, young adulthood, or middle age. As I write, the oldest known living person, Kane Tanaka, is 118 years old; that means she has been old for almost half her life.

For Kane Tanaka, old age has lasted nearly six decades. It was while I was mulling over this potentially very long chapter in our lives — not to mention in this book — searching for a meaningful way of thinking about the different phases of old age rather than seeing it as one monolithic chunk, that I came across the work of an American psychologist called Bernice Neugarten. A specialist in adult development and the psychology of ageing, in 1974 she coined a new term: the 'young-old'. 'That's it,' I thought, 'that is the paradox at the heart of chapter five.'

In her pioneering paper, 'Age Groups in American Society and the Rise of the Young-Old',[3] Neugarten identified a new 'meaningful division' she saw appearing in the life cycle, 'namely, a division between the young-old and the old-old'. I like the way she qualified this when she wrote, 'Although chronological age is not a satisfactory marker, it is nevertheless an indispensable one. So, at the risk of oversimplification, the young-old come from the group composed of those who are approximately 55 to 75 — as distinguished from the old-old, who are 75 and over.' In this I heard her saying what I have also found; that chronological age is deeply inadequate as a way of thinking about the life course, but there is no way around it. More important for this definition than age, however, are the qualities of this young-old cohort which are, according to that 1974 paper, 'markedly different from the out-moded stereotypes of old age'. The young-old are 'relatively healthy, relatively affluent, and they are politically active', she wrote. They might opt for early retirement or choose to continue working beyond 65, with some — like Kemi — changing careers after the age of 40; they want cultural enrichment and political involvement; and they could seek to create 'what might be called an age-irrelevant society in which arbitrary constraints based on chronological age are removed and in which all individuals, whether they are young or old, have opportunities consonant with their needs, desires and abilities'. She differentiated this group from the 'old-old', those over 75, later defining this demographic as 'persons who are in need of special care', while also acknowledging, in that paper, that 'some 80-year-olds are obviously more vigorous and youthful than some 60-year-olds'. [4] She called for us to 'return older people to the human race by ignoring age differences wherever possible and by focussing on more relevant dimensions of human differences'.

I hungrily gobbled up her papers during a visit to the British Library, and the more I read the more convinced I became: I need to interview this woman. I wanted to ask her what it felt like to define this phase in life; did she have to go through a period of soul-searching, like Arnett with his emerging adulthood? Are the young-old more or less adult than the old-old, these persons 'in need of special care'? What opportunities does she think this life stage presents when it comes to growing up? On my way home from the library, walking along the Regent's Canal and watching the elegant swan and fluffy grey cygnets floating by, I imagined how she might look and sound in my mind, picturing a psychologist version of Judge Ruth Bader Ginsburg. The next morning, sitting in the garden in the dappled shade with my cup of coffee and my laptop, I googled her to find out her contact details — and that's when I came across her obituary, in the *New York Times*. It begins: 'When Dr. Neugarten began her research on aging at the University of Chicago in the 1940's, she discovered very little scientific literature in the field, but many stereotypes, which she proceeded to shatter.'[5] I read on and felt such loss. She sounded like a very cool lady — a Jewish woman from Nebraska who had changed the way people thought about ageing. She had died at age 85. I drank a mouthful of coffee and read on. I read about her daughter, Dail, who had also done research into old age and I thought: 'All is not lost! I will try to interview Dail, and see what she thinks about the question of adulthood and the young-old, and how she experienced her mother in old age. It will be even better!' I then read that Dail too had died, shortly after reaching young-old age herself, of muscular dystrophy.[6] I felt an ache in my chest as I read this, learning of the early death of a woman I had never known, or had even known existed until a few moments earlier. But I didn't dwell on that ache; I drank a mouthful of coffee and read on, scrolling through the search results. I came across a paper delivered at a symposium called 'Tributes Celebrating the Life and Scholarly Vision of Bernice Neugarten', written by a Robert H. Binstock[7] — a professor of ageing in social sciences. He summarised her ideas and demonstrated their extensive influence, describing her with real warmth and admiration as a clear-thinking and generous woman, who seemed to have been a kind of mentor for him. I googled Robert H. Binstock: also dead. At that point I sat back in my chair, pushed my coffee and my laptop away, and thought, I'm doing something here. What am I doing?

I thought for a little, and then I understood something. Instead of experiencing the pain I had that this inspiring, fascinating woman had died and I would never be able to speak to her, instead of staying with that ache in my chest and trying to allow it into my mind where this loss could be felt, thought about, and mourned, I was manically running around, in my head and on Google, trying to find other interviewees who could replace her. Running away from accepting reality and mourning the loss, running away from the opportunity to wrap my mind around this realisation that death means that people are lost forever, that they cannot answer any more questions, that life continues until it ends, and then it's really, truly over.

I sat back in my chair, closed my eyes and felt the breeze on my face. I tried to think about the fact that this woman is no longer alive. I have her writings, yes, but I am not going to speak to her, I am not going to hear her voice, I am not going to experience her as a generous mentor, I am never going to know her thoughts about what it means to grow up later in life, if she thinks that is possible. Tears pricked my eyes, and I thought, 'This hurts.' Something hurts, and it's important that it does. Something I learnt way back at the start of our search floats into my mind, an idea that touched me. I remember it was a thought I had while speaking to Natterson-Horowitz, whose understanding of adolescence in animals changed my view of my own teenage years. That growing up is painful and hard, and that it has to be painful and hard in order for us to learn and change and grow.

This life stage which Neugarten called 'young-old age' in the 1970s, and which in the 1980s was famously termed 'the third age' by the historian Peter Laslett, was known much earlier, in Early Modern England, as 'green old age'; it is a time of life characterised, Thane writes, by 'fitness and activity with some failing powers'.[8] It has a long history, but this is the life stage of the moment. *The Economist* named the 2020s the decade of the young-old — or as the editorial called it, as if we don't have enough names for this demographic, 'the yold'.[9] The peak of the baby boom was 1955 to 1960, so, with boomers hitting their mid-60s in the 2020s, there were estimated to be 134 million 65- to 74-year-olds in rich countries in 2020, making up 11 per cent of the population, up from 8 per cent in 2000 — the fastest growth of any large age group.[10]

I ask Professor Alexandra Freund, Chair of Developmental Psychology: Adulthood, at the University of Zurich, to describe what we mean by 'young-old' today. She begins by telling me about how the stereotype of an old person has changed over her lifetime: 'When I was a kid, an older adult was stereotyped as a stout, grey-haired woman with a perm, all puffy and coiffed, wearing a shapeless dress. They were a little big, but sort of nice and harmless — that was the granny stereotype of older women. As for older men, well, they didn't talk much. They might have been grumpy, and they had a walking stick, and if you weren't behaving, they shook their stick at you. That was the image — and that has changed dramatically.' The difference, Freund explains, is that now, the stereotype of people approaching this stage is that they are healthy and active, and if they have the ability and — 'big caveat — the money' — many people enter it, thinking, 'Now I'm going to do what I always wanted to do,' which is why she calls this the bucket-list life stage. Her research shows this bucket list also exists in reality — not just in stereotypes — and can be observed across the socio-economic spectrum, though what's on the bucket list might change: while rich people might plan to travel in luxury, the less-well-off list less costly joys such as gardening in a community garden. Other bucket-list items include getting involved in charity projects, exercising, relaxing, reading, and spending more time with friends and family.[11]

In her paper coining this idea, Freund puts the shift partly down to the increase in our longevity, which appears to be almost universal, and which she calls 'arguably the most dramatic demographic change over the past centuries'. It is true that the parameters for old age have not changed much over millennia, and that able old people have always existed — Thane writes that the Venetian doge Enrico Dandolo was 97 when he led the Fourth Crusade in 1204 — but what has changed is that in the 20th century, for the first time in history, it became normal to grow old. It is no coincidence that this same time period saw the international development of a new specialisation in medicine: geriatrics, a term coined in 1909 by the Austrian-American doctor Ignatz Nascher, who had to fight for the medical treatment of older people to be taken seriously. Thane writes, 'Nascher believed, correctly, that doctors paid insufficient attention to the ill-health of older people: since they had not long to live, it was not thought worthwhile trying to cure them.'[12] Then almost halfway through the century in 1948 came the NHS, providing free healthcare for all in the United Kingdom; now, more of us grow older, and more of us spend more of our old age in good health — although of course this is more true for the more privileged in society, and health inequalities remain a stark injustice. This expectation of a longer life might lead us to postpone our 'bucket list' of enjoyable activities until after midlife, as until that point we are consumed with the highly demanding tasks of pursuing a career and raising a family, Freund theorises in her paper. This segregation conforms, she writes, to 'a Western cultural script following the Protestant work ethic of delaying gratification by pursuing obligatory goals first (work, family)' — only then do we 'turn to "play" after retirement'.[13] It is as if only once we've had our main course, and we've eaten all our vegetables, do we allow ourselves dessert. So now when we hear the word retirement, rather than thinking of people who have given up looking after themselves, turned grumpy and curmudgeonly and decrepit, we see a very different image in our mind's eye. Looking at TV portrayals and advertisements, which, Freund says, is a good way to see how images and stereotypes have changed, 'We see the salt-and-pepper-haired George Clooney types, an attractive older man. And the same goes for women; they may be grey-haired but not necessarily, and they don't have a lot of wrinkles.' They are nicely dressed, and portrayed as active: cycling and hiking, on a cruise ship or walking along the beach. Even Viagra adverts follow this theme; while the images allude to biological age-related changes, they still do it in a way that portrays people as sexually active, fit, and attractive. All this influences how we perceive this life stage. Freund is quick to acknowledge that these are adverts, not documentaries: 'Of course, that's not what it's really like. Of course you still wake up feeling tired, you don't feel like working out. You still have to clean your house and do your dishes. It's not always sunshine on the beach.' But these images do tell us something important about how we think about early old age today: 'I think a lot of people look forward to it in the way it looks in the adverts.' In the fantasy of many of us, she thinks young-old age looks like it does in the ads that we're all familiar with — beautiful, fit, and healthy people always having fun. That is the fantasy, but I am left wondering, what is the reality? And how might that fantasy get in the way of growing up?

At the opening of her book, *Successful Aging as a Contemporary Obsession: global perspectives*,[14] Sarah Lamb quotes one of my favourite authors, Haruki Murakami: 'One of the privileges given to those who've avoided dying young is the blessed right to grow old. The honour of physical decline is waiting, and you have to get used to that reality.'[15] When I reread these two sentences in Lamb's book, I knew they bore a significance that went beyond my immediate understanding. I made a note of it and held on to it in my mind.

As a Professor of Anthropology at Brandeis University in Waltham, Massachusetts, Lamb tells me she studies ageing through a particular lens, 'looking at ageing not just simply as biological processes, but also as people's beliefs and attitudes about what ageing means, how it's experienced, how it relates to ideas of what it is to be human'. She asks questions about how we change over the life course: what do these changes mean? Do we embrace them or do we deny them? Is ageing good or bad? What kinds of stigma might be attached to it? How does it relate to gender and family and work? At the core of her work, she says, is the principle that 'ageing is a fascinating part of the human condition, that one goes through if they're lucky to live long enough'.

I speak to Lamb online, and although I can see her face, one of the first things I notice about her is her voice. She sounds optimistic and energetic, and her manner is very warm and friendly. It sounds like the voice of someone who might think that ageing is always sunshine on the beach, but in fact she takes a much more thoughtful approach. When I ask her my opening gambit, if she is an adult, she tells me, 'That's interesting. I guess I do feel like I'm an adult, but it took me a long time. For one, I fit into your "young-old" now. I've been studying ageing since I was in my 20s, and I just turned 60 this year. I started saying to more people, and to myself, "I'm getting old now."' She didn't think she was an adult until around the age of 35 or 40; she kept feeling like she was young, perhaps too young to be a professor or to be chair of her department. But now she does feel that she has reached adulthood 'and the beginnings of oldish age'. Despite considering ageing as an honour and a privilege in theory, quoting Murakami on the first page of the book, even Lamb struggles to escape from negative stereotypes of what it means to grow old, now that she has started putting herself in that category: 'When people say they're old these days, the connotations are — in our public culture, and it seeps into you — that you are less vital and growing, that you are stopping to grow up and learn. I do think those stereotypes are there, so it's hard to embrace that concept of old for oneself.' This conflict is fundamental to thinking about ageing and growing up, I think, and it leaves us with an important question: what do we — we as individuals, as a culture, as a society — do about the fact that we don't want to grow old?

One answer to this question can be found in the 'successful aging movement',[16] and Lamb's analysis of it. As soon as I read those words, successful aging, I felt I intuitively knew what was meant by them. Even if like me you have no idea about prevailing gerontological theory in the USA, even if you have no background in sociology or health or old age, you might still have an idea of what it means to age successfully, to age well — and it may look like George Clooney walking on the beach. Lamb writes, 'Successful ageing envisions inspirationally that the negatives of ageing can be pushed further and further away, or even made to disappear, by medical technique and individual effort,' adding that it can be found underlying all our 'attempts to eradicate the kinds of declines, vulnerabilities, and dependencies previously commonly associated with old age'.[17] It seems to me that successful ageing is the doctor-approved version of the more cosmetic-sounding anti-ageing; it is fighting ageing to the death, in all respects. It stems from and nourishes the fantasy that we can exercise, sudoku, and moisturise our old away. It is nonsense, of course; one of the earliest lessons we learn as children through the game of peekaboo, is that something doesn't go away just because you close your eyes to it. I had to laugh recently when I saw a newspaper article with the headline 'Ageing process is unstoppable, finds unprecedented study,'[18] as if this was news. The subhead was equally comic to me: 'Research suggests humans cannot slow the rate at which they get older because of biological constraints'. I look forward to reading the equally groundbreaking news story, 'Bear shits in woods'. However, Lamb says the successful ageing ideology 'is very widespread and internalised and part of the culture' in the USA, and she adds that while some aspects of the movement are 'peculiarly American', its influences can be felt in other countries and cultures too — with the terms 'healthy ageing' and 'active ageing' more common in Britain and Europe. The successful ageing mindset can be seen in the popular self-help books with names like *Younger Next Year*, *Live Young Forever*, *101 Best Ways to Feel Younger and Live Longer* — and so the list goes on; it can be seen at gerontology conferences, where half the sessions will be about successful ageing; and as a cultural imperative, it can be seen everywhere around us in the Western world, in expensive anti-wrinkle creams and our wish to buy them, in '60 is the new 40', in the rudeness of calling someone old, in every aspect of our youth supremacist society.

We are so steeped in this attitude to ageing that it can be hard to see that it reveals something specific about our psychology and culture, as opposed to reflecting the apparently objective fact that Old Is Bad. Of course there are many benefits to the successful ageing paradigm: if we exercise more and eat a Mediterranean diet, that is better for our health; if we see this phase as a time of energy and passion rather than being put out to pasture, we may feel inspired to lead more creative and fulfilling lives. But there is nothing particularly healthy about dyeing your hair, and there is something particularly unhealthy about refusing to use a walking stick or a hearing aid if you need one. Lamb tells me, 'A lot of these things we call healthy ageing are just the denial of ageing, because "ageing is bad". You can still try to be healthy, but also try to accept that old age is part of life.' Part of the anthropological project, Lamb says quoting the anthropologist Horace Miner, is not just 'making the strange familiar', not just going out and looking and trying to understand other cultures, but also 'making the familiar strange' — trying to see our own society clearly and lucidly, as a culture with its idiosyncrasies, prejudices, and lies it tells itself. In this respect, and others too, anthropology is a lot like psychoanalysis. Only when we make the familiar strange, by developing the capacity to hear our mind's background noise made up of the lies we tell ourselves, can we hope to change and grow. And it is particularly important to see the strangeness of what has become so familiar when it comes to how we see old age, because, Lamb writes, 'The contemporary paradigm of successful aging is not the only way, nor necessarily the best, most humane, or most inspirational way, to imagine aging and what it means to be human.'

Graham has a gentle voice, which carries a sense of unsureness and diffidence. It means that during our interview, I am frequently caught unawares by the devastatingly precise emotional truths he speaks; at moments I breathe in sharply, taken aback by the depth of feeling he conveys in his slow-paced, slightly hesitant speech. I begin, as I often do, by asking him, are you grown up? 'Not really,' he replies. 'I'm 65, a month short of 66, which is grown up in numerical terms I suppose, but I must say I don't really feel grown up at all.' Yet there is something about Graham that does feel grown up to me, in a way I can relate to, that I could see myself growing into, that doesn't feel so out of reach. Perhaps it's because he seems so very conscious of his not-grown-up parts. He tells me he is very aware of a childlike part of himself, and he always has been, though he hasn't always known how to make space for it. He worked for 40 years — he recently retired — as a lecturer in an academic institution where, he says, 'It was very important to put on a front. You had to appear to be knowledgeable and authoritative and very resilient to survive in it. When I was doing that, I was always trying to overcome this inner child, who isn't like that at all, who is quite vulnerable, shy, and reticent.' For 40 years, in order to survive, he says, 'I was constantly overriding this person who I really was.' This makes sense I think, when I consider his voice and the way he speaks. One part hesitant, unsure, shy child; one part eloquent, lucid, incisive adult. I am intrigued by this sense of never feeling able to be himself, of always covering up the person he really was. I can really connect with this in some ways — I feel I have covered up who I really am too with my adult-looking carapace — but the difference between us is that I have blocked out this vulnerable part so effectively I do not yet know who is underneath, whereas something tells me that Graham does. Who is Graham?

We start at the beginning. He was born in Liverpool Central Hospital and spent the first five years of his life in Bootle, a working-class area of the city, surrounded by a large extended family of aunties, uncles, and grandparents. 'I think it was quite typical of living in the North at that time, where there was quite a lot of poverty,' he says, remembering a happy childhood, mainly spent visiting relatives, visits which continued long after his father, a teacher, had saved enough to move to the more affluent area of Crosby. 'Being in Liverpool and being close to the port had a major influence on our lives, we'd walk down to the coast to look at the ships coming up and down the River Mersey,' he remembers. I ask him to share any strong memory from his childhood and he tells me about when he was three and a half and his sister was born, and he was given a present: a guitar. 'It was a plastic guitar, and it came with her. I found that quite inspiring — it was music all around us at that time in Liverpool, that was when the Beatles were taking off.' When he was a teenager he formed a rock band at school with friends, playing in local church halls.

After rebelling against his father and teachers, growing his hair long, and spending all his time practising with his band instead of doing schoolwork, Graham messed up his O-levels and ended up studying for what was called an Ordinary National Diploma in business studies at a local college. It wasn't what he had hoped to do — he had really wanted to study music — but, in a surprising turn of events, he developed an avid interest in industrial relations, and he was good at it. There followed eventually the 40-year career in lecturing.

In his mid-30s, he took all the adult steps he was supposed to — buying a house, marrying, and becoming a father — but the marriage broke down when their daughter was 7. For the next decade, he says, 'I decided to try to be as positive as possible and to devote myself to my daughter and to work.' As a working single father, he had little time for himself — for his own self-exploration, or for other relationships — and it sounds like his personal life at that time was on hold. 'After the divorce, I just felt kind of, completely sort of … I wasn't in the land of the living. I thought that marriage would be there indefinitely, but it wasn't.' At some point he thought, 'I'm going to have to throw myself into some sort of situation here, or I'm just going to sink.'

The big grow-up came when he was in his early 50s and he heard that an Irish folk centre near where he lived in Bristol was looking for violin players. 'I'd not played violin since I was about 10, at school. But I picked it up again and it was remarkably evocative, the feeling, that texture, playing it again.' I ask him, what was that feeling? I find his response quite moving for its beauty: 'It felt, it felt … what did it feel like? There's something very tactile about musical instruments, and there's an excitement. What sound can you get out of this? And the wood, the wood has this beautiful resonance and shape. I've felt that when I've seen any instrument since I was a child. For me now, musical instruments are the most … I'd rather touch or see a musical instrument than a BMW or whatever, I find them much more exciting. But when I picked up that violin in Bristol, it transposed me back to when I'd been playing the violin at school.'

The first time he picked it up as an adult, he couldn't really play it, and he didn't think he would keep going. 'But I have kept going now for 15 years. And it's been a remarkable vehicle, this violin.'

Eventually, Graham moved to London and joined the East London Late Starters Orchestra; now after moving back to where he grew up, he has joined Yorkshire Late Starters Strings, two arms of a charity which offer adult beginners the chance to learn how to play and be part of a community. His violin has 'not only been a great instrument for making music, but also for making friends', Graham says, enjoying the pun. 'There's such a beautiful informal way of interacting, of communicating, which doesn't use words, among like-minded people.' That wasn't always the case in academic life, where it was always about one-upmanship, being clever and highly articulate. 'With a musical instrument, you don't have that. It's communal. There's a great kind of chemistry and beauty that comes from it.'

Listening to Graham as he speaks of his relationship with music feels like a gift; he is sharing something so personal and I can feel the aliveness in his voice. I tell him I think it is very interesting that he would bring this up as part of his story of growing up in later life, because it sounds like it was really about connecting with his childhood and the more excitable, youthful part of himself. This was the part he'd had to squash down as a lecturer, when part of the job description was to be the adult in the room. 'That's it, that's absolutely right,' he says. Joining that Irish folk group, he feels, gave him the opportunity of becoming who he actually was, through a reawakening of the childlike part of himself; that was the feeling when he picked up the violin again. 'There's something about childhood which is to do with the discovery of new things and wondering about the universe, and thinking there might be something magical about things. It's quite naive. I recaptured that.' He sees himself as an unusual grown-up in many respects because he is not hardened as many adults seem to be; he is still vulnerable. 'Music is connected with that, there's a very strong and immediate emotional impact with music, and it's to do with the unexplored, and something wonderful.'

Picking up his violin again opened new possibilities for a different kind of relationship with himself, and with others, and so began, step by step, what he calls 'the reconstruction of my life after the divorce'. This was a growing-up in later life that he desperately needed. It started off by making new friends, and that really helped with his self-esteem; he realised that people actually liked him, and that women actually found him attractive: 'I never thought that happened before, really.' This was in his early- to mid-50s, 'when it's more about friendship and being funny and being stimulating, not being too overbearing'. Gradually, incrementally, over time, he found he was able to 'pull things together', to 'reconstruct myself'. But he was not the same man he had been before. 'I found myself as a different person, more comfortable with myself. I got to the point where I thought, I'm just going to be who I am, and not try to be someone else in a home which is constructed for me. I'm going to just be who I am.' What a grow-up.

Three years ago, at age 63, he met his partner, who is at the same young-old life stage, and not just in terms of age. 'I think we've both arrived at the point where we don't really care what people think that much, we're not really competing with them, we're not trying to prove ourselves to each other.' Even lockdown has been quite positive for them in some ways, because all the added complications and external influences have been removed, and it's become 'a very simple life', he says. 'I think with relationships at this age, there's a kind of Indian summer effect, where there's not so much pressure to perform or to be anyone. For my daughter's generation, maybe your generation, there's so much pressure to have to be someone, to present an image, and to interact all the time, and lots of it I think is quite artificial.' I feel a wave of relief wash over me as he says this, that feeling that I have come to associate through my analysis with somebody saying something true. I wish I could escape from that external and internal pressure to present an image — from that bullshit artist in my head that child and adolescent psychotherapist Ariel Nathanson described in chapter one — but it is so pervasive, and so insidious, that I am only just developing the capacity to recognise it. Still, that's progress, I think. Graham explains that he and his partner are building their relationship in a new and different way that works for them, with no external pressure and no assumptions about how they'll live: 'We've got differences, because we've both been single for so long. So the way we organise the relationship is to have times together, and times apart. I've lived so long on my own and I have to keep certain aspects of space and time to myself to do things I want to do.' They live in different places, but visit at weekends and do things together, still retaining the elements of single life that they both really enjoyed. It seems to me that something about this life stage has meant that Graham has felt able, finally, to grow up into a man he feels comfortable being.

It was at around the same time he met his partner that Graham retired from his career in academia, and left London for the North-West, near where he grew up and near where his partner lives. It is still early days, and he does miss elements of work, he says. 'But I've always been someone who likes the slow pace of life, who doesn't want to be in the thick of it all the time. I'm doing quite comfortable things, and not being pushed to do things — but also being very constructive, and finding activities that I have always wanted to do.' Although the Yorkshire Late Starters Strings can't play together over lockdown when we speak, he is enjoying playing musical instruments on his own, teaching himself piano and violin and how to read music, reading books he really wants to — at the moment he's reading *Middlemarch* by George Eliot. 'I never had a chance to read those sorts of works of literature before. I'm walking, doing exercise, eating well, and that type of thing. I don't know how long it's going to last, but I'm really enjoying it.'

This might sound like Graham has drunk the 'successful ageing' Kool-Aid, experiencing young-old age as his own version of sunshine on the beach — but that is not the case, as he makes clear. 'The other inevitable thing about growing up is physical deterioration and mental deterioration. Illness. I'm relatively well off as far as that's concerned, but I was diagnosed with type two diabetes, which I didn't know I had.'

After taking more care of his health, which he didn't do when he was working, he went into remission. 'I think that's a very important thing about growing up; realising your mortality and the nature of life. You can't just override physical problems; you've got to take care of your body. There's inevitably deterioration, and I think part of growing up is accepting that deterioration. You're not as fit and you're not as active. A lot of people don't want to accept that, and want to think they can just keep going. But I'm not the same person I was when I was 22, at all, in any respect.' I share my thoughts about the anti-ageing mentality with Graham and ask if he has any thoughts about it. He tells me, 'When you see a young person on a bike, or you listen to people talking, you realise that the deterioration process is absolutely inevitable and highly significant. It happens to every aspect of your body and your mind. You're not as quick at picking things up, particularly things like technology, you forget things, people's names. I like to think it's not happening, but it is.' He thinks he probably has a relatively active mind, because of his academic career, and he is careful to make sure he does regular exercise too — 'but there's no two ways about it, there's decline. And it's about just keeping things afloat, being healthy enough, not trying to fight it, not trying to pretend you're 20 or 30 or 40, because that is just impossible. Some people fight against it, but my feeling is that there is a significant deterioration, and the best thing to do is try and be comfortable with it and accept it and operate within all the constraints. I just wouldn't go along with this trying to pretend, to deny that you're ageing. It's impossible really.'

But that doesn't mean it is easy to accept these changes, and part of that is because of the way society treats people at this life stage. 'I think the negative element to being this age is that you feel marginalised and you feel quite redun—' he coughs, as if the word sticks in his throat, still painful, although he is making peace with it, 'redundant. You feel like it doesn't matter if you exist or not, because you're out of all that, out of all the loops, out of the communication networks. I think there is a great deal of age discrimination which is not really addressed in the discourse about discrimination to a great extent.' Never more so, he feels, than during the pandemic. He and his partner are classed as vulnerable, so as the rest of the UK began opening up after the first lockdown, as the measures protecting those who had shielded were withdrawn, they both stayed home.

These are some of the losses that Graham is having to face. And it is painful. It may seem easier to pretend that none of it is happening. But, he tells me, that would rob him of so much. By experiencing this life stage for what it is, seeing the truth of it rather than pretending to himself and others that it is something else, he is giving himself the chance to experience the uniqueness of young-old age. Part of this is to do with his circumstances; he has met his partner, he has enough income not to have to work, and so they have the time to enjoy themselves, and, as he puts it, 'not feel guilty about that'. He explains it is very easy to feel a sense of guilt, especially if you've been working for 40 years and you have a certain view of how to organise the day which is highly structured — there is a feeling that you should be occupied every minute and doing something constructive. 'I'm still getting over that. I think you have to arrive at the realisation that there's time, that you don't have to rush, and you can have times just sitting around doing nothing. We've both got to that point where we owe it to ourselves to enjoy the moments while they're here, and we don't owe that to anyone else.' Music helps with this. 'One great thing about playing music is it's absolutely in the moment, whatever standard you are, you're enjoying it in that moment. There are very few things like that, I think.' Work was always about deferred gratification — that something was going to happen, some article was going to be published, a grant was going to be won. 'That was endless. You have to arrive at a point where you enjoy what's happening in the moment. I think that's probably the main thing about music — everything else is excluded.'

It reminds me of what psychoanalyst Josh Cohen said about being in the middle of life, and of when psychologist Oliver Robertson said,

'Maybe, one day, you can sit down and think, I'm not going to compare myself with anyone any more, I'm just going to be here. It's all right here.' It sounds very grown up to me; I wonder if it does to Graham. He tells me, 'It's hard because I still don't really know what growing up means. I have always felt very young in my own psychology for my age. I think everything has contributed to that — the music, being a lecturer, because you've got to keep playing with new ideas and dealing with young people. So I've never felt old and crusty, I've always felt quite youthful and open to new ideas.' He reflects on this and says, 'If growing up is getting to be at peace with yourself — then that has happened.' As definitions go, it's as good as any I've come across.

Getting to be at peace with yourself. Is there an attitude that could be more at odds with the anti-ageing state of mind, or rather, state of no mind? To me that mindset seems more like a war of attrition. Because while there are undoubtedly some health benefits that come with signing up to successful ageing, I'd argue there is a serious risk of side effects: you could end up with a healthy body but a stifled mind, seeking not to develop and change but to stay the same — to becoming a person who grows in age only, who never psychologically grows up. I think of the child and adolescent psychotherapist Ariel Nathanson, and how he described the way some adolescents take refuge in experiences that seem to stop time, so they can feel in control of what is happening, as if they are the boss. Graham seems to have done something very different, accepting that his body, his mind, and his life are inevitably changing with the passing of time, and this acceptance has brought with it a deepening, enriching awareness of who he is, and a greater capacity to embrace the paradoxes of being young-old.

Inherent in the adherence to 'successful ageing', we could argue, is a fear of something that might be called failed ageing. Lamb has seen something of this in her research in America among the young-old, and she is keen for me to understand that successful ageing 'doesn't only have to do with the way my body is going to look or not, or attractiveness or not, but with such a discomfort with dependence'. This discomfort is cultural and tied to notions of individualism and independence; the idea that 'the individual should make it by themselves, succeed, and take care of themselves'. It strikes me that this is something we experience unconsciously at every life stage, not just at old age, whether young-old or old-old. I think I glimpsed it in Sam as an adolescent who has proved himself so independent; I can see it in myself as a young adult who cannot bear being the patient rather than the therapist; I think I might have heard it when Rose described how, as a first-time mother, she struggled to express her needs; and I can feel it in Alex as a middle-aged man who told me he can only weep alone, in the early hours of the morning, about the loss of his father decades ago. Perhaps we can even see it in the baby who weans herself. One person I did not see it in was Graham.

It seems to me that we are all, in some way, dependent on each other, we all have needs that we cannot fulfil ourselves, and yet we do not want to acknowledge this. So what do we do with our dependency? In the course of my training and my analysis, I think I've understood something about that. Everyone seems to know the word 'projection', one of the first 10 psychological defence mechanisms adumbrated by Anna Freud in *The Ego and the Mechanisms of Defence* in 1936,[19] and one of the most famous words to come out of psychoanalysis. And — in a beautiful example of projection — everyone seems to think it's everybody else who does it. One of the most uncomfortable things I have come to see over the last few years is that most of us do it, most of the time, unconsciously. It is a way of disowning the parts of ourselves we do not like, and attributing them to others. For example: it is the very old who are dependent — not me. I think this might be what Lamb saw in action when she visited a retirement residence for her research: there was a real segregation between those who had started to show signs of dementia and who couldn't eat as well so might have to wear a bib, and those who had not. 'The people who were more fit and who didn't look old did not want to eat "with those other people",' she says. The healthier residents would say things like, 'When I first moved in here, everyone was walking. Now look at all those walkers lined up in the dining hall. That's really bad, I don't want to live in a place where there are all these walkers.' It is easy to judge that kind of talk, but I can empathise with the terror of facing the dependence to come, and it is human nature to want to deny it, to make it only those people over there who need a Zimmer frame, and to want to distance yourself from them as much as possible. As a patient in psychoanalysis, I have had to see something of my own dependency and I can tell you, I do not like it. I hate it. It is absolutely awful to see your own needs and just how dependent you feel on somebody else. Perhaps that was one unconscious reason for locking myself in the adult department when I was a child — it meant I didn't have to see the vulnerable, dependent parts of myself that got locked out. I often try to get away from those parts by looking after my analyst — as if she's the dependent one, not me. I do everything I can to blind myself to my own need, and yet I also know that acknowledging it is absolutely fundamental to seeing the truth of myself.

I put my thoughts about our horror of dependence to Lamb and she tells me, 'I think that's a huge part of this whole anti-ageing, successful ageing, healthy ageing paradigm: there is a cultural understanding of what it is to be an adult, a good adult. More successful means that you can care for yourself, you don't need care.' Again I find myself thinking of Boru, and his definition of an adult as someone who has their shit sorted out; of Adam and his realisation that growing up means learning to take care of yourself. There is a lot of truth in their words, I think, but that truth can be twisted and perverted and stretched out of shape into a cruel, superego edict; being an adult means not needing anyone else to take care of you, not needing anyone else's help. Dependency may be just about acceptable to us in childhood — although not to children themselves — and in people who we see as the elderly. Always other people, those people over there. The thought of someone experiencing dependency as an adult, that it might be part of the grown-up experience, seems to be absolutely intolerable for many of us. And by intolerable, I mean it cannot be tolerated, so it must not be experienced, and so it is denied. Anti-ageing makes age deniers out of all of us, and if Oil of Olay could sell anti-dependence creams, they'd make a killing. The irony is there is something deeply un-adult, thoroughly not grown up, quite toddler-like, and quite dangerous, about not accepting that sometimes, like the infant struggling to roll over at the opening of the last chapter, we need help.

Lamb is more aware of her own phobia of dependence than many of us will be. Just after she turned 51, she was diagnosed with cancer. Doctors told her husband there was a 75 per cent chance that she would die within two years. She remembers lying in a hospital bed after having a tumour removed and telling her nurse, 'You know, a few days ago I ran the Boston Marathon.' The nurse suggested she wear her marathon jacket in hospital to make her feel better. Lamb recognises in this story her own need to show an image to others — and to herself — that, as she puts it, 'I actually am fit and vital — this is just a temporary aberration.' She too had come to associate dependence with weakness and failure, she says: 'I'm sort of aware of my culture because I'm a cultural anthropologist, but I'm also part of it, so you absorb things.' On the one hand, she celebrates her age: 'I tell my students I'm 60, I don't want to hide from it, and my husband and I were going to have a big party until the pandemic happened,' — but on the other hand: 'It's embarrassing to turn 60 in a way. Part of me thinks it would be better to be 40 or 50.' This conflict of feelings, this ambivalence to ageing, is what makes that Murakami quote so meaningful. Lamb tells me why it resonated so much with what she had been trying to think and articulate: 'It is blessed to grow older, and that does entail usually — well, for everyone — some kind of physical decline. We should try and think of that as something one could learn and grow from, that has some meaning.' The quote conveys how if we can think of the whole life course as part of being human, 'then we can embrace all of it, learn from all of it, make the most of all of it — even dying'. This is something Lamb felt deep in her bones when she fell ill and then recovered: 'I got such an intense sense of joy for living and appreciation of living and life — even just the way that the leaves on the trees look so intense. It's already fading for me now, but it helps you realise, I think, that one thing that gives life some of its precariousness and sense of urgency, and its preciousness, is that it can't last for ever.'

This is what we lose if we buy into 'successful ageing' wholesale and turn away from the fact that our bodies and minds are deteriorating; if we try to anti-age ourselves out of the painful reality that ageing brings losses as well as walks on the beach. It is one thing to exercise to keep healthy; it is another to try to unconsciously stave off old age by running away from it, or to unconsciously believe or hope that your marathon jacket can protect you from cancer. The two things may look the same: it's just a person in their 60s going for a run — but one can be a meaningful appreciation of the value of health as Graham described it, while the other can be a manic flight from the reality of mortality. We all desperately try to cover up the losses we face in life from time to time — say, by frantically replacing one dead interviewee with another. I think this is what really gets me about the more insidious, quotidian symptoms of the successful ageing ideology, those self-help books that say you can be younger tomorrow, and the anti-wrinkle cream ads that demonise any signs of ageing. They seem to suggest that you can grow older without loss — and that, I think, is endorsing growing older without growing up. Growing up hurts. That's why the young-old life stage shouldn't just be sunshine on the beach; if you want to keep growing up, it has to hurt. Anything else is a lie.

When you think about it, babies and children have to deal with some extraordinarily profound losses very early on in life, even when things go well. Going to nursery or a childminder or school, having to share your parents with a new sibling, realising that your mum and dad spend time together without you. Before I started my training, it never occurred to me how huge these experiences are, how painful they must be, even if nursery, the childminder, or school is fun and exciting, which might distract from them. But the losses really begin far earlier than that — as soon as the baby leaves the womb, in that movement from being inside the mother's body, to existing outside the mother's body. I still struggle to get my head around the idea that on the inside, nourishment is provided continuously through the umbilical cord, there is constant protection from the cold outside because air never touches the baby's skin, and the baby is never not being held and supported by the mother's body. How, at the separation of birth, the baby leaves this state where, in a healthy situation, nutrition is constantly provided and enters a state of being in need — in need of food, of warmth, of holding. No wonder birth can be such a complicated, difficult, and painful process; I don't think I'd want to come out either.

During my infant observation, I saw how as the months pass, over and over again a baby will have the experience of wanting a feed, of having a feed, of a feed coming to an end, and then of wanting to feed again — and each time, this will involve experiencing hunger, need, satisfaction, and loss. And then, at some point, the infant is weaned, like the baby at the opening of this chapter. With weaning, there is a more permanent kind of loss, and it is not only about milk. It is extraordinary to think about how complex this experience must be for an infant; Melanie Klein wrote of weaning — both from the breast and from the bottle — in her influential paper 'Mourning and its relation to manic-depressive states': 'The object which is being mourned is the mother's breast and all that the breast and the milk have come to stand for in the infant's mind: namely, love, goodness and security.'[20] I can almost feel my mind creaking when I try to think about how huge a task it must be for an infant to make sense of this loss — but it is a very necessary one. Different babies react in different ways. Some are inconsolable; some may appear to take it in their stride; either way, psychoanalysts have found that ultimately, future psychological development rests on the capacity to gradually accept this loss and to mourn it. That is no overstatement: this is a most significant grow-up for an infant.

Klein saw, in the infant observations that she conducted, that this is a gradual process, with fluctuations between the depressive position and the paranoid-schizoid position. In the depressive position, the loss can be accepted and the breast can be experienced as a good thing that is missed; in the paranoid-schizoid position, all loss is denied, and so nothing has to be missed at all. I reread what she wrote about the core characteristics of this paranoid-schizoid response to loss — denial, omnipotence, triumph, and idealisation — and in them I see a new meaning. Our society seems to me, in its 'anti-ageing' attitude, to share these exact characteristics: denial of change, the power to hold back time, triumph over loss, and idealisation of ourselves and others who manage to stay forever young. Denying loss and triumphing over it instead is the opposite of mourning it and feeling the pain. I am criticising this way of being — but I would like to make it very clear that I am a frequent visitor to this state of mind. I did it when I searched for one interviewee after another without pause, and I did it when my analyst was on her summer break and I signed up to gym classes every morning in her absence. Many of us will recognise this manic avoidance of loss — and there is ample opportunity to do it even more in early old age, when the losses begin to mount. But there is another way. Instead of denying these losses and running away from them, we can mourn them.

Mourning hurts, but what I have learnt through my training, and through my own analysis, is that it is fundamental to psychic health, and to growing up. Klein wrote, 'Any pain caused by unhappy experiences, whatever their nature, has something in common with mourning. It reactivates the infantile depressive position, and encountering and overcoming adversity of any kind entails mental work similar to mourning.'[21] And although the work is hard, and it is painful, it is worth it. She continued: 'The phases of work in mourning when manic defences relax and a renewal of life inside sets in, with a deepening of internal relationships, are comparable to the steps which in early development lead to greater independence.'[22] In her words, I read that mourning can lead to a renewal of life, to a deepening of our relationships with the different parts of ourselves as well as with others, and at every life stage no matter how old we are, this can lead to a kind of development and independence that constitutes a fundamental grow-up.

It is through mourning that we can take baby steps towards growing up, whatever our age: that to me has real truth to it, real meaning. It is the opposite of phrases like 'age is just a number', as if growing older should have no meaning. Although I have written that age does not necessarily correlate with adulthood, that it is not the most important factor when it comes to growing up, I do not believe that age is just a number. I think if we tell ourselves that ageing means nothing, then we deny ourselves the meaning that age brings. The essential grow-up at this life stage is to see yourself as you are — not as you wish to be. To understand where you are in your life — closer to the end than the beginning — and to understand the reality that while deterioration is inevitable, growth is still possible. This, it seems to me, is what Graham has managed to do. Of course, it is easy to be seduced into cutting oneself off from that truth; the lure to believe in the myth that death can be omnipotently escaped and triumphed over is powerful. We can see it in the Ancient Greek myth of the philosopher's stone, with its power to delay death indefinitely, and in the *Harry Potter* book of the same name, which topped the bestseller charts centuries later.[23] Our obsession with escaping death and evading ageing has long, long roots. But if we give in to that seduction, if we cut ourselves off from that truth and what it means — if we are anti-ageing in our approach to life — then we cut ourselves off from the nourishment that truth can bring, of what can grow from it. This is what I heard in Murakami's quote: 'One of the privileges given to those who've avoided dying young is the blessed right to grow old. The honour of physical decline is waiting, and you have to get used to that reality.' If you don't get used to that reality, you deny yourself the honour, and the privilege, of growing up.

Why is it that some of us deny ourselves that honour and that privilege? I was recently reading another book by Murakami, his novel *Killing Commendatore*, in which two characters talk about ageing: "'Who was it that said, 'The greatest surprise in life is old age'?" he asked. I couldn't help him with that one. I'd never heard the saying. But it was probably true. Old age must be an even bigger shock than death. Far beyond what we can imagine.'[24] The shock of change must be far beyond what I, at this stage of my life, can imagine. But I wonder if it is possible, even from my position of ignorance, that although I cannot know what this is like, I can still empathise with the shock and with the wish not to have to change. Professor Freund says that while some people are capable of withstanding that shock and continuing to grow up throughout life and into old age, this is not the case for everyone. 'Not everybody. Not everybody takes these chances. There are people who basically shut down at some point in time and they don't want to change any more. I think they take away something from themselves in stunting their growth.' I think I have done that to myself at many times in my life — my hope is that psychoanalysis is helping me to open up again. There was something else that Freund told me, when I asked her about the process of growing up and becoming an adult, that comes to mind now as I write this. She said that fundamental to this shift is the realisation that 'This is it. This is not a trial run. This is *my life*. It's not that it will start at some point in time. Many people walk through life until the end, sort of waiting until it starts, until it truly starts, without realising that they are in the midst of it. There is no other life coming up for them.'

I think this is me. I think I have been waiting for adulthood to come, thinking that is when my life will begin. What blindness! Part of growing up for Freud 'is this realisation: it's me, and this is it. It's not a trial, it's not a game, this is it.' That realisation, she says, can propel you into a more grown-up state. It is the realisation of 'Oh, my God, I'm really going to die.'

There is something in how Graham builds up his picture of what it means to grow up, in his arrival at the phrase, 'getting to be at peace with yourself', together with the realisation Freund speaks of, 'I'm really going to die', that puts me in mind of the social psychologist Shinobu Kitayama and his fascinating research. We meet on Zoom, and I feel instantly at ease in his virtual presence. He sits relaxed in his office chair, and on his open face, under the professorial glasses, there is a natural, unforced expression that seems to carry a mix of curiosity, intelligence, and kindness. I get the feeling he has a good sense of humour. We do not have long to speak, so I am rushed, but he is not; as he generously shares his reflections on his own journey to adulthood, and what it has meant for him to reach young-old age, I wish we could have longer. As Professor of Psychology and Director of the Culture and Cognition Program at the University of Michigan, Ann Arbor, Kitayama has, for decades, been researching cultural differences and similarities in mental processes between people in Asian countries and in America.[25] It was in midlife, when he turned 50, that he thought, 'Oh my gosh, I have been doing this research on culture, maybe I can't dwell on it for the rest of my life and just keep doing something similar — that would be fun, but it's not terribly exciting. All this made me feel that I needed to do something different.' He asked himself a very important question: 'If I want to do something instead of dying, what would that be?' His answer was neuroscience. 'That made sense,' he explains, 'because as a researcher in culture, I am always trying to show that culture can get under the skin, very deeply, in some way. Obviously the brain, heart, and cardiovascular system are under the skin, so it seemed like a good idea to tap into the brain and the internal dynamics of physiology as a function of cultural forces.' This was a transformative time for Kitayama: 'Fortunately I didn't have any crisis, but this was a kind of converging of several things which happened around that time, and lent themselves to some kind of change. I became more multidimensional, and probably that's not a bad thing. Gradually, I think I have developed in some way. Growth can be documented. I managed to do something which I can interpret as evidence for growth.' I think that means he grew up.

Now, aged 62, he has been thinking about what it means to grow old, and how the young-old life stage differs in Japan, where he was born and where he still visits, from America, where he now lives. He believes the American way — which, from his description, is a close match with how we've been thinking about successful ageing — is deeply rooted in the culture. 'I really like the Bob Dylan tune "Forever Young",' he tells me — the song Dylan wrote as a lullaby for his son in the 1970s. 'He was maybe describing the time and place, but that song also shaped the time and place as well; that's dynamic art, the reproduction of culture.' In his recent paper, 'Culture and well-being in late ddulthood: theory and evidence', Kitayama explains, 'In writing this song, Dylan also underscores a central tenet of American culture. America is a country for those who are independent, active, and positive. These features would require youthful energy and enthusiasm — thus, a cultural imperative of staying "forever young".'[26] Or to put it as he did to me: 'Americans work so hard to fool themselves that they are young, even when they are not.'

There are some aspects of this that he thinks are positive: 'I do enjoy it in part because in interacting with my graduate students, I define myself as an equal, just like those crazy young guys — we work together, and to do that, you really have to be energetic, on top of things, and really committed to this particular research project or experiment.' You have to be a little bit crazy, he says, to care so much when an experiment result shows a 20-millisecond reaction-time difference; it's only with the benefit of youth that one can feel excited about such a small shift. 'As you get older, you get greater wisdom, and you come to realise that "Oh my gosh, 20 milliseconds difference in two conditions won't change the world, and who cares?"' These are among the positive aspects of American socialisation, he feels: 'Even when you are not young any more, you stick with the youth, with the energy of youth, and you maintain some sort of frontier spirit, and that helps you to work with young people and, maybe, to stay young.' In Japan, it's another story. 'Now, Japan is very different; if you are old, you are old, so what's the point of fighting against this biological reality? Once you get older, you are in the place where you can find meaning in its own right, and therefore it doesn't make sense to try to be something you are not.' Instead, the focus changes to crafting your life, to cultivating your new role: 'You have to realise what you want to see from the perspective that you've gained over the years — and, necessarily, you will end up doing something different.'

In his paper, Kitayama proposes — and shows evidence to support the idea that — the American ideal of preserving youth, in other words the anti-ageing approach, gives rise to an important mismatch between personal aspirations to stay energetic and youthful, and the reality of ageing and age-related decline. In mainstream American culture, he explains, there aren't really age-graded social roles — you just keep going as a young or middle-aged adult for as long as you can — unlike other cultural traditions such as Buddhism and Confucianism, where later life is structured quite differently. In East Asian cultures there are clear, differentiated, age-dependent roles and tasks, divisions when activities like paid work or vigorous exercise are replaced by looking after grandchildren and lighter physical therapy sessions. This, and the deference towards older adults in families and communities, might be a protective factor in helping Asian older adults adjust to later life, he suggests, whereas Americans might face 'passivity, alienation, and disengagement from social life'. He posits that these two different approaches to ageing — finding meaning in where you are, or finding meaning in trying to stay where you have been — have a profoundly different impact on our experience of old age.

I wonder what Kitayama makes of these two different ways of thinking about entering old age, as someone who is both Japanese and American. He says, 'I'm in the United States right now, and I enjoy working with my graduate students, and I am surrounded by all these colleagues who pretend that they are young when they are not. When I go to Japan there is, I feel, a greater pressure to shape me into some roles that I'm supposed to be in, so that's the negative aspect.' And there is also a positive aspect: these age-graded categories of growth may help to maintain meaning in life, 'because you don't have to be pretending to be someone that you cannot be. Culture provides you with age-graded roles, so as long as you're happy to live with that, it's far easier to cultivate some meanings.' If you are brought up in an East Asian society, he says, in that kind of a framework, conformity to ageing roles may not come across as repressive or suppressive; 'It's the natural way of how things are … that's not necessarily repressive but it can be construed in that way.' Of course, he is discussing entire cultures, rather than the individuals within them, who will all be unique and have their own experiences; 'You really have to be careful. I don't like to paint an entire group as better or worse just by looking at the data — any data or study might be concealing other aspects of a place,' he says, and he mentions that Japan has a very high suicide rate. But if we do tread carefully, aware of the potholes of stereotyping and generalising that threaten to trip us up, these two approaches to ageing can help us to think about what it means to grow up: 'Those are two prototypes which are very different, and even if they don't exist in pure forms in either place, thinking about them can help us understand some very different patterns of ageing and growth.'

As I let these paradigms, these two approaches to life, roll around in my mind, my thoughts return to Graham, and to his decision, in his young-old stage of life, to move back to the area he grew up in as a child. I ask him what that has been like and he tells me, 'There's a feeling of coming home,' he says, but in a 'double-edged' way. He describes how 'There's a great feeling of nostalgia — seeing a building which I last saw 50 years ago, how it evokes my childhood and the elements of comfort and excitement,' and how at ease he feels being back in the industrial North. 'My formative experiences were in the Port of Liverpool, so I really enjoy the industrial architecture, I like these terraced houses, they're so cosy. I used to visit grandparents and aunties in these terraced houses and I always felt like a little cosy embryo'; I understand he means 'coming home' in the most warm, reassuring, womb-like way. And yet, 'There's also a feeling of being a bit let down by it, because it doesn't stand up to the memories. In many senses you can never go back to it; it's hopeless to think you can go back or try to recapture it, you can never go back to previous relationships and previous friendships.' I am reminded of Victoria, and how she felt going back home after her first term at university, moving back in with her family, but discovering that everything felt so different from before. For both Victoria and Graham, I think growing up means accepting that loss, but also finding a way to hold on to something of their past in a meaningful way; finding a new meaning for the word home. I think this is what Kitayama is talking about when he speaks of the age-graded social roles he has observed in Japanese culture. I think it is also what Graham is talking about when he tells me, 'I'm conscious the reason I came back was not just to come back home, but to be with my partner, and to take up new activities here — the orchestra, and the new relations associated with it. That group has been very welcoming, and when I met them for the first time, it felt like I was coming home to them.'

Before moving out of his flat and back to the North-West, Graham went through a process of decluttering — which he wants me to understand was both external and internal; 'physical objects relate to psychological objects, you cling on to things because they're remnants of the past,' he says. He had to go through every single object he owned and make a decision. 'It's a very difficult process — you look at something and you think, I should throw that away, and then you look at it again and you think, no, I want to keep it because it could be important, or it's meant something to you.' He eventually realised that the criteria for what to keep had to be about what he wants now: the books he wants to read, the music he wants to listen to, a record player. 'No high-tech devices. My life has become quite stripped down; I'm just concentrating on the things I enjoy.' It has felt good 'to take these objects to the tip and see the back of them'— to let go of the things from his past he no longer needs. The process he describes strikes me as a wonderful metaphor for understanding some of the grow-ups we face as we enter early old age. This is why, I think, Marie Kondo and her books about decluttering have been so popular; the questions of what we want to keep in our life, and what we struggle to let go of, are ones that haunt us throughout life, but especially at times of transition, and perhaps especially as we near the last chapters of our lives. Graham explains, 'Sometimes I get wound up in negative relationships, or in the redundancy process — but then I say, it doesn't matter, forget it, let it go. That all happened during those two decluttering processes, the physical and the psychological, in parallel. It's important to chuck out stuff that you don't need ... but it's very, very, very hard to let things go.'

This is it, I think — this is the key grow-up of early old age, although it has its roots in adolescence and every stage of adulthood. I think of Tochi letting go of his feelings towards his parents for their response to his sexuality; I think of Adam letting go of his desperation to succeed at all costs; I think of Amy letting go of her expectation that she should become a mother; I think of Alex and the weight of his father dropping off his shoulders; I think of me trying to let go of my need to hold everything together. This is the grow-up that the anti-ageing mindset tells us we do not have to face, but one that Japanese culture values as absolutely essential. Letting things go.

Kitayama is clear that in his research, he was not seeking to judge either culture, but to study both of them to try to understand them better; nevertheless I find myself, despite myself, pulled towards idealising Japan and denigrating Europe and America. That is not what Kitayama was trying to do, and he says that both American and Japanese people were a little bit offended by the study. But I do think there is something that some aspects of Western culture get very wrong, and which perhaps Graham and some aspects of East Asian culture do not get quite so wrong — or at least, do not get wrong in quite the same way — and that is the assumption that it's bad to feel bad. This is linked to what Oliver Robinson called the pathologisation of feeling bad — that sometimes mental health professionals seek to treat feeling bad as if it is always an illness to be cured. This may well sound peculiar at best, masochistic at worst, and contradictory in the middle — at least, it did to me: it was not until I was a couple of years into psychoanalysis that I finally began to see just what an assumption it is, that it is bad to feel bad. That feeling pain, for example, is A Bad Thing. It is something that it has taken me a long time to get my head around. At one point, when I was going through a very difficult time, I remember my analyst saying to me, 'Perhaps you don't want the pain.' I was shocked into realising that there is another way to think about pain; to see it as an important and significant experience; to respect it. It is so intuitive to assume that feeling sad or unhappy or being in any kind of pain is a bad thing; I am asking you to put that assumption into question. And so is Kitayama. He has done studies on this too.

He explains, 'Western civilisations have a very strong commitment to a linear idea of sadness and happiness. Sadness is here,' he says, gesturing with one hand, 'happiness is here,' he says, marking the distance with his other hand, 'and the transition is pretty linear; if you go in a constant direction you are on the right track, you are all set, but once the trajectory goes the other way, you are in trouble. Physical pain is bad — you are in bad shape! — psychological pain is also very bad — you are in bad shape!' This is so obvious as to go without saying — except that it does need saying, because although it might be obvious to us, although it may feel like a stable, solid, self-evident truth — it isn't true for everyone. East Asian philosophy is very different, he says. 'The full moon is the last thing you see before it begins to lose its full state the next day; that's a good metaphor for caution when you are extremely happy. If you are in love with someone, if your love is like the full moon, you have to be careful, because it may go down tomorrow.' To this, my grandpa would have said, 'It's being so cheerful keeps you going.' But extending the same cycle theory to happiness and sadness may provide some psychological protection, Kitayama argues: 'You may be miserable right now, but as long as you are surviving, as long as you are eating and getting enough sleep, the day could be better tomorrow. So there's an element of hope in the misery.'

Feeling bad is a different prospect in America from in Japan, Kitayama theorised, and he designed a study, 'Feeling bad is not always unhealthy', to see just how deep 'under the skin' this cultural difference goes.[27] He did this by linking the emotional experience of sadness with the physical symptoms of feeling stressed and under threat, postulating that when feeling sad, people in America would show more physical signs of feeling threatened than people in Japan. 'What is threat?' asks Kitayama, thankfully not expecting me to answer. Evolutionarily speaking, he explains, threat is the expectation that your body may be damaged — for example, if we suddenly find a big bear in front of us, we feel threatened, because our brain has somehow acquired the knowledge that this big animal can kill us, so the visual stimulus alone is sufficient to initiate a series of different reactions, including inflammation. Inflammation is the body's first line of defence to fight bacterial infection following an injury, and it always has been; whether you are a cave man afraid you're about to be bitten by a big bear, or whether you're walking along while reading an email on your phone and not looking where you're going and you fall over and cut your knee, inflammation will help your body to fight off any bacteria that might enter through your wound. Humans and monkeys have evolved with this system to respond to the threat of physical injury, and it is a 'very primitive biological reaction, ingrained into this human system of social interaction'. But inflammation doesn't only occur in response to the threat of physical injury; it also occurs in response to psychological stress, and when psychological stress doesn't go away, inflammation can go from being a helpful, timely way of fighting infection to a chronic problem that causes damage to the cardiovascular system. In his study, Kitayama demonstrated that 'Feeling bad is not always unhealthy', by surveying a group of American and Japanese participants. He found that in the Americans, there was an association between the experience of so-called negative emotions and increased inflammation (among other biological markers of threat), but this was not the case among the Japanese: 'Negative affect is a very potent threatening stimulus for Americans, but not for Japanese. That's the story of our research.' He believes these results can be explained by the fact that in America, being in pain is more stressful, because feeling bad is a 'source of threat to self-image', whereas in Japan, it is understood to be 'natural and integral to life'.

What this research does is make the familiar strange. We assume that feeling bad is bad — and it is, in a way, for many of us in the West. But it is not true in Japanese culture; in Japanese culture it is not good or bad, it just is. What I have learnt through having and studying psychoanalysis, and through how much my relationships are changing as a result, is that what matters most is the truth. Suffering, feeling bad, feeling pain, feeling loss, feeling needs that cannot be met — this is all an inevitable part of life. At some points in our lives we will experience these feelings, and they will hurt. It is okay to hurt; it is not bad for you. What is bad for you is trying not to feel bad when you do feel bad, pretending to yourself that you don't feel bad, or telling yourself you mustn't feel bad, or trying to get rid of the badness into other people by making them feel bad instead, or using drugs or alcohol to numb the bad feelings — that's what does the damage. Patients (including me) often hope only that therapy will take away their pain — but equally important, writes the psychoanalyst Wilfred Bion, is for the 'analytic experience to increase the patient's *capacity* for suffering'.[28] To get better at feeling bad. Because feeling bad is not actually bad, getting old is not actually bad — but kidding yourself that you can stay young forever to avoid feeling bad about getting old, well, that might actually make life quite difficult when it turns out not to be the case. When we are unable to face up to the truth, the painful truth, of our situation, we deny ourselves the chance to mourn and develop. Although feeling pain hurts, it facilitates growth. When we avoid it, we shrink away from growing up.

Prior to my analysis, I had no idea how often I would protect myself from knowing things that were true about me that I did not want to know. But in my analysis I have had to face up to some pretty cold and unpleasant facts. I can be manipulative; I can be envious; I can think I am superior. I cannot bear being a patient; or being a child; or accepting something from someone that I cannot provide myself; or accepting that I need something from someone that I cannot provide myself. I am actually wincing as I type this. I have seen my capacity for unconscious racism, ageism, misogyny, cowardice, destructiveness. It has taken me three years of therapy to begin to be able to hear some of these hard truths about myself, and I am still in that process. I find it very painful. But I have to believe it's worth it. I believe that we either know about these parts of ourselves, or we choose not to — and if we choose not to, we are far more likely to act on them. And I believe that it is only by understanding these difficult, painful truths that I can hope to grow up.

The task of the psychoanalyst is understanding, said the famous analyst John Steiner in a recent lecture.[29] This is why it is so different from other forms of treatment like cognitive behavioural therapy or medication, he explained; the cognitive behavioural therapist's task, the psychiatrist's task, is to help. That is part of the reason that the psychoanalytic stance taken by some therapists can feel so alienating — we are used to thinking of therapists as people who will be helpful and sympathetic and reassuring. It can be extremely difficult, and require a lot of discipline on the part of the therapist, not to reassure patients — and this is something I have been learning to do over the course of my training. It is important, I think, because trying to help and reassure your patient can really get in the way of trying to understand; to understand the truth of their emotional reality. If someone has a problem or a negative belief about themselves and you try to reassure them that they are okay, you are not really listening — you are forcing your view on them and saying yours is more valid than theirs. If you tell that person what to do — if you try to help — your advice might happen to be helpful or it might have consequences that are deeply unhelpful, in this particular situation. But if you can understand their problem, if you can explore where that belief comes from in their past and how it lives on in their mind, and understand the emotional truth of what is going on for them and communicate that truth in a way that they can hear it, then you give them the chance to understand their situation and make their own decisions for themselves. It is a liberation. In one of the most beautifully simple lines I think I've heard in a lecture, Steiner said, 'Understanding is therapeutic.' Understanding not simply as empathy, but as awareness in opposition to ignorance. This is something we do not have a scientific explanation for. It's just true. It is the difference between feeling our pain and sensing where it comes from and being able to put it into words, or being overwhelmed by a heavy, foggy, fragmentary experience which brings to mind Wilfred Bion's expression 'nameless dread'.[30]

For Wilfred Bion, truth was food for the mind. He wrote, 'Healthy mental growth seems to depend on truth as the living organism depends on food';[31] 'without it, the mind dies of starvation', wrote his wife Francesca Bion in her memoir.[32] After reading some of his work — most of which, at first at least, I found completely impenetrable — I began thinking of psychoanalysis as a journey we go on with truth as our compass, with understanding as our destination, although that destination is constantly moving as we are diverted by forces within us — defences — that throw us off course. Perhaps in this sense, it shares something with the journey we are on in this book. Wilfred Bion believed that every session was shaped and coloured by the patient's and the analyst's capacity to bear the truth of things — or whether either had to shy away, to turn their back on truth because they could not tolerate the pain of it. This is what we do when we find ourselves caught up in the successful ageing, anti-ageing mindset, I think: we deny the truth that we all die, and that some of us — the lucky ones? — get old first. If we can accept this, at least some of the time, then we have a real opportunity to grow up, and, in Graham's words, the chance to make peace with ourselves. But first, we have to mourn the losses. The terrible terrible losses. The mistakes we made, the things we did not get to do, the people we let down, the relationships we stayed in but wanted to leave, the relationships we left that might have survived. There is something, I think, about reaching early old age, touching the doorway of later life for the first time, that can, for some people, make that more possible than it was before.

I think that is what happened for Sheila. When I first spoke to Sheila, she told me how when she was in midlife, her husband had left her and their young son, suddenly, for another woman. She was completely broken. But some years after that, she met a man she fell in love with, and they married just over a decade after her divorce. Sheila seemed so fearless in her commitment to trying again, even though it hadn't worked out for her first time around, and I was struck by her resilience and her determination to live fully whatever pain she suffered. I thought this was what our interview would be about — about growing up through a second marriage later in life. But those questions didn't seem to be so relevant, somehow, when I interviewed her for this book. In fact, she had something quite different to tell me.

I ask her when she became an adult and she tells me, 'I'm quite clear: I would say 15, because I left home at 15, in the clothes I stood up in, with nothing.' There is no doubt in her voice when she says, 'I grew up almost the minute I walked out the door.' Now age 64, she is very conscious that she is entering a new life stage, which she feels is best described by the phrase young-old. 'I want to try and keep healthy, so we do a lot of exercise, my husband and I.' They do barre, HIT, yoga. 'We've collectively decided that it is a bit of an insurance policy. I never had the time before because I had so many responsibilities with work, running the house, my son, balancing everything. Now I have more time.' The big question she faces now is, when should she retire? 'I could retire financially on the basis that I now draw a pension and we don't have any mortgage, but I enjoy my job. So there is the question of when do you say, right, this is the time I'm going to stop so I can travel before I'm too old or too unwell? Well, that's the crystal ball.' It doesn't sound to me like she is that close to retiring — she has just been promoted, and she speaks about her career with such interest and energy that it is energising to hear — nevertheless, I can hear that she is very alive to the fact that health risks are on the horizon. She is keeping fit not to escape old age, but because she knows she won't be able to carry on for ever.

Before this, before she talks to me about her job and her exercise, I ask her about her experiences with growing up and she tells me about something much more painful. 'I lost a baby to cot death, and I never ever talked about it. It would be interesting …' she says, and then she drifts off. And then she tells me her story, beginning with the end — with a woman she interviewed for a job at work. This candidate had hobbies on her CV, including the usual ones like yoga and Pilates, and she also listed that she was a psychic. Sheila explains, 'I said it sounded really interesting, and asked if it was something she'd learnt, or if it was a gift. I had never wanted to train as one, but my husband always says I'm very intuitive, and I do pick up on things that perhaps other people wouldn't.' The candidate got the job, and some months later she and Sheila were on a train to London for a meeting, talking about business, when suddenly the new employee said, 'Do you mind if I ask you something?' She asked Sheila if she had had a child who had died.

Sheila says, 'I was so taken aback. I was shocked. There is nobody left living that knows that about me. I hadn't … I couldn't bring myself to visit the grave, and it had happened over 40 years ago, and nobody, not even my best friend knew, not my son, my ex-husband, or my husband. I'd never talked to anybody about it.' But when her colleague asked her that question, something shifted. She was understandably shaken and spooked in that moment — but the impact of that question went far beyond that moment. 'Pandora's Box was opened.'

She tells me her story from somewhere nearer the beginning. 'At 15, I left home with nowhere to go because I couldn't stand the verbal abuse of me and my mother by my father. It all came to a head one day and that was it, I left and never went back.' She thinks that her father most likely had a mental health condition and could not control his behaviour, but at the time she could only experience him as cruel. 'He was incredibly difficult, controlling, unpleasant, and really ugly sometimes in the things he said, and then so remorseful afterwards.' She remained close with her mother, but never moved back home. She moved in with her boyfriend and his family, and fell pregnant. She was 16 when their son Peter was born in October 1972. He died in January 1973.

'It was a cot death. It was so traumatic, it was just so awful, the trauma around it. We had no money, we had nowhere to live really — we were living with his mother. We didn't have enough money to bury him, we had to borrow money and pay the funeral home off week by week, and that went on for months,' she says. Her relationship with Peter's father deteriorated, and they broke up not long after. 'With the trauma of losing Peter, not having any stability in my life with parents or a boyfriend, I was completely on my own. I just had to get on with my life, I couldn't dwell or think, I just shut it all away.' Over the years, on the anniversary of Peter's birth and death, she would think of him, remember him. 'But I never went back to the grave. I hadn't visited the grave since the day Peter was buried.'

After this conversation with her colleague, though, something changed. 'I thought, I want to go to the grave. I want to visit Peter. I just want to do that.' Her colleague's question on that train journey 'opened up the chains, and the lock came off the box'.

I ask her if she felt she had ever grieved for Peter's death. 'No, I definitely didn't, I definitely didn't. I suppose there's guilt there, because his life was so short. It was all so upsetting for everyone, it was just … unimaginable. It's so devastating. I certainly wasn't prepared for it, I didn't know how to deal with it, so the only way I could deal with it was to shut it all down and just get on, just not talk about it. It's just easier not to talk about these things.' For the first time in her life, after her colleague asked her that question, this was no longer true; it was no longer easier not to talk about Peter. 'It gave me the opportunity to open up. I decided to tell my husband. I questioned whether I wanted to share it with him and I thought well, why shouldn't I? I want to visit the grave, he's my friend, he loves me, he won't judge me. I wanted to share the day and the decision with him.' She continues, 'We went to visit the grave. I didn't know, but it's engraved with his name and the date that he died. But because this was in 1972, a lot of the letters have fallen out. It was a real mess. I wanted to put new stones on it, and to do the lettering. So I bought some really beautiful stones, they're black but they glisten. It looks very lovely, the grave now. It was powerful. It was a relief, almost.' She didn't just go to Peter's grave. She also found the grave of her ex-boyfriend's mother, who she had lived with, and who had helped her care for Peter when he was born. That grave was in disarray as well. 'I want to tidy that grave up too, because she was so, so good when Peter was born, I was so young, and she helped me a lot.' I am very moved when Sheila says this. It feels, all these years later, like something very important is taking place. Mourning, reparation.

It seems to me that two things needed to happen for this box to be unlocked. It wasn't just her colleague asking that question — it was also that she asked that question at this particular time in Sheila's life, as she enters this young-old life stage, with old age approaching, and less time ahead of her than she has behind her. She tells me, 'I buried that particular thing because it was so traumatic, I buried it, but then I opened it up again and dealt with it. I'd felt a bit ashamed about not having gone to the grave, but I understood why I hadn't gone.' I ask her if she thinks her age played a part in this process, and she replies, 'There's something about being in your 60s … When you get into your 60s, you become more aware of how fragile life is. You've already started to lose close friends, you've witnessed things that bring huge trauma and sorrow to people, whether its death or redundancies or divorce. I also have grandchildren now and that's been a huge gift to me, and a huge emotion, because I didn't know, I hadn't anticipated how I would feel about my grandchildren.' And, she says, at this time in her life, she has started to look back. 'I miss my mum, I think about her a lot, she died in 2011, and we were so close. So you think about what's happened, what's in the past, and also when you are going to die yourself, and is everything in order. I can honestly go to my grave thinking I've done everything I could for the people I loved.'

I am coming to understand that there is something about the awareness of death and its ever-increasing proximity, particularly in the young-old life stage, that makes mourning — and therefore growth — more possible. Facing her loss more than 40 years after it happened meant that Sheila could finally begin to mourn the terrible trauma of her young adolescence. And with that, she found a way towards making peace with herself. To me — I don't know that she would think of it this way, but to me — this was a kind of growing up.

When I first became interested in the ideas of psychoanalysis, before I really knew — or rather, thought I knew — anything about it, I read a book called *Inside Lives: psychoanalysis and the growth of the personality*, by a wonderful author, psychoanalyst, and Member of the British Psychoanalytical Society called Margot Waddell.[33] It is such a beautiful book, beginning in early infancy and ending in old age, quite unlike anything else I'd read before; it is a journey into the inner worlds of infants, children, teenagers, adults, and older people, exploring how we shift and change psychologically over the course of a life, the way different psychoanalysts have thought about development. There are some books that point you in a different direction, reorientating you in your own life, and this one did that for me. This book also gave my friend and me a bit of a crush on, as we called her, 'Queen Margot'. I was delighted and terrified when our queen agreed to an interview, a couple of months before the first lockdown began. I suppose for other people, this might be like interviewing Harry Kane or Beyonce. Sitting in her exquisitely chaotic sitting room, books piled up on every surface, I asked her, 'Are you a grown-up?' 'Absolutely not,' she replies. 'No. I've always been … very uncertain about myself.' She is 73. And she has never even heard of contents insurance.

'I think the honest thing would be to say to you that I'm still struggling with growing up.' She has children, step children, and grandchildren, she says, 'and I do have to feel like a grown-up. But I … I don't think one ever does. I just don't.' She still feels that she has everything to learn. 'I feel that I'm growing up, that I have to grow up all the time. I don't think one's ever something called a grown-up.' We can only hope to be in a state of growing, not grown, she seems to say — present tense, ongoing, as opposed to something in the past, completed. In fact, she says, 'A grown-up is somebody who has the internal capacity to know that they could always develop further, and that there is no end of the road in life as they live it. Some people get nearer the end than others. So I think it is a grown-up who can bear that, and not disappear under the shackles of "Oh no, I haven't done it" — who can go on accepting their inadequacies, let's say, and offering their children the best they can. I don't think there's an ultimate state called being grown up; it's a process, which with luck, can be sustained.'

I feel fireworks going off in my mind as I hear this. I was so hoping that through writing this book, I would learn how other people grew up, and what it means to them to be an adult, and then be able to do it myself. That ... does not seem to be happening. I have listened to others who have also struggled with growing up and spoken to experts from all different fields, and although I find their stories and their studies fascinating, I am left with the rather distressing realisation that they cannot help me — or at least, not in the way I wanted them to. I cannot force myself to grow up. In my analysis, I have come to see that it is quite likely that I have been using the writing of this book as a way to avoid my own dependence on my analyst — trying to deny my need of her and to grow up outside of my analysis, rather than engaging fully in the process that might help me to see the truth about myself. That was an ouch. But through these realisations, even as adulthood feels further out of reach, I do feel that I am changing, growing. There is a process that is ongoing in my mind, in my analysis, in this writing, and also in living through the pandemic. I think it's to do with being able — from time to time, but by no means consistently — to see the truth of things a bit more clearly. I may not have grown up, but I'm understanding a bit more about why, about what that means, and at times, I am able to be a little more forgiving of myself. That has to be better than not understanding it. Typing out Queen Margot's words, I understand that I am going to have to let go of this idea of adulthood as an answer to a question, as a state I will one day reach, when things will be sorted. It is painful to let go; it was comforting to be in search of an answer, to be reaching for a something which I thought would solve everything, or most things at least. To be the infant reaching up to my grandfather's keys. Mourning this wished-for state is a sore grow-up indeed. There is some consolation, though. This new version of adulthood I am discovering is not only more terrifying, but also more interesting.

'It's so difficult,' I say to Margot, and she responds with the kindest words I think I have ever heard. I take a photo of the transcript and send it to my friends, and I keep it for myself to look at from time to time.

And now I'm giving it to you.

Moya: It's so difficult.
Queen Margot: It's very difficult.
Moya: It's really hard.
Queen Margot: Yes, it is.

Chapter Six
The last chapter

'I Contain Multitudes'
Song by Bob Dylan

A baby is communicating. She sits on her father's lap as he turns the page of her favourite book, and she gazes up at him and touches his chin with her hand. 'Baa baa aah,' she says, and he replies, 'Yes, you like this bit, don't you?' He continues reading her the story of the bear who wants his hat back, and as she sees the mischievous rabbit who stole it, she bounces on his knee, hitting the book with the palm of her hand, shouting, 'Ah ahhhh, ah ahhh ahhh!' 'That's right,' her father says, with laughter in his voice, 'it was the rabbit, wasn't it?' She smiles broadly at him and replies, 'Uh uuugh, ng uh wuuuuh.' He responds: 'Mmhmm. I think so too. Shall we turn the page?' She reaches her arms up towards his neck and says, 'Agagaga,' and he gives her a cuddle, echoing 'Agagaga.'

She turns back to the book, he turns the page, and their conversation continues.

Last week, my father had the coronavirus vaccine. He was 86 years old. He had not left the house and garden, other than for medical appointments, for more than nine months. When I found out he would be getting the jab, I was overwhelmed by a surge of feelings and at first I couldn't make sense of them, I just wept. Looking back now, as

I try to put them into words, I know there was relief and happiness of course, but also something close to devastation. It made it all real — all the death, the closed schools, the strange indoors life. But I think the biggest feeling at that moment was an intense sense of gratitude.

My father was among the first in the world to have the vaccine outside of a clinical trial. The first was Margaret Keenan, who said it was the best early birthday present she could've hoped for — she turned 91 the following week. When I watched the news and heard the interviews with the people aged over 80 who were being vaccinated on that first day, I felt warmth and hope swell in my chest. There was something very moving about the fact that it was these people who were the first to be offered this gift of the vaccine. It felt right. It felt like this was something we as a country could be proud of, that we were prioritising those most vulnerable to the virus, rather than those who have the most money and power.

But I know that warm feeling of pride covers up a much darker truth. The truth is that this age group was failed terribly during the pandemic. The then UK Health Secretary said in the House of Commons that the government threw a 'protective ring' around people in care homes, but the reality is that Covid-positive patients were sent from hospital into these care homes, where the virus spread, killing thousands of residents.[1] As individuals, many younger healthy people got caught up in something very deadly, I think, which it was hard to be conscious of at the time. Right from the start of the pandemic as it unfolded in this country, as the first deaths in the UK made the headlines, the newsreaders would tell us the number of people who had died — and then tell us their ages, or the underlying condition from which they suffered. The anthropologist Sarah Lamb noticed this in America too: 'When they reported the deaths in the news, there was always mention of a pre-existing condition, or that they were older, this or that,' she says. She thinks some viewers would then think, 'Oh, those are other people, I'm going to be okay.' And if the deceased didn't fit into one of those categories, if they weren't old or ill — 'then it was alarming, because then it could be me'. The children's author Michael Rosen put it well in an interview on the *Today* programme, which took place as he was recovering from coronavirus. He was speaking, as a person in his early 70s, of his experience of the atmosphere as the pandemic began, before he became terribly ill: 'I sat there already having a sense that around the country, people were talking as if, well, this is an old person's illness, so it doesn't matter as much. I seem to remember that I wasn't saying that people were *actually* saying that old people don't matter as much, but it *felt* as if they were saying that. Now, in retrospect, looking back at it, I think they *were* saying that. People *were* thinking in those terms, as if somehow or other, there's a sort of watershed moment, you're 70, and then we can junk all that lot ... because they're going to die soon anyway. I think the moment you start thinking that sections of the population don't matter as much, I find that absolutely lethal, and of course horrifying. I hope that I would think it was horrifying if I was age 30; I obviously find it horrifying as I am 70-plus.'[2]

I think he's right. If I am really honest with myself, in a way that makes me feel a bit sick, I can recognise that in the early days of hearing those news reports, amongst the sadness and empathy, I did feel something like relief in hearing that it was an older person who had died, rather than a younger person, like me, although I wasn't conscious of that feeling at the time. This, despite the fact that I have two parents in the at-risk category, about whom I was desperately worried. And I do find it horrifying, utterly horrifying, to acknowledge that ugly, self-preserving side of myself, of humanity, that hides behind the more acceptable side. The part that has the capacity to treat some lives as worth less than others. I know it wasn't just me who had this unconscious reaction, though. Lamb pointed out the same conflicted, contradictory phenomena in many countries that have suffered from the pandemic: 'In many societies, people have been willing to discard the old, and not get as concerned that they're the ones dying. But on the other hand, there's also talk about performing care — saying you should all wear a mask and be vigilant because these are beloved people in your lives, you should be careful for the sake of the elderly. People are performing both — that it's okay to discard the old, and that they're valuable.' I think this hypocrisy reveals something of our profoundly split and ambivalent view of old age and older people — the way in which in our society we revere and raise up older people on the one hand, and on the other, we belittle and dismiss them, speak to them as if they are toddlers who have not grown up. Only when we see the truth of this messy dissonance, only when we see what so many of us get so wrong about this, can we really begin to understand the true meaning of these years. In writing this book, in writing this chapter in particular, I have seen for the first time how the final years of a person's life are just as precious as all the rest of it, if not more so. It is such a mistake to see these years as less valuable than those that have gone before. Different, yes; less valuable, absolutely not. Because, apart from anything else, there is such a lot of growing up still to do. And this is the last chance to do it.

This final stage of life, referred to in academic literature as the fourth age, or by Bernice Neugarten as 'old-old age',[3] is now a reality experienced by more of us than ever before. A striking illustration of this is the likelihood of reaching one's 100th birthday. Pat Thane writes in *The Long History of Old Age*, 'At all times a few people have lived to 100 or a little beyond. At the beginning of the 21st century more people than ever before lived to their century, but it is still rare to live much beyond that, although there are occasional examples of survival to around 120.'[4] In Britain at the beginning of the 20th century, an average of 74 people a year reached 100; at the end of that century, it was 3,000; in 2019, that number was over 13,000.[5] The same trend can be seen in America and Australia too. When I was a child, I remember learning that when people were 100 years old, they received a letter from the Queen — now it is no longer quite such an unusual event. The combination of the development of geriatrics, the impact of the

NHS, and the timing of the first baby boom that followed World War I, means that the proportion of people living into old-old age has soared. In 1966, there were 2.4 million people aged 75 and over in the UK; in 2016, there were 5.3 million.[6] The number of people aged 90 or over almost tripled over the three decades to 2019.[7] In America, in 2016, the 85 and over population was projected to more than double from 6.4 million to 14.6 million in 2040 — a 129 per cent increase.[8] In Australia, in 2017, there were under 500,000 people aged 85-and-over; it was then projected that in 30 years that number would triple.[9] I cannot bear to think how much these numbers might change as a result of coronavirus. Simply surviving to old age, of course, does not necessarily imply good health — but neither does it imply the opposite. Thane explains that as a result of the development of geriatrics and the NHS in the UK, while many of those who recovered from acute conditions which would have killed them in earlier times did go on to succumb to chronic disorders such as arthritis, diabetes, or Alzheimer's, the majority of people surviving to their 80s and 90s at the end of the century did not suffer from acute illness and regarded themselves as in good health and capable of independent activity, though of course this varied by age, class, and gender.

When I talk to Professor Klaus Rothermund, Chair of General Psychology at Friedrich-Schiller-Universität Jena, he picks me up on my use of the terms 'young-old' and 'old-old'. He tells me, 'Although I am aware of this young-old, old-old distinction, I personally don't use those terms so much.' He prefers to ask simply, what changes when we are growing old? He accepts it is important to acknowledge that there is something like the first part of old age and the second part of it; 'But I would not draw a true, strong line between the two, because you will typically be young-old in one domain and already old-old in another.' If you've lost your job and there is no way to re-enter the job market, in the domain of work you would be considered old-old; but you may, in other domains like leisure, health, or personality development, still be very much young-old. It reminds me of neuroscientist Sarah-Jayne Blakemore's description of how our brains mature, developing in some areas before others, and at a different pace in every individual. This brings me to an important point: beware the misleading unambiguity of chapters. It may be a bit late to say this, but I'll say it anyway: chapters are lies. If this book were truly representative of the life course, there would be no chapters, but uninterrupted text, swirling forward to adulthood and old age then back again to adolescence and further back to infancy then forward again to midlife and round and round we go. Fortunately for all of us, I have sacrificed experimental literary form in the hope of achieving something like clarity and readability. Nevertheless, I recognise this is not without cost, and I think Rothermund puts this well when he says that using the terms young-old and old-old as if they refer to two distinct and separate chapters of life also can convey a judgement on both: 'Using this young-old — old-old distinction comes with a strong evaluative component that young-old is good and old-old is bad. So I would prefer to talk about, what changes? A lot of things change when you grow old.'

So let's talk about the changes. 'There are changes in the opportunities you have; in the resources you have; in the functional capabilities you have,' says Rothermund. 'You probably lose something while growing old in this regard. On average, at least, people become less fit, less healthy, and they have memory deficits. Taking into account the huge variability we have, this is the global trend.' Psychologically however, it is a different story, and not only one of loss. Older people 'are more interested in generativity, in transcendence, in moral standards. These are the things that are more important — whereas young people are focussing on doing something now in order to reap the benefits later.' The long-term goals that some young people might have, to achieve a big ambition in their career for example, 'lose their meaning in old age, because your future time perspective becomes narrower. So people switch to other types of goals that are already meaningful in themselves, where at the very moment you act, you already see the meaning of your action.' Trying to find this different kind of meaning, I think, is key to growing up in old age. And as we began to see in the previous chapter, if you are too focussed on ageing successfully in young-old age, you rob yourself of a very important time to prepare for this, Rothermund argues: 'Anti-ageing is fighting the negative variant of ageing — but of course phrases like this show us that the negative image of ageing is the most prominent one. And giving people the illusion that they could avoid becoming old kills any incentive to create positive images of ageing. By distancing yourself from old age or older people, you might perhaps have more difficulties in mastering the developmental tasks that are inevitably tied to becoming old. And you will become old sooner or later — most of us do.' If you don't wish your old age away, if you face it, if you think about it, if you have ideas about it, then you can prepare for it. 'If becoming old is just bad, just a threat, well, there is nothing you can do about it except try to prevent becoming old. But then sooner or later, the point will come where you can no longer deny that you have grown old. And you have not prepared for it. You have not developed any plans. You have not done the things that are necessary to live a good life.'

Rothermund has done a lot of research[10] comparing the goals of older people with the goals of younger people, designing experiments which show that people of all ages change their goals when they imagine that their lives might end imminently. His findings have led him to conclude that this change in what brings meaning to later life has to do with what he calls the 'narrowing of the future time horizon'. This is the defining feature of old-old age, perhaps the most important factor that differentiates it fundamentally from earlier life stages: you are, without a doubt, in your last chapter. He explains, 'The crucial thing is if time is limited, that immediately makes you aware that you cannot do everything. You have limited time and you have to be highly selective, and when you have to be highly selective, you focus on what is most important.' I am reminded of Graham and his external and internal decluttering. Rothermund is keen to emphasise that this is not a panicked reaction to anxiety about death; it's the realisation that time is so precious because it has a limit. It is not awareness of death that provokes this change, he says, but awareness of time's limits. At first, I thought this was an inconsequential point to make, because after all, death is what limits time. But I think he is right to emphasise it because there is an important delineation to be drawn: the difference between something being urgent, and something being important. Rothermund continues, 'It's different when you're young, when you can still try out everything. You can do things just because you want to do them, because you can do the important things later. But when you're old, doing the unimportant things first means you might never do the important things, might never face the important things.' This honing process, this sieving and sifting of what matters most — this is a key grow-up of old-old age, I think — although perhaps it has roots much earlier in life. I think of Victoria's realisation that if she wants to get things done, she can't spend all day on social media; of Roxy Legane finding her mission in life with Kids of Colour; of Alex choosing to be the tortoise rather than the hare; and of Sheila visiting her first son's grave. At this life stage this grow-up has even more importance, resting as it does on another grow-up: understanding the fact that your life is coming to an end. These are the grow-ups that define this life stage, and they are essential for growing up through old age, rather than shrinking away from it. As Rothermund puts it, 'This is a shift, a developmental achievement, and it is a kind of growth. Living in a way that you focus on what is truly, lastingly important.'

I felt more nervous than usual when I rang the doorbell of Rabbi Jeffrey Newman's house. I am a liberal Jew, and growing up, I used to go to classes at synagogue on the weekend to learn to read Hebrew and meet boys (not in that order). I think it was then that I came to see the rabbi a bit like a head teacher, so maybe that had something to do with my nerves. Plus, this was one of the earliest interviews I conducted. It was back before the pandemic hit, when going into someone's home was a perfectly normal thing to do, when I had no idea that it would soon become illegal.

Weeks earlier, I had watched a video taken at an Extinction Rebellion protest which had gone viral. In this video, against the backdrop of noisy protestors and police, a rabbi in his 70s, wearing a suit and his kippa and tallit — the Jewish skull-cap and prayer shawl — is carried through a London street by police to be arrested. I felt moved, seeing a religious man breaking the law in this peaceful way for something he believed in, and I wanted immediately to find out what this man had to say about growing up in this final phase of life.

Now as I sit at the kitchen table many months later, I try to clear my mind of the to-do list rattling around my head and to allow any memories and feelings from the day of our interview to float into view. I remember sitting down on the brown leather sofa in Rabbi Newman's living room and taking out my dictaphone, pressing record, double-checking I'd pressed record. I remember the wooden flooring, the packed floor-to-ceiling bookshelves, the bay windows, the dim lighting. I remember feeling nervous, and then almost immediately at ease, relaxed by the low pitch of his voice, the very slow, deliberate pace of his speech, the long silences as he reflects on my questions and weighs each word of his answer. I listen to him as he talks about his life, and in the way he speaks I can also hear him say, without words, 'Please do not rush. We must take our time, this is important.'

He begins to speak about growing up. He was born in 1941, early in World War II. He talks about the Latin teacher at school who bullied him so badly he wanted to kill himself. He describes the psychological breakdowns he has endured over the course of his life, and how therapy and medication have helped him to feel more grounded. He talks about the death of his father. He speaks of his family — his wife, his children, his grandchildren. He tells me about his early first marriage which ended in divorce, and how he blamed his mother for it — she found it so hard to let him go, he says, that he was left with no choice but to marry young to separate from her. He tells me about the afternoon when he and his mother were alone in the house together and the idea for a healing ritual came to him; he wrapped his tallit around her shoulders and cradled her as she sobbed and cried. All of this was him growing up, he says. And it is still happening — the process is ongoing.

I want to know, what does growing up feel like for him now, at age 78? Well, 70 was a big birthday, he says. 'I was scared. I was very scared of becoming 70.' He references Psalm 90:10, the significance of three score and ten; and it is only now when I look up the psalm that I make the link to his fear: 'The days of our years are threescore years and ten; and if by reason of strength they be fourscore years, yet is their strength labour and sorrow; for it is soon cut off, and we fly away.' For him, reaching 70 meant, 'You can't escape it any longer. From 70 onwards you can't escape the fact that you're elderly. At a certain moment, you have that opportunity of being elderly.' I am reminded of the Murakami quote about the privilege, blessed right, and honour of growing old. I ask what difference it made to his life, when he reached that certain moment, that opportunity, and he says drily, 'Nothing then changed. The good thing sometimes about going through these barriers is to come out the other side and to realise actually, it's just another day.' For him, the change in fact began a decade earlier, when he stopped working as a community rabbi — the leader of a congregation in a particular synagogue — when he was 59. I ask if he would describe this as retirement, and he shakes his head. 'No. Change.' This was when his daily life was transformed; he had the freedom and the time to be able, as he put it, 'to work out what I really care about'. To work out what was really important to him. A vital grow-up. Since then, 'It's been a very, very exciting period of my life.' I think of Rothermund's explanation of how life goals change in old age when Rabbi Newman says that now, his life is 'about learning even more about living in the moment and discovering what it means to be of service'. His and his wife's bodies are changing, they are having to experience the ageing process, to deal with physical problems; 'And yet, what I think we are both finding is that we need to ensure this part of our lives is not merely about hospital visits and seeing doctors, which happens inevitably more than it did 20 years ago. That's not what gives meaning to life. Meaning comes through a deepening of engagement. So I think that's what's happening at the moment.' This is what 'being of service' seems to mean to him. 'Everything has, now, a reason for me to learn about it, in order to try and see, what do we need to do to bring about change? To help the world to be a bit more how we would like it to be?' This is something he has been trying to do in different ways throughout his adult life, and he has been fighting climate change for decades, but the difference is that now it has become his sole focus. This exploration with others, with young people and older people in Extinction Rebellion, is 'a very fertile place to be' for him at this time. It is through these explorations he has come to think of his current life stage through a different lens, and a different name: eldership.

'Eldership has been lost in the West,' he says, 'and I think it is absolutely essential that we rediscover it.' I ask what eldership means, and he doesn't have a clear definition to give me; it's something he is still thinking about, still working out — just like with me and adulthood. But he does have some pointers. 'It isn't that you suddenly feel you're an elder. Within indigenous cultures, you are chosen — others initiate you into eldership.' He was invited to help form an eldership group in Extinction Rebellion, and he attended a conference which brought together indigenous elders from 17 different parts of the world including Colombia, Peru, Mexico, North America, India, the Philippines, New Zealand, Australia and the Arctic areas. Through all his thinking and meeting, discussing and reflecting, he has arrived at a few different characteristics of being an elder: 'Obviously it's got something to do with wisdom. And that's why you wouldn't ever say or think that you're an elder, because it's also got something to do with humility. All that you can know is that you're working towards it, not that you've ever got there. It's got something to do with curiosity, with kindness and awareness, sensitivity, courage. Some of the people who might be accepted as being elders may not have all of them, but you've probably got to have a good cluster of them.' All that you can know is that you're working towards it, not that you've ever got there; with a sigh, I understand that what is true of eldership is true of growing up, too. The keys my grandfather dangled in front of me disappear further into the distance.

I wonder what Rabbi Newman makes, as an elder, of the younger end of the climate movement, from Greta Thunberg to the children missing school for the climate strikes, the despair they feel. He tells me the following, and I think it is important to quote him at length:

I think what happened is that it has touched a very wide awareness. That awareness is especially carried by young people who are, like I suppose many of us at different times when we're in our adolescence, very idealistic. We see injustice, we see nuclear arms, we see Vietnam, we see poverty, hunger, violence, the Iraq war. And we protest, with everything we can, to try to bring about change. The young people here and now see a world of potential deadness. They see the animals, the insects, drought and fire and hunger. They may know about the 'just in time' society that we live in, that could be very quickly affected by crop shortages or energy shortages in other parts of the world. They may have scientific recognition of feedback loops and cascades and the speed at which changes are taking place, far beyond what the authorities, whether cautious scientists or politicians, have ever predicted.

He also sees all this. And he also has hope: 'We never know how bad things are going to be, and, equally, sometimes there are unknown positives. There is a lot which is happening in the world, in different places, which, in different ways, could bring about positive change.'

I ask him about his arrest and in the way he talks about it, I can see it was a profoundly significant experience for him; in the aftermath, he realised it was an initiation ceremony of sorts into elderhood. I understand that it was an act of service, and not only because an arrest would have a much less damaging impact on his future than on a young person's future, and as a white, middle-class older man, he could feel safer in the hands of the police than others might. He was afraid, he says, but 'It was something I needed to go through. I have never been in trouble with the police — I am scared of authority. It was about being prepared to step out.' That's where the courage comes in, I suppose; feeling afraid, acknowledging it, and nevertheless, doing what was needed. That is the courage of being an elder. He tells me something about what happened that day, as he and fellow Extinction Rebellion members joined the protest in the City of London. They arrived at the area where the police had corralled the protestors, and Rabbi Newman read out something called the Solemn Intention: 'It's a very powerful, very short piece written by someone in Extinction Rebellion, that is used sometimes before an XR meeting to ground us in this moment. It's something like: "Let us take a moment, this moment, to recall why we are here. Let us remember this beautiful world, this planet which feeds and nourishes us, and let us think of our need to protect it, not for ourselves but for all." It's not much longer than that.' He read it out loud at the protest, and as he started reading, it echoed, as everyone around him echoed it phrase by phrase, 'And it became very big. The police stopped hassling us and trying to get us across the road, and the whole area was full of the sound of the solemn intention. And when we finished, I just knew that all I needed to do was to be on the ground. It was tarmac, but it felt like the earth. And I sank down and I had no intention of moving.' A policeman came up to him and gently and politely informed him that he must move on or he would be arrested. 'And I said yes, I know, thank you, I'll be arrested.'

It is a bit of a curveball to find that for a 77-year-old rabbi, the most significant grow-up of his life stage was getting arrested. This was one of the many, many moments I have had while writing this book where I found myself more confused about what growing up really means than when I started. But now that I know I have to let go of the idea that I'll ever arrive at a clear, solid, permanent definition and state of adulthood, I seem better able to embrace its contradictions and paradoxes, as well as my own. This was an important grow-up for me, I think. I feel more comfortable and tolerant of its complexity, that growing up means different things at different life stages — and different things at the same life stages. It means being able to be a separate and independent person — but also a person who can accept his or her own dependency and need for others and for their help. It means developing an internal motor to be self-directive, to become the person you are rather than the person that others want you to be — but it also means accepting that some things cannot be changed, that much is out of your control, and that losses have to be mourned. It means taking responsibility for yourself and making your own decisions rather than blaming your mistakes on others — but at the same time, recognising that we are not omnipotent, that we are also subject to the decisions of others and that we are not responsible for those decisions. I liked the way Rabbi Newman talked about eldership — we can think about adulthood in the same way, I think; the idea of a cluster of characteristics; the understanding that the working towards something is the closest you can ever get to attaining that thing; the qualities of wisdom, humility, kindness, awareness, sensitivity, and courage — it is as if he put into words the ideas that have been building in my mind, through all these chapters and interviews, of what it means to grow up.

I find a good cluster of these qualities in Pog — her nickname is an anagram of her initials and a shortening of pogo stick. We speak for two and a quarter hours over Zoom one morning, and I can tell from the moment she starts speaking that I am going to enjoy our conversation. It has something to do with a bounce in her voice, a rhythm in the way she speaks that feels determined, stimulating. She laughs a lot and makes me want to laugh — it's not that she's cracking jokes, but much of what she says is laced with a teasing, humorous spice. It is exciting to listen to her talk about her life in the past and in the present. At times, it feels like I am talking to a young teenager who enjoys being mischievous and knows she is getting away with it.

I tell her a bit about what the book is all about, or at least, what I think it's all about, and I ask if she's interested in these sorts of questions, in what it means to grow up, in the possibility that people who look like adults — even older adults — on the outside, might not be grown-ups on the inside. 'I would love to explore it with you. I really would. Because, now that I've started thinking about it, I'm quite shocked really,' she says, with an amused look on her face. 'I truly do not consider that I have grown up. And I'm 90.'

She continues, 'But one thing that really pleases me, to the extent of being a bit smug about it, is the really childish pleasures. You know, where you sort of clap your hands and say, "Oh! Look at that!" And somehow I've still got that, and I love it. It can be completely trivial things.' I don't think smugness is quite right the right word — she sounds to me like the cat who got the cream and is rather enjoying it, or like she has a secret super-power. 'I'm so grateful for it. And that's my main conclusion — which isn't exactly deep, is it?' she adds, dismissing herself. I can see why she thinks it's not deep; it's one of those thoughts that can very easily be turned into a vomit-inducing, meaningless cliché on a mug or on a pencil case: 'It's the simple pleasures that make life worth living!!!!!' But I think she's talking about something quite profound. It is so easy to take for granted the childlike ability to feel amazement at everyday life. But when we are depressed or anxious or grieving, and that ability vanishes, it is such a deadly, deathly thing. I have had mornings, as I imagine most people have, when I have woken myself up crying, when I have had to grit my teeth to get out of bed for feeling such inexplicable pressure, when the feeling of sunshine on my face or the smell of fresh coffee or the touch of a loving partner, these easy pleasures that ease us into the day, evoke nothing. Nothing. And when you notice those pleasures return, when something grows in you and you find yourself once again spontaneously fascinated, like a child, by the intricate beauty of the veins on a leaf or by the lethal precision of a spider trapping a fly in its web or the divine comfort that comes from sucking the tea out of a dunked chocolate Hobnob … it is a feeling of coming alive. This seems to me to be what Pog is talking about — and it brings to my mind the thought of Graham playing his violin, of Kemi at her sewing machine, of Hemal flicking his kids' ears, of Legane so engaged and alive in her activism, and of Boru on one of his Sunday bike rides, the cows whizzing past him as he speeds down those country lanes. All of the people I've interviewed have spoken about this, in some way; they have helped me to see that whatever life stage you find yourself in, the question of being more or less grown up, of being able to continue growing up or of stalling somewhere along the road, has something important to do with how we relate to the younger versions of ourselves that we hold inside us — the concentric circles in our tree trunk, as Gianna Williams put it. Whether we can hold on to them, find a way to live with them and look after them, to keep them alive in us, so that they can keep us alive.

Pog was born in Malta, where her father was a Chief Engine Room Artificer on a submarine in the Royal Navy. She says proudly, 'I still cannot believe this, but in 1929, my mother decided she wanted to go and see my father for a holiday, so she made her way by train across Europe and, as she delicately put it, "If it hadn't been for that Maltese sunshine, you would not have arrived."' Several months later, 'She made the journey again, pregnant, alone, to be with my father when I was born. From what I remember, and also from what family have subsequently told me, they were crazily in love.' But just before the war, when Pog was 9 years old, her father was killed in an infamous submarine disaster when HMS *Thetis* sank during sea trials in 1939; he was one of 99 men who died. 'It was an early loss. The sad thing was that it affected my mother's mind, waiting three days to see if they got them out.' When Pog was 13, her mother was diagnosed with schizophrenia and was, in today's terminology, sectioned in a psychiatric hospital. Pog was adopted by a cousin. I ask how she feels these losses affected her. 'They made me extremely grateful for the stability I subsequently found in marriage and motherhood. The memories I have are only of being loved, of never not being loved. That's about all I can say about my childhood.'

She met her husband, Brian, at church, where she sang in the choir. Before they married, she says, 'We had relationships that went on for years, and either one of us would get fed up with it and go off and be with somebody else, because in those days when I talk about "being with" it doesn't exactly mean what it means today, because having intercourse before marriage was just not on. You might do everything else — which is damn good training, because you learnt about foreplay. But you didn't actually have sex.' Eventually, after years of this, they were in love, 'And so we got married, like you do.' They had three children, and when I ask her about the best time in her life, she talks about being a mother. 'The kids as teens — oh God, they were menaces. They were right rebels. But my God, they were such fun, and they still are. Motherhood I've enjoyed throughout, I still am enjoying it, and I feel mighty privileged to have these three adults that I really like as well as love. They are all three completely different, but they are three adults that I genuinely like, so that's really what my life is all about, I think.' I seem to be unable to read this without tearing up. I wonder if it might be because Pog puts me in touch with the part of me that wants to know and experience that love first-hand — the love of a mother for her child.

Although these were all growing-up experiences in different ways, there is a more recent one that Pog wants to talk about. 'The thing that happened was my husband getting Alzheimer's,' she says. 'That's when I learnt some very unpleasant things about myself. I lack patience, I lack empathy. That was … yeah, that was a pretty serious growing-up time. The awful thing is that everybody says, oh, you were marvellous, you were so good with Brian. But I know the truth, Moya. And that was serious growing up.'

Brian lived at home for 8 years following his diagnosis, and Pog became his full-time carer. 'I lost Brian gradually, the real Brian,' she says, 'The cardboard cut-out looked immaculate; he was nicely dressed, kept himself clean and tidy, and looked the same as he ever did. In fact everybody would say, doesn't Brian look well, you must be looking after him well, Pog. But the real Brian took eight years to go. They call Alzheimer's the long goodbye, and it's a very, very accurate description.' Life caring for Brian became harder and harder, and her children were worried this was such a strain on Pog that he would outlive her. 'I now know they were plotting among the three of them to get him into a home. Towards the end, I wasn't able to get out at all.' Except for having a weekly hairdo — that was her therapy. 'I'd think, well, if Brian does something dreadful while I'm out, then I'll jolly well have to live with the guilt, but I've got to have a bit of a life, otherwise I'm going to crack up. But I'd only be out for an hour and then I'd dash back.'

Brian never did go into a home; he died 5 years ago, when Pog was 85. She talks about his death with touching dark humour. 'Bless his heart, we went out for a meal with friends and he upped and died. His famous last words were "Scampi and chips please". And he literally died. Badum. He hiccoughed and died. If there is such a thing as a good death, that was it.' It was as good as it could have been for Pog, too: 'I was amongst friends in a restaurant and I know the owner, and he came and cuddled me and organised hot tea, and my friends cuddled me. It was just incredible. I do regard it as a beautiful death, and the fact that I was there, I saw him die, not too many people get that. And I think it is wonderful to be there when your best beloved actually dies, It's amazing, absolutely amazing.'

I have not heard somebody speak in this way about death before, and I want to understand. What was amazing about it? Pog explains: 'Well, the flesh and blood is still there. So I cuddled him and spoke words into his ear, hoping that, as hearing is the last thing to go, that they might go through. I don't know if they did. But it's closure, it's real closure, isn't it? You have seen them die. You have seen them being taken into the ambulance as a corpse. That's it, I think, looking back. It's closure.' It does sound quite amazing, when she puts it like that.

I am struck by how honestly Pog talks about her situation and the confusing, overwhelming mess of feeling that swept her up after her husband died. 'The awful thing is that I was so grateful for his death. That's the difficult thing, coping with the mixed emotion afterwards.' Again, she found herself in a situation with everybody telling her, 'Oh, Pog, you were marvellous, you turned your life around.' 'And I'm thinking, well, I was just so grateful because I didn't want to put Brian in a home, but I also didn't feel that I could carry on any longer. It was a ghastly state to be in and it was all solved by his death. Oh God, it's an awful thing, but it's just recognising that we're not perfect, anybody looking after somebody with Alzheimer's is going to have some really bad moments, when, quite frankly, they'd be willing to kill, because of the sheer frustration of it. And to have all that taken away, to go home that night and know that I would not be woken up several times … She pauses, and looks at me. 'Do you want me to witter on about this?' she asks. I tell her yes, I do, that I think it's important. I tell Pog I think if more people could be honest about how difficult the experience of being a carer for a loved one can be, and of how complicated it makes the experience of grief, then it might help people feel less alone, less guilty, even though their experiences might be different from hers.

She continues, 'After he died, I began sort of, living my life again.' But this wasn't how she was supposed to feel; 'You're supposed to be mourning and prostrate with grief and all that stuff. But it wasn't a difficult time because I had this overwhelming gratitude that I didn't have to live that life any more.' When she talks about how people idealised her, portraying her as some kind of saint, I wonder if it is our way of sanitising what is a really horrible experience because the rest of us cannot bear to see the truth of what it means for some people to struggle to care for a loved one with dementia day in, day out. The truth is Pog isn't a saint, that this brought out some parts of her that she really didn't like, that she is brave and honest enough to recognise, rather than trying to deny or push away. 'Oh yes,' she says, 'Oh yes. I've always known those parts were there. We do know ourselves, if we've got any sense at all, don't we, and we know the bits that lurk in the dark corners. At least, I do for myself.' Pog has come to know these dark corners on her own; I need my analysis to try to get to know mine.

It wasn't until 18 months after Brian's death that the grief came. 'Suddenly everything changed. My very perceptive neighbour suddenly said, "You've changed, Pog, you're completely different."' Pog describes what took place, and what was noticed by her neighbour, as 'a complete softening of my personality. I think up until then, there'd probably been a sort of shell that was put on for outside viewing'. Thinking of my tortoise shell, my carapace, I ask her if this shell was there just for the 18 months, or for her whole life. 'I think possibly my whole life. You know, I was the person who was keeping it all together, and I do like to appear to be in control of the situation. Certainly, then, I was putting on that show, and not realising that I was putting on a show.' Until, suddenly, she wasn't. 'I was grieving. I was doing all the bits, you know — crying at sloppy feelings and sloppy tunes and stuff like that, having memories. I truly mourned. I'm very grateful that I did, because now I do feel normal about it.'

She mourned, and then she grew. That mourning was so important because it meant that, in the years since, she has been able to live a good life. 'It took time to get used to the new situation, but it's been wonderful. I have had a new lease of life.' I ask her how this shift changed her day-to-day experience, and she says, 'It's a sense of freedom', which meant

— pre-coronavirus — more 'socialising, a lot of eating, a lot of drinking. Yes, definitely a lot of drinking, and going to shows and movies, music festivals and things like that.' She does not mean freedom in the sense of going on wild adventures or travelling to far-flung countries, nor new hobbies or activities — although there have been a couple of holidays with family. 'I've just so enjoyed being able to read in peace, to be able to eat what I want, when I want. Brian was meat and two veg and everything fried; I'm salad, not much meat, and nursery food like tomatoes and poached eggs on toast. So that's been lovely. It's a sense of freedom, of being entirely selfish. I've enjoyed it.' Even over lockdown, she has not felt lonely most of the time. 'I do like living alone, and of course, in our day, you didn't, you just didn't — you went from the parental home into the marital home, it wasn't until widowhood that I've had the experience of living alone. And it is new and exciting. It really is.'

The mourning process was a period of growth for her, she says. 'I do think I have grown up as far as that's concerned. But for God's sake, how old was I? 85! It was one hell of a stage, and I didn't do it until I was 85!' Do you think that's when you really grew up, I ask her? She replies, 'I wouldn't think it is a complete process. There's still a long way to go. I'm sorry, but there is.'

I tell her that according to academics I have read, she is now in the life stage called 'old-old age', and she replies wryly, 'That figures.' I wonder if that matches up to how she feels. 'The only thing that is different now — and it's not because of Covid — is I am very conscious of my own mortality. I think it's since they diagnosed this heart problem; it's not a real problem, just an enlarged heart and an irregular beat, but I'm very conscious that I could shuffle off at any time. And I'm not that bothered by it. Because there's an acceptance that things are not going to get better … they may not necessarily get worse, but they're not going to get better.' From time to time, a new feeling washes over her, unlike anything she has felt before. 'There is sometimes a tiredness. It's a really funny feeling, Moya; it is quite strange, and sometimes I think to myself, are you depressed without knowing it? I don't think I am. But there is, sometimes, a tiredness. It's not that "I can't be bothered" feeling; it's quite weird and I haven't really processed it myself.' It is tied up, this feeling, with her approach to life: 'It's a completely different attitude to the one I had, say, three years ago, when you're still assuming that life will go on for ever. Now I'm conscious that it won't. It's quite an unusual state, I've no idea whether other people go through it. It's not the sort of thing you ask, is it?' She smiles. 'You don't go around saying to your friends, and how're you feeling about dying?'

I am delighted she's said this, because it's exactly the question I want to ask her, and I do: 'How are you feeling about dying?' She replies immediately: 'I don't want to. But I now know positively that I'm going to. I don't assume anything any more. It doesn't mean that you don't look forward to things or make plans for the future, but I don't assume or take it for granted that I'm going to be there to do it. And then something happens and you think, oh goodness, you really do want to go on living.' She muses, 'Perhaps, I don't know, is humility the word? I'm not sure. As I said I haven't really processed it myself.' It is a privilege to listen to Pog, to witness this fluctuation between on the one hand, being able to face the reality of mortality, to get her head around the fact that death is real and imminent and not just something that happens to other people — and on the other, feeling just how much she doesn't want it to happen to her. I think being able to experience this in the way that she describes is quite an enormous achievement; it seems to me the only way most of us get through the day is by pretending on some level that we aren't going to die. She tells me, 'Well, you take it for granted that you're not going to, don't you? I always have, anyway.' This is the major change for her: now she knows it's inevitable. About 18 months before we speak, Pog laid out what she calls 'Pexit' — Pog's Exit. 'It's entirely up to them what they do with my funeral, but I've told them what music I would like played, and I want a live band if we can get one.' This sounds like a very valuable experience, a facing up to the facts of life and death and a finding meaning in bearing their reality. I ask her if there are moments when she feels ready. 'There are moments ... I can't say I feel ready, but there are moments when I don't mind. It's part acceptance of the inevitable, I guess. And in its way, it's extremely comforting. I'm not afraid any more.'

I wonder what Pog makes of this assumption in our society that growing up and being an adult is tied to age — that at some point in your 20s, or your 30s, you do become an adult and you do grow up; how what I'm finding through writing this book and speaking to people like her is that this is not how it works; that it seems to me we all have experiences throughout life through which we grow up or we don't, that we can sometimes inhabit quite grown-up states of mind, and that sometimes we cannot. I wonder if she feels that she has grown up now — if facing death and accepting it is a real moment of adulthood, of facing the truth of things and not living in a fantasy world where we can live forever. She says, 'The real sort of inside growing up, the mental attitude, I don't feel I'm there yet. I think there's still stuff to do — though I'm not sure what. Circumstances may throw it up; if my health deteriorates an awful lot, if I end up, God forbid, bed-bound, that will be something else to cope with, to increase my mental maturity. There's stuff to learn — I don't mean coping with Zoom and stuff like that; Heavens to Betsy, that's been a wake-up call — but, what do I mean? It's inside of you. I don't know exactly what I'm trying to say, but I don't feel that for myself, the process is complete. I think there's still stuff there which I haven't yet learnt.'

I am very moved by listening to Pog trying to puzzle this out and think it through and have a conversation with herself and with me about what it is that she's reaching to say. What I understand from the reflections she shares is that she may be 90 and she may have experienced a lot of loss and mourned it, and had some wonderful experiences and some frightening experiences and some sad experiences, and she may have come to know quite a bit of herself, but she still feels there's more work to do. I ask her if she thinks it is a process she will complete in her lifetime, or if it will be ended by death but never finished? She replies, 'Can I say that I hope it is not finished because in a way, that's almost a sort of immortality, isn't it? While I may accept the fact I'm going to die and all that stuff, if there's still a tiny spark which says, there might be something more to learn, isn't that something to look forward to?'

I ask her what she feels are the main ways in which her mind feels different now from earlier in her life. 'I'm not sure I can answer that without thinking about it,' she answers. I tell her to, please, take the time she needs, and after some moments pass, she tells me, 'Peace, I suppose. And not having ... not having to strive any more. Not really keeping up appearances. I don't mean clothes but ... tranquillity. Peace is the word, I think. That's about as far as it goes. All I can think of is that word, peace, I just can't get away from it.' This is what it means, for her, to be in a grown-up state of mind, I say. 'Yes,' she says, 'yes. Truly accepting what you are and what you've become.'

When I began thinking about this chapter, I wondered if, for a person to enjoy the privilege of growing up in old age, for it to be possible for psychological development to continue in tandem with inevitable physical and cognitive decline, if that person would have to be more or less well. I wondered if this privilege was reserved for people like Pog, or if those suffering from dementia as her husband did might still be able to experience some kind of growing up at this life stage, and what that might look like.

Gill Livingston is Professor of Psychiatry of Older People at University College London, and she is also my aunt — I am married to her nephew. She is one of the most admirable, impressive, and sensible people in my life. She is the woman who I instinctively want to phone in a crisis, because she will know what to do, and her response will be kind and efficient. She does have two children of her own who have children of their own, and nine nephews and nieces (plus their partners), not to mention an ever-expanding brood of great-nieces and -nephews, so I only call when it's really, definitely serious. She is also quite busy, as she happens to be one of the most respected authorities on dementia in the UK. If anyone I know is a grown-up, it's her. The first question I ask her is if she is an adult, and her answer comes immediately: 'Yes.'

Livingston (it feels very, very strange to call her that) did not go into psychiatry wanting to specialise in dementia, but when she learnt more about it, she says, 'I realised that it encompasses everything that I'm interested in. I'm interested in people's intellectual ability and in their family relationships. I'm interested in their mood and experiences. I'm interested in physical illness. And those factors all come together in this illness and what happens with families. It drew me both because I thought I could be useful, but also because I was really interested in how these things interacted, and how people manage, and how different it can be, depending on the illness but also the illness in the context of individuals and their families.' Often when we use the word dementia, we use it to mean one illness, but in fact there are different types of dementia which have different symptoms — and dementia itself is a term for a collection of symptoms which are caused by different diseases of the brain. Not just that, but it affects different parts of people's brains at different times, and goes at different speeds, so each patient is affected in their own individual way. At the most severe stage, she acknowledges, the symptoms are not individual, and the disability experienced by sufferers looks very much the same. Until that point, 'One person can have it and can be very cheerful and enjoy their life, and another person can be very miserable, and it's not necessarily what you'd predict — and it's not what they would have predicted either.'

The most common disease to cause dementia is Alzheimer's, in which, Livingston explains, 'Lots of brain cells die, and they get tangled up, so you get these tangles of the outside of cells. And because the cells are dying, your brain shrinks, so you've got less brain.' There is also a deposition of a protein called amyloid, and around the brain cells that are left, there is a lack of the essential chemicals — neurotransmitters — which allow brain cells to pass information between them and communicate with one another. Vascular dementia, another disease, 'is just like a heart attack in the cerebral cortex; there hasn't been enough blood and a bit of it has died — or maybe quite a lot of bits'. The next most common is called Lewy Body dementia. 'Well, that wasn't even described when I first started studying it.' Lewy bodies are the name given to abnormal clumps of protein which form inside brain cells, which are also found in people with Parkinson's. Most people who develop Parkinson's, about 12 to 15 years later also develop dementia, as these Lewy bodies spread to the cerebral cortex — this is the outer layer of the brain, the grey matter, which plays a key role in perception, thought, and memory, among other tasks. All of these diseases, among others which are less common, lead to the collection of symptoms we know as dementia.

Livingston was asked by the esteemed scientific journal *The Lancet* to lead their Commission on Dementia, bringing together scientists from around the world to research and work together to find out more about the causes of dementia and how we can prevent and treat it.[11] In the commission's most recent meeting in 2020, Livingston and her colleagues found that about 40 per cent of all dementias in the world were potentially preventable. Of all the findings, she says, 'The thing that surprised me most, that I wasn't expecting when we began, is hearing aids. Studies show this is the highest risk factor in a population and in individuals.' I find myself thinking about this long after our interview. It seems very meaningful. The risk factor is not hearing loss, but *not* using hearing aids; there have been studies showing that individuals who have hearing impairment, who use hearing aids, have no excess risk. My assumption is that the damage comes not from the fact of being deaf, but from the effects of losing the ability to hear — the social isolation, the loneliness, the inability to engage and connect and communicate with other people as before. Livingston and her colleagues' research, confirming findings of other studies, found that exercising regularly, eating a healthy diet, not drinking too much, not smoking — all of that helps a lot to reduce your risk of experiencing dementia, as you'd expect. But not as much as using a hearing aid if you need one.

I wanted to find out who invented hearing aids, and fell, for a very enjoyable period, into a Wikipedia hole.[12] It was a man called Miller Reese Hutchison, born in Alabama in 1876. It turns out he also invented the Klaxon car horn, and reading Hutchison's obituary in the *New York Times* I learn that Mark Twain is alleged to have told him, 'You invented the Klaxon horn to make people deaf, so they'd have to use your acoustic devices in order to make them hear again.'[13] He developed the first hearing aid in 1895, when he was 19 years old — he gave it the far more exciting name of acousticon. And do you know why he started working on it? He had a childhood friend, Lyman Gould, who lost his hearing from scarlet fever. Perhaps it was a childhood wish to help his friend communicate that led this remarkable man to invent a device that would help protect millions and millions of people from the impact of hearing loss — not to mention the dementia which can result from it.

When Livingston began studying dementia, she did not know that one day, both her parents would suffer from it. She thinks her research affected her own experiences, in that she knew the practical steps to take — like asking them to sign power of attorney when they were still well — and that she didn't experience the denial that some families do; she saw the reality, perhaps before others, that it was no longer safe for her mother to drive or to live alone in her own home. 'I think a lot of people were not as aware of the dangers. So instead of thinking this is a one-off, and maybe it won't happen again, I knew it was only going to get worse, we can't allow it.' She thinks all the work she'd done might have helped her to accept the situation. Her mother changed dramatically, and that meant adjustments for the whole family; Livingston would tell them, 'She is whoever she is now. Okay, she's different, but whoever she is now, that's really her. This is really a legitimate part of her life. Not a bit that she's chosen, not a bit that she wanted, but it's her life, and it's legitimate. And I think that helped.' I ask her if she thinks that people with dementia can continue to develop, to grow up, in tandem with the cognitive decline they are experiencing. 'I don't think they're growing up,' she says, 'No.'

Johanna Wigg is a social gerontologist — a sociologist of old age — and she also runs a care home in Maine in the USA called The Vicarage by the Sea.[14] I was researching in the British Library when I came across a paper she wrote with the intriguing title, 'Intimacy among the socially dead: examining intimacy among institutionalised elders with mid to late stage dementia'.[15] Some weeks later, we speak on a video call while she waits in the car to pick her six-year-old daughter up from football practice. In her tone of voice, in its rhythm and cadence, I can hear the decades she's spent caring for people with progressive neurological conditions; everything she says reverberates with clarity and generosity. It is just a pleasure to listen to her, especially when she talks about her previous residents and their lives, her work and the fulfilment it brings her. Her mother was a psychotherapist and her father a doctor, and innate in both those disciplines as she sees them is intellect and caregiving; this is what she finds in her work as well, running her own care home — in the combination of researching and designing a model of care that is intellectually rigorous and robust, and delivering that care in a compassionate way. But she also brings herself to it, in a way that is just her own: 'I feel such reward from being engaged in physically supporting people, caring for them in the most menial of ways, in the toileting, in brushing their teeth, shaving.'

Her approach to all this was shaped by her grandmother. 'She was an artist,' Wigg says, 'a sculptor. Very in tune with the natural world, with the aesthetics of life, and colours. Extremely kind and gentle. She and my grandfather were of Swedish lineage, they were first generation. She was just an incredibly gentle soul.' She began showing the symptoms of dementia, and when these worsened, she needed more help at home. This was at a time, in the early- to mid-90s, when in America the only alternative would have been what Wigg describes as 'large-scale institutional care. And by that I mean large nursing homes with locked doors, long corridors, very sterile, heavily influenced by medical protocol.' Unlike her older siblings who had their own families, Wigg, then a student, had the time to care for her grandmother, who was in her 80s, through to the end of her life. 'What I realised in that care was that my grandmother was present 'til the very end. I couldn't get over how her appreciation of the natural world continued. She may not have been able to articulate clearly in language what she was wanting to convey. But she could say enough for me to hear the essence, her spirit, what was happening around her.' There is a story about her grandmother that Wigg loves to tell. They were sitting at a table, along with several of Wigg's friends from graduate school, and her grandmother out of the blue started singing 'Happy Birthday'. One of Wigg's colleagues said, 'Esther, Esther, whose birthday is it?' And she replied, 'I have no idea — but let's have a party.' For Wigg, 'Those pieces of her spirit radiated through, even with the enormous cognitive challenge.' That experience of caring for her grandmother shaped her world view and it has shaped the Vicarage.

At the time when she set up the Vicarage, Wigg says, dementia was taboo in America. 'Really taboo. People were ostracised. People were put in wings, doors were shut. It was horrible, what happened. There was a tremendous amount of fear, that we were all going to get this, that you become a shell of yourself, that there's really nothing left.' She wanted to do something very different when she set up her own care home 20 years ago. 'The goal was to destigmatise it; to say to the families that come for care — and I still say this every day in my work — "I'm so sorry that you've had such horrible experiences trying to have your loved one treated in a humane way. This is a different reality.'" Her thinking is shaped by the Eden Alternative, a movement which supports the de-institutionalising of long-term care settings for older people, as well as by the work of the dementia-care pioneer Tom Kitwood. His was a model of person-centred care based on the core idea, as Wigg puts it, 'that our sense of personhood is far more resilient than our use of language, our physical ability, even our psychological stability'.

Instead of medicating the symptoms of dementia — symptoms like wandering around, repeating things, asking lots of questions, looking for people who have died — Wigg has designed a care home and a structure to normalise, adapt to, and fit around the needs of her residents. So what does that look like in reality? Take the symptom known as wandering; in many care homes, doors are locked to keep residents safe, but this can also be very distressing for them as they can't go where they want to and don't understand why. In the Vicarage, there are no locks on the doors; instead, there are motion detectors, and whenever one goes off, the staff are alerted by a buzzer vibrating on their belt, and they go for a walk with the resident who wants one. The staff have also fine-tuned their approach to wandering, tailoring it to every individual resident, Wigg explains: 'If you learn the rhythm of the person's day,' — which they can because it's an enormously intimate environment, with only eight residents, so staff are very involved in their daily lives — 'you get to know when that person is going to want to go for a walk. So we schedule a walk into their day before they begin to get anxious, and then they come back and they relax. So you don't have to work so hard against a need that wasn't addressed in the moment that it needed to be addressed.' It's about getting to know the rhythms, needs, and personality of the individual, she says; something that large-scale, institutional care is not set up to do. 'This is the sociology of the piece: you have to understand institutions and how they function and then how to deinstitutionalise.' Staff don't wear any identifying clothing:

'We're all family, which reduces the sense of hierarchy and makes people feel more comfortable; like it's their grandchild or niece that they're relating to, as opposed to somebody in charge who's going to tell them what to do.' Of course, this all comes at a cost, and although the fees are comparable with more medicalised institutionalised settings, many families are unable to afford to send their loved ones to the Vicarage. Those who can become a part of the Vicarage family. 'For 20 plus years,' Wigg says, 'I've been trying to create a model of care that creates a culture that allows these individuals to live as normal a life as they could, with dignity, good care, and normality, and then let life carry on. And that's what's happened.'

I find her way of speaking about her residents compelling, but I struggle to wrap my mind around the idea that dementia might not take away someone's sense of personhood — I feel I've seen that happen. Wigg is not surprised by my struggles. She quotes the medical ethicist Stephen G. Post who coined the term 'hypercognitive society' to describe the way in which our culture places such tremendous value in cognitive ability. This helps explain why when a person begins to experience dementia, their social network will often distance themselves and pull away — meaning a dementia diagnosis can also be, in effect, a social death sentence. But what Wigg has found in her work is that this social death does not stem from the dementia itself, it is not a symptom of the illness; intimate relationships, friendships, and romances can emerge between people with dementia, and they frequently do. In that first paper I read by her in the British Library, she presents observations from her work providing evidence of rich intimate relations between residents with mid- to late-stage dementia. I ask her about this and she tells me, 'Look, we care for people with dementia who fall in love. And you can't deny it. You watch it happen; you see them across the table, they hold each other's hands, they won't let go of each other. They do everything that your teenagers are doing, that you do when you're falling madly in love. Every aspect of intimate interpersonal engagement is represented.' She talks about two previous residents, a lobsterman and a woman from the local community who had raised a big family, both in their early 80s. 'From the time their eyes locked, it was a very authentic lust and then love between them.' They would go into the bedroom and shut the door, and when concerned staff cracked the door open to check what was going on, 'they had gotten down to their undergarments and were just spooning together in bed holding each other. It was the most beautiful, loving expression of finding somebody who could make you feel good during a very challenging time.'

The social death sentence is handed down, Wigg has concluded, by well people who do not have dementia, and who can sometimes struggle, quite understandably, to relate to their loved ones who do. 'What I am constantly encouraging families to do is to redefine their relationship with their loved one so they don't have to lose that relationship,' she says. She has cared for many people who, when they lost their cognitive function to the degree that they could not interact with loved ones as they used to, then lost their families, who could not bear the loss, and let go. 'They don't visit. They don't spend time. It is too uncomfortable, it is too painful.' That can be hard to watch, she says — but it doesn't always go that way. She has cared for plenty of families who, with encouragement and support, 'can realise that that person is still present; there are just other means of communication that we must engage in, be it touch, be it facial expression, be it tone of voice'. Even if someone with dementia cannot understand exactly what a loved one is saying to them, they can hear the rhythm of the words and the sound of their voice and recognise it, and that, Wigg says, is communication. She sees it as part of her job to do her best to help loved ones to understand this. This can be particularly powerful when a spouse learns to communicate with their partner in a new way. 'I say, I want you to be able to be a partner again. I want you to be the loved one, and not have this hierarchy of care provider, care receiver. And when you see that finally happen, you realise that the loved one is able to reunite with the essence of that person who they so loved for so long.'

She says when this works, it means that loving relationships can be sustained, and sustaining, until the very end. She tells me about a woman they cared for, who had been a teacher, and who was almost mute. 'I have this sense that she was a quiet woman anyway for most of her life, very demure,' she says. 'Her daughter would come and sit at the feet of her mother, she would sit on the floor, this middle-aged daughter. Her mother, sat very straight on a cushion on a chair, just stroked her hair. You got the sense that this mother was a matriarch, that's who she was, and this daughter was giving her some normalcy, some respect, creating this engagement that let her mother know that she was her daughter.' This daughter would let her mother stroke her hair, and then talk to her and show her pictures of what was happening in the family, pointing out who people were. 'But she never asked a question. She never expected something in return. She was just present with her mother, allowed her mother to take in what she could. For all we know, her mother was understanding a great deal, or she was understanding very little, but what was happening was a mother-daughter loving engagement. You could not deny that on any level. She knew it was her daughter. It was beautiful.'

I ask her to tell me about some of the other people who have lived at the Vicarage. She says the youngest was 55, and some have been in their early- and mid-60s, but the majority are aged 80 onward. Most of them are very healthy — except for their dementia. They have family who have the time and the energy to find good care for them, and they can afford it. Most of them are educated, some very highly educated. When she tells me these facts and figures, she sounds like an academic sociologist. But when I ask her about their personalities, if she can tell me what her residents are like, she talks with the energy and excitement of a child talking about all the friends she's made at school. 'The personalities run the gamut,' she says, smiling broadly. 'I have over the years cared for just so many interesting characters. Many of the people we care for have led these very productive, esteemed lives, and have these tremendous histories.' She cared for a woman who worked for the CIA back when not many women did, 'and yet you'd ask her about it and she'd say, "Oh no, there was nothing very odd about it."' One woman resident was the first organic farmer of Nova Scotia. 'And a gentleman who passed not too long ago was part of groundbreaking work as a paediatric cardiac surgeon, and he saved many, many babies' lives back when children really weren't surviving cardiac issues at birth.' Many of the residents share certain characteristics, she says. Some are fairly obsessive; some quite concerned with schedules. 'And so you see these patterns that obviously fed their lives in their professions, and in their homes caring for children. But at the same time, they have a depth to them.' The dementia does not take away their individuality. She tells me about one resident who was a famous author: 'You would give him a book and he would read, and you just knew that words were what had built him and sustained him. He could not necessarily have a linguistic conversation with you specific to what he was reading; he couldn't explain it, but hearing him read and then watching his mind grapple with it all was very, very powerful. You could see the innate humanity of who that person was.' Of course, because people are as diverse with dementia as they are without it, she explains, 'There have been people that were very challenging to care for. I don't mean to suggest that every person we've cared for in their rawness has been beautiful and loving.' But regardless of the residents' behaviour, Wigg tries to understand their distress and listen to where it might come from.

And then she says something that seems to connect profoundly with what I've been trying to reach for: a sense of what growing up needs to mean for me and my tortoise shell, for all of us as we grapple between what is false and what is true. 'I can't get people to buy this yet, but some day, perhaps it will happen. I feel that one of the beautiful effects of dementia is that the social cocoon that we develop throughout our lives to survive our social lives — and it starts at infancy, really, that's when we begin to learn how to get through this crazy world — that social cocoon slowly gets peeled away. And before you know it, you see this incredibly vulnerable, raw, very real humanity in these people.' And so it was with that resident who had been a paediatric cardiac surgeon. When the manager at the Vicarage had a baby who she brought in to introduce to everyone, Wigg says, this retired doctor 'immediately asked for a stethoscope and held the child like he would have held all of the babies that he probably saved, and he proceeded to listen to the child's heart. Not because anybody asked him too, but to check her child's heart, to make sure that he could look at her and say, "You have a beautiful, healthy child." So the essence of who that man was, was so present to the end of his life.' I cannot explain it but every time I read this story, I start to cry. Perhaps it is something to do with the kindness and generosity of this man, of the proximity of old age and new life, of the paradox of a mind that, in its deterioration, retains something true and beautiful.

It seems to me that Wigg feels like she is part of a secret world, seeing all this humanity where others cannot. 'When you see stuff like I have, you just gasp. These people are written off all the time, and it's so unnecessary,' she says. Two decades after opening the Vicarage, 'I feel it 100 times stronger, that the humanity of these individuals is ever present.' I tell her that I am moved by what she has told me, and that I think her work really gets to the heart of what I am trying to find out. How we often seem to think that growing up is something that happens in childhood and adolescence and young adulthood, that once we are — officially, anyway — adults, and especially when we reach old age, our story is purely one of decline. But what she is saying when she talks about layers getting peeled back, when she speaks about humanity being ever-present, it seems to me, is that running in parallel with these losses, we can also perhaps read a story of a movement towards something true within ourselves. That this process can continue in some form, in Wigg's view, for some in their experience of dementia. 'Can this be a kind of growing up, in a way?'

I ask. It's a leading question, I know, but Wigg bites: 'Absolutely, absolutely,' she replies, 'it is.'

I wonder what she makes of the idea, which can be found everywhere from Shakespeare's 'second childishness' to the way many people use the same voice to speak to babies as to speak to older people, that rather than growing up, people with dementia are returning to infancy. Infantilisation is very, very dangerous in this population, she says. The distinction is that her residents 'have lived big lives, many years of life — periods of education, of child rearing, of caring for their own parents. That doesn't just go away while I'm caring for them.' So while she knows they need her help, she never perceives them as if they were her daughter and had not reached adulthood. 'This was true when I cared for my grandmother. I never perceived her as a child, even when she was babbling and not speaking clearly. I could hear enough in what she was saying to know what she was referencing. She was a religious woman, she had faith, and she would do this chanting as she'd sit and watch the birds, which she loved to do. She'd say, "Bird-bird bird-bird bird-bird; bird-bird bird-bird bird-bird." It was very rhythmic, sort of spiritual, and it was very in tune with nature. So it never sounded like babble to me.' She believes that if you can contextualise a person's behaviour, which requires a deep understanding of who you're engaged with, it is very hard to infantilise that person. 'It's never been something that I've experienced, and that's probably because I've been interested in who the person is and was.'

And yet, a common sight in the Vicarage is of the older male residents holding baby dolls as if they are their own child or grandchild. 'Sometimes it's very hard for families to see their 80-year-old father or grandfather cuddling a baby doll, cooing to it, stroking it, telling it how beautiful it is,' she says. But for Wigg and her colleagues, it is very moving. 'When you talk about how people continue to grow and evolve, even with dementia, you cannot convince me that a display of an 85-year-old man with a life-sized baby doll treating it as if it is real and doing all that he probably did to his own children, to his own grandchildren, is not continued human growth.' These men will share the baby doll with one another, carry it around when they're doing other tasks, and they engage with this doll as if it is a real baby. 'And in that, you see the depths of their humanity.' This is, she says, 'at its core, the beauty of humanity that we get to experience all the time'.

Listening in the way Wigg listens to her residents is a radical act. It is also the oldest and most instinctive act of compassion. It is similar in shape and feel to the kind of listening I describe at the opening of this chapter, between a father and his baby daughter. I say this not because I think Wigg's residents are like infants — but because I think the way a parent develops the openness and compassion to tune in to their child is not so far from the openness and compassion that we all need to develop to listen to each other. It is the opposite of the kind of non-listening that characterises our contemporary world — the opposite of a Twitter storm, or a self-help online step-by-step programme to 'improve your mental health'. This kind of listening and understanding that Wigg describes is very similar to the kind of listening that I experience from my analyst, and that I try to provide for my patients as a psychotherapist. It is a kind of listening where you are trying to understand not only the content of what is being said, but the meaning that is delivered in the way it is said, and in the silences. This is what gives you a sense of the atmosphere of a person's inner world. It is a refusal to see a person as if their brain and body is a bag of symptoms; it's a commitment to meeting a person from the position of wanting to understand.

I needed to write this book, like I needed my training, like I need psychoanalysis, because I did not know how to listen to myself. It seems to me that psychoanalysis is like a very special kind of acousticon; a hearing aid that allows you to hear, to be in communication with yourself and with others in a new way. I started writing this book because I wanted to know what it meant to be an adult and to find out why I wasn't one yet, hoping that I would become one by the end of it — that this would be my happy ending. I wanted to make myself grow up. Now I can hear that I was asking the wrong question — or, rather, that question has changed. Now the question has become not why haven't I finished growing up, but how can I keep growing up, throughout my life? I wanted to find a definition of what an adult is, what it means to grow up. Now I understand that this definition will be different for every individual, and that it will change from moment to moment for each of us, depending on the grow-up we are facing. I do now know, through this writing, through my analysis, through my patients, through speaking to so many fascinating people, that the work of growing up never stops — not if you're lucky. Not until the very end.

When I learnt from Thane, the historian, about the rapid increase in people surviving to 100 years old, it touched that childhood fascination in me with becoming a centenarian. I don't think of myself as a royalist in particular, but I confess I did wonder about my chances of one day getting a letter from the Queen. It turns out there is a website for that, where you can find out your odds of living to your 100th birthday — thanks Office for National Statistics.[16] I type in my sex, my date of birth, and I click 'Calculate'. The answer: I have a 21 per cent chance. Sometimes an answer is so much less interesting than a question. My response is 'meh'; it doesn't feel real. But that is not the only information on my results page. I read: 'Your average life expectancy is 90 years. This is 56 years from now.' 56 years of life left, I think to myself. That feels real. It is bracing. I know it is just an estimate, but it makes me realise as if for the first time, again, that my time here is limited. This is what Rothermund was talking about — the narrowing of the future time horizon. I write a note to myself: 'I really do not have long left. This is my life. I need to live it. I cannot wait for adulthood to come, I cannot live my life for other people, or

be who other people want me to be — I need to live for me, to be who
I am. But who is that?'

It's not that I think there is a 'me', some essence, some true adult self,
out there or in here, waiting to be discovered. But there is certainly an
idea in my mind of a self who I must try to be — a 'should-be-me' or an
'I-should-be'; a pretend me, covering up something more real. Just like I
don't think there is such a thing as one truth — but there is certainly such
a thing as lying, or as pretending, or deafening yourself to something
because you cannot bear to hear it — and when you stop doing that, you
are left with something more truthful. Psychoanalysis-the-acousticon is
helping me to hear these lies I tell myself, big ones, small ones, and each
time I can hear one it is a painful — but vital — grow-up. It occurs to
me that perhaps the reason I didn't feel adult was because I had this very
adult-looking tortoise shell and I was constantly trying to live up to it;
I thought that's what being an adult was. As the months have passed in
this pandemic and lockdowns have come and gone, over the course of
writing this book, as my training has progressed, and with every session
and with every break between the sessions in my analysis, I have come
to sense a qualitative difference in my everyday existence. For one thing,
I am so absorbed in my work that I have far less need for the app that
stops me accessing Twitter — I am not even tempted to log in most of
the time. And there are moments where I feel more separate, more at
ease, less panicked when alone. This is not a constant, one-directional
march of progress: at times, I am able to feel more in contact with my
own wants and needs, with my contradictions, my love and hate and
anger and fear, my desires and aggression; at others I am not, and I
bury my distress in the internet; this is the pinball-machine, Mr-Messy
theory of psychological development after all. In the weeks after I write
that note to myself, I have another revelation. It surprises me. It is this:
my life has value simply for being mine. I have value simply for being
me. I have always been a bit jealous of other people, wanted to be like
them — wanted to be more beautiful like this friend, to be better read

like that colleague, to be more successful like that person on Twitter. And so on. Now I finally get it, and it feels like a wave of freezing sea water crashing down over my head, reinvigorating me down to my bone marrow: I have been trying to grow up into somebody else. I need to hold on to the recognition that this is my life, my only life. I need to be as truthful to myself as I can to find out who I am and stick with me. I don't need to reach for my grandfather's keys any more. It is time to let them go. My life on this planet is limited, and it is always running out. And so is yours.

Afterword
What's next

'My Back Pages'
Song by Bob Dylan

The doorbell rings, and it is Boru. It has been 23 months since he last came to my home. When I open the door, I notice that the ponytail, the black nail polish, and the slightly hunched posture have gone — and he has a lot more tattoos. He does not fold himself into my sofa, or seem weighed down by the heaviness that quietened his voice in our last interview. He sits relaxed and solid in himself, smiling an easy, unforced grin as he tells me, in a voice that resonates with energy and life, 'I'm in such a different headspace from last time. It's so weird. I was thinking about it when I was coming over and I was like, she's going to think I'm a completely different person. Yeah, I've changed a lot since then. Well, grown a lot. I'm looking forward to talking.'

I do not actually think he is a completely different person. I recognise the same thoughtful, self-reflective silences; the same hunger to speak about his feelings and to precisely articulate his internal experience so that I can understand; his generosity and his gentleness. I can still sense his tenderness and vulnerability, too, but these parts of him are not vibrating off the surface of his skin as they once were — they seem more thoroughly integrated, woven into him in a more complex way. I can still see child and man in him, but the proportions and the relationship between the two are not the same as when we last met. He feels to me as he says he feels within himself: 'a lot more grown up'.

We sit, and we talk. He tells me that over the last two years: he has stopped taking cocaine, stopped smoking weed, even stopped smoking cigarettes. He has got a job as a cycling coach at the velodrome where he used to train, and he has big plans for his future career in coaching. He has saved his money instead of spending it on drugs and is about to move out from his parents' and into a rented flat with friends. He is planning a trip to Rwanda for a cycling race with another friend, and he is cycling more than ever, because it brings him joy and peace, meaning and fulfilment. All of these developments seem almost miraculous to me when I think back to our last interview and the droop of his shoulders, how hopeless he sounded, how defeated he looked, how he could see no way forward for himself. I ask what he now makes of his definition of an adult as someone who has their shit sorted, and he laughs and tells me, 'Yeah, that's what I've been trying to say without saying it; I've not got all my shit sorted, but I've definitely got more shit sorted than I did, and I feel more of an adult. So that means something. I'm still 22 years old — I'm not saying I've finally reached this nirvana of adulthood. But I'm a lot clearer of the path and the journey than I used to be.'

It is a profoundly emotional experience for me to listen to all this. Not just to see him so much healthier and happier in himself, but also to witness the kind of development, of growth, of adulthood I have been reaching for in this book — to hear it articulated and to see it embodied in Boru. He and I seem to have come to similar conclusions about adulthood over the last couple of years, although our experiences have been very different. Instead of running away from himself, using drugs to replace his thoughts and feelings, he now uses cycling to digest his emotions: talking about when he's on his bike, he says, 'I feel much more engaged with the world when I'm out there. Instead of removing myself from the world, I'm putting myself into it.' He talks me through how that works: 'So at first, you might switch off for a little bit, not think about anything. And then you get into the lanes, and if it's a nice day, you start appreciating everything; sometimes you're riding along and a little bird will fly in the road in front of you, and you think, I'm going to try and keep up with this guy. You notice the flashing sunlight as you go through the trees, the shadows on the ground. And then you start thinking about things, about situations that you're in and how you can best navigate them, rather than just putting it off. It's like a meeting with yourself.' A meeting with himself. He has found his acousticon — and it has two wheels.

And this grow-up has come in tandem with many others: 'I definitely know myself better,' he says. He understands how his mind works, so if he feels he is going in an unhelpful direction, 'I can recognise that and say, ah, we've been here before, this isn't something you want to do. And that helps you navigate that journey a little better than you did the last time. You might not get it right — I mean you probably definitely won't get it right. But at least you're going to do it slightly differently, because you understand yourself more.' That understanding, that getting to know himself, has been crucial in helping him to grow. 'I used coke so much because I convinced myself that when I had it, I felt how I was before I was depressed,' he says — that was the Happy-Go-Boru he was constantly in search of. But now that he has stopped trying to go backwards, he has been able to take a giant leap forwards in his life and grow into himself: 'I'm not trying to aggressively pursue the Boru that I wanted to be. I just let things take their course and I found a different kind of happiness that isn't like the one I was searching for before.'

I point out that on his T-shirt is the text, 'Break Free', repeated over and over again, and I tell him I think it's a great symbol, because it took real courage to break out of the stuck place he was in and to grow up. He replies, 'You know what though? It wasn't, "Oh, now I'm liberated!" or like I managed to escape these shackles that held me back, restricted me, debilitated me.' No, he is clear that breaking free is not the right way to think about this process; 'It's not like I'm super-confident now — I still get nervous as shit if I'm ordering something in a restaurant, that's still there. But it's not holding me back in the way it was, and it's not causing anything worse to happen as a result of it.' He didn't make it through these grow-ups through some force of will; there were many times where he did try to make himself grow but he remained stuck where he was, just as there were many times he tried to stop taking drugs, but couldn't. (While others may not relate recovering from addiction to growing up, for Boru the two are intertwined; 'Getting better is what made me grow, so I say those two things interchangeably.') Nor has he reached some state of supreme, self-confident adulthood — and he recognises he will go through hard times again in the future, although he now seems more open to seeking help if he does. What he describes instead is a much less dramatic, more nuanced, and finely balanced process of reaching a point where, he says, 'The dissatisfaction of my life finally outweighed the short-term feel-good nature that those things gave me.' The process was out of his hands, he seemed to be saying, but it propelled him forward once he was able to let it, and now he feels okay.

Realising this in my own life has been perhaps the biggest grow-up for me over the last two years. Finally understanding that I am not in control of my adultness or non-adultness, that I cannot use psychoanalysis to turn me into the adult I have always wanted to be, that I cannot grow up by telling myself off, by forcing myself, nor by writing a book to make it happen.

And yet, when I finished the last chapter of this book, I reflected, and I thought to myself that I had grown up a bit. I noticed I had been feeling more and more okay, day to day. For starters, I felt much less at the mercy of the internet; although I still fell into a Twitter hole from time to time, I was better able to fish myself out. The thought of having a child — while still quite terrifying — did not feel quite so beyond me, beyond us, as it once did. I even bought contents insurance. I thought to myself that if I were to start writing a book today, it would not be this book; I could not write a book about not feeling like an adult now — it's not that I now feel like one, so much as that I no longer feel sufficiently not like one. It doesn't feel like such a big deal any more.

And then, approaching the end of my psychotherapy training, I was offered a job in a psychodynamic talking therapies service. It's just like child and adolescent psychotherapist Ariel Nathanson said, back at the start of our search: 'You only know where you are at a certain point … and then it changes.' As soon as I received the allegedly good news, I was flung back into insecurity, terror, self-doubt. I accepted, and then I regretted my acceptance. I wanted to retract it, but I didn't — instead I spent the night watching TV and scrolling through social media, trying to fill my head up with fluff so I didn't have to feel so scared and inadequate. But there was a quiet voice in the back of my mind that said: 'Maybe you will feel different tomorrow.' I thought again of Nathanson and his moving description of surviving grief: 'The adult can hold their breath, knowing that after this wave, there will be some air.' This stands for more than the specific circumstances of bereavement, I think. The adult in me, the more forgiving superego in me, allowed me to watch TV, to get through that night, and then to wake up feeling a little better in the morning, when I was more able to think about things. I kept breathing, and I kept the job.

And so the grow-ups continue.

Boru tells me he thinks our last conversation played an important role in his growing up, and I ask what it was that he found so helpful. He says, 'I think it was admitting things to someone where you don't feel judged. Saying things out loud that you then realise and accept. I was able to say things a bit more truthfully and think about things more. I think that's why our conversation had such a lasting effect; it was just so different from any time I had spoken before about those thoughts and feelings.' Following that interview, he says, he still took drugs, but, 'I took a lot less after that — it made me really start cutting down. It kick-started this whole series of events, where I admitted that I can't be like this for ever, that I want to get my shit sorted.' A couple of months later, he set himself a New Year's resolution to start cycling once a month — what he considered to be a very low bar — to let himself feel good about something. And about a month after that he took hard drugs for the last time — that was well over a year ago.

Boru gives our conversation more credit for his grow-ups than I would — this all has far more to do with him of course, with the fact that he needed to have that conversation, that he wanted to. It strikes me that the way he talks about our conversation is similar to the way I talk about my analysis. I wonder if he was ready to face up to these truths and so that's what he used our conversation for, and then he continued that conversation afterwards within himself, and he continues to do so every time he takes off on his bike. Putting the truth of his situation into words meant, as Boru put it, he stopped trying to distance himself from himself. Instead of taking drugs so he wouldn't have to think about what he calls 'all the negative stuff', he was ready to become more reliant on thinking and turning towards the truth, to engage with himself in a different way. 'You start to have those conversations with yourself, and you become more of an honest person. I don't feel like I'm hiding from anything because I'm not hiding from myself.'

Not hiding from himself. This is it really, isn't it? That's what growing up is, that is what it means to become an adult, this is what I've been trying to say for the last 100,000 words. Whether you're a beginner adult in the 'weird limbo' life stage, or if you're a young adult in search of contents insurance, or if you're thinking about (non)parenthood and facing down the ghosts in your nursery, or if you're finding your way on a path through a dark wood 'Nel mezzo del cammin di nostra vita',[1] or if you're young-old and rising, or if you're in your last chapter. This is what it means to exist in a state of separateness from your parents and family; to shed the carapace of false adulthood and instead look after every single one of the different circles within your tree trunk; to want something better for your child than you have had and to bring something better to your child; to get used to the reality of 'the honour of physical decline'; to find your own acousticon and to use it to listen to the multitudes that you contain. This is what it means to live in peace. I understand this in a new way when I learn from my rabbi that the root of the Hebrew word for peace, *shalom*, is the same as the root of the Hebrew word for completeness or wholeness, *shalem*. The roots of these words are the same in Arabic. This is a truth that courses through the veins of humanity and always has done; we cannot live in peace while we are in hiding from or at war with parts of ourselves.

Not hiding from yourself is different from the notion of finding yourself, as the old cliché goes. Finding yourself implies there is a solid, coherent, single, and unchanging self to be found; a happy ending. Trying not to hide from yourself is to be engaged in an ongoing process, to accept there is no end but death, and to be open to a completely different way of being, one I am still grappling with. So I will keep going to analysis, I will keep listening to patients, and trying to listen to myself, and I will keep writing, and I will keep living — though no longer in the safety of dreaming about some magical key that my grandfather held. No longer on the same quest in search of the same answers. No longer an adult in search of adulthood — not because I've found it, but because I no longer need it in quite the same shape. Just a person, listening, talking, writing, breathing, open to seeing what I find when, if, I can stop hiding from myself.

> '*God reach out to us in tenderness, and give us the most precious gift: the gift of peace.*'
>
> *Jewish prayer, translated and interpreted by my rabbi*

Author's note

There are some points I would like to note.

First, I am aware that there are many nuances and experiences of growing up which I have failed to explore in my book, and this may leave some readers feeling excluded. These are among the many limits to my work, and should this leave any readers feeling unseen, I am sorry for that.

Secondly, I also want to emphasise that everything in these pages — my interviewees' life experiences, my experts' academic work, my own reflections, all of it — these are all moments in time that I have done my best to capture and think about. So much may have changed for many of my interviewees, and for myself, between the writing of this manuscript and putting it to bed. So please do think back on this book with Ariel Nathanson's words in mind: 'You only know where you are at a certain point … and then it changes.'

Thirdly, as I first encountered some of the interviewees in this book through my work as a journalist, there will be a little overlapping material in my articles previously published in various magazines and newspapers. The scenes of infancy at the opening of each chapter did not take place in reality but came from my imagination.

And finally, if you are curious and would like to find out more about psychoanalytic psychotherapy and psychoanalysis, you can find further information at the British Psychoanalytic Council: www.bpc.org.uk, and at the Institute of Psychoanalysis: psychoanalysis.org.uk.

Acknowledgements

I would like to express my deep gratitude to the following people, without whom I would not have been able to write this book, and who have helped to shape it into something which, I believe, has some value.

My interviewees. Some 45 academics, clinicians, authors, and case studies are quoted in this book, and many others also gave me their time and their thoughts in the course of my research who I was unfortunately unable to include. To my experts: it really has been an extraordinary experience to listen to people at the top of their fields, who care so deeply about their work, and who are so good at it, and who are expanding our understanding about ourselves and our world. I am especially grateful to Josh and Carine, from whom I have felt such support for this project. And to my case studies: your honesty, generosity, openness, and emotionally rich inner lives have enriched my own. Every one of you has helped to grow this book, and helped me to grow, and I am in your debt.

I also want to make it clear that any misunderstandings or errors are my responsibility alone, and I apologise for any that remain despite my best efforts to hunt them down. (Hello, superego.)

Rebecca, my agent, and Molly, my editor. It has been the privilege of my writing life to have your brilliant minds at work on my work. Thank you for shaping it into something I feel proud of. Thank you also to Anna, whose beautiful mind created this cover, and to Laura, Adam, and all at Scribe who worked on my book, and to Emma at Janklow and Nesbit.

My parents, for everything you have given me, and for the safe and loving home I grew up in.

My friends and family, many of whom generously read early drafts and have given their thoughts, reassurance, and invaluable criticism. I am particularly grateful for the extensive reading and crucial reflections from Andrea, Brendan, Conor, David, Dom, Jeff, Laura, Leila, Rose, Sam, Sarah, Sarah's writing group, Sharron, Shaun, and Tom. Tom, your infectious creativity has a propelling motor force of its own, thank you for directing it towards this book. Thank you also to Niki.

Emma and Jack, thank you for giving me space when I couldn't write without it, and for your friendship.

My supervisors, tutors, fellow trainees, David's Beyond Bion reading group, Leila's psychoanalytic book group, and my course reading group, my infant observation family, and my patients, from whom I have learnt so much.

My favourite psychoanalysts, whose brilliant and penetrating thinking has furthered our understanding of what it means to be human. Thank you to Sigmund Freud, Melanie Klein, Wilfred Bion, Neville Symington, Donald Winnicott, and the many others whose work has informed this book and changed my life. I have done my best to credit ideas appropriately, and hope I have not unconsciously veered into plagiarism.

My analyst … It's complicated. Thank you.

And finally, and most importantly, my husband. Thank you for reading this book so many times. Thank you for your belief in me, for your love, and for the light that never goes out.

Endnotes

Introduction: Beginnings

1   Francis, G. (2018) 'First time buyers average age has risen by seven years since the 1960s, survey finds', *The Independent*, 7 March. Available at: https://www.independent.co.uk/property/first-time-buyer-age-increase-1960s-housing-market-cost-property-ladder-a8244501.html (Accessed: 17 September 2021).

2   Statista (2020) 'Estimated median age of Americans at their first wedding in the United States from 1998 to 2019, by sex'. Available at: https://www.statista.com/statistics/371933/median-age-of-us-americans-at-their-first-wedding/ (Accessed: 17 September 2021).

3   Australian Institute of Family Studies (no date) *Births in Australia*. Available at: https://aifs.gov.au/facts-and-figures/births-in-australia#:~:text=Age%20of%20new%20mothers&text=Nowadays%2C%20the%20late%202020s%20and,2011%20and%2048%25%20in%202016 (Accessed: 17 September 2021).

4   Office for National Statistics (ONS) (2016) *Births in England and Wales: 2015*. Available at: https://www.ons.gov.uk/peoplepopulationandcommunity/birtsdeathsandmarriages/livebirths/bulletins/birthsummarytablesenglandandwales/2015 (Accessed: 17 September 2021).

5   Hamilton, B. E., Martin, J. A., Osterman, M. J. K. (2020) *Vital Statistics Rapid Release — Births: Provisional Data for 2019*. Available at: https://www.cdc.gov/nchs/data/vsrr/vsrr-8-508.pdf (Accessed: 17 September 2021).

6   Ogden, T. H. (1992) 'Comments on transference and countertransference in the initial analytic meeting', *Psychoanalytic Inquiry*, 12(2), pp. 225–47.

7   Ibid.

8   Bick, E. (1964) 'Notes on infant observation in psycho-analytic training', *The International Journal of Psycho-Analysis*, 45(4), pp. 558–66.

9   Shakespeare, W. (1978) *King Lear*. in *The Complete Works of William Shakespeare*. London, UK: Abbey Library, pp. 883–916.

Chapter One: The weird limbo

1   Sarner, M. (2019) 'Abandoned at 18: the young people denied mental health support because they are "adults"', *The Guardian*, 20 March. Available at: https://www.theguardian.com/society/2019/mar/20/abandoned-at-18-the-young-people-denied-mental-health-support-because-they-are-adults (Accessed: 17 September 2021).

2   'Gillick v West Norfolk & Wisbech Area Health Authority' (1985) *Weekly Law Reports,* 830.

3   Ibid.

4   *The Children Act 1989* (c.23). London, UK: The Stationery Office.

5   Ibid.

6   Appleton, R., Elahi, F., Tuomainen, H. et al. (2020) '"I'm just a long history of people rejecting referrals" experiences of young people who fell through the gap between child and adult mental health services', *European Child & Adolescent Psychiatry*, 30(30), pp. 401–13.

7   Blakemore, S.-J. (2018) *Inventing Ourselves: the secret life of the teenage brain*. London, UK: Doubleday.

8   Keats, J., Gittings, R. (Ed.) (1975) *Letters of John Keats*. Oxford, UK: Oxford University Press.

9   Ibid.

10 Winnicott, D. W. (1971) *Playing and Reality*. London, UK: Tavistock Publications.

11 Ogden, T. H. (1986) *The Matrix of the Mind*. London, UK: Karnac Books (1991).

12 Winnicott, D. W. *Playing and Reality*.

13 Schüll, N. D. (2012) *Addiction by Design*. Princeton, N.J., USA: Princeton University Press.

14 Chu, S. W. M., Clark, L., Murch, W. S. (2017) 'Measuring the slot machine zone with attentional dual tasks and respiratory sinus arrhythmia', *Psychology of Addictive Behaviours*, 31(3), pp. 375–84.

15 Sarner, M. (2019) 'Am I addicted? The truth behind being hooked on gaming, sex or porn', *New Scientist*, 11 September. Available at: https://www.newscientist.com/article/mg24332470-700-am-i-addicted-the-truth-behind-being-hooked-on-gaming-sex-or-porn/ (Accessed: 17 September 2021).

16 Gambling Commission (2018) *Gambling participation in 2018: behaviour, awareness and attitudes*. Available at: https://www.gamblingcommission.gov.uk/PDF/survey-data/Gambling-participation-in-2018-behaviour-awareness-and-attitudes.pdf (Accessed: 17 September 2021).

17 Twenge, J. M. (2017) *iGen: Why Today's Super-Connected Kids are Growing Up Less Rebellious, More Tolerant, Less Happy — and Completely Unprepared*

for Adulthood — and What that Means for the Rest of Us. New York, N.Y., USA: Atria Books.

18 Sohn, S. Y., Rees, P., Wildridge, B. et al. (2019) 'Prevalence of problematic smartphone usage and associated mental health outcomes amongst children and young people: a systematic review, meta-analysis and GRADE of the evidence', *BMC Psychiatry*, 19 (356) https://doi.org/10.1186/s12888-019-2350-x.

19 Sarner, M. (2018) 'Meet the tech evangelist who now fears for our mental health', *The Guardian*, 15 March. Available at: https://www.theguardian.com/technology/2018/mar/15/meet-the-tech-evangelist-who-now-fears-for-our-mental-health (Accessed: 20 September 2021).

20 *Riley v California* (2014) 134 S. Ct. 2473.

21 Sarner, M. (2018) 'The age of envy: how to be happy when everyone else's life looks perfect', *The Guardian,* 9 October. Available at: https://www.theguardian.com/lifeandstyle/2018/oct/09/age-envy-be-happy-everyone-else-perfect-social-media.

22 Winnicott, D. W. (1960) 'Ego distortion in terms of True and False Self', in *The Maturational Processes and the Facilitating Environment.* London, UK: Hogarth Press, 1972, pp. 140–52.

23 Freud, S (1893-1895) 'Studies on hysteria' in *The Standard Edition of the Complete Psychological Works of Sigmund Freud.* Vol. 2. London, Hogarth Press.

24 Natterson-Horowitz, B., Bowers, K. (2019) *Wildhood: the epic journey from adolescence to adulthood in humans and other animals.* London, UK: Scribe, (2020).

25 'Albatross sex ed'. Available at: https://www.wildhood.com/videos/albatross-sex-ed (Accessed: 16 October 2021).

26 Hobson, P. R. (2018) *Consultations in Dynamic Psychotherapy.* London, UK: Karnac Books.

Chapter Two: Contents insurance

1 Henig, R. M. (2010) 'What is it about 20-somethings?', *The New York Times Magazine*, 18 August. Available at: https://www.nytimes.com/2010/08/22/magazine/22Adulthood-t.html?pagewanted=all (Accessed: 20 September 2021); Steinberg, L. (2014) 'The case for delayed adulthood', *The New York Times Sunday Review*, 19 September. Available at: nytimes.com/2014/09/21/opinion/sunday/the-case-for-delayed-adulthood.html (Accessed: 20 September 2021); Beck, J. (2016) 'When are you really an adult', *The Atlantic*, 5 January. Available at: https://www.theatlantic.com/health/archive/2016/01/when-are-you-really-an-adult/422487/ (Accessed: 20 September 2021).

2   Shakespeare, W. (1978) *The Winter's Tale.* in *The Complete Works of William Shakespeare.* London, UK: Abbey Library, pp. 323–53.

3   Arnett, J. J. (2000) 'Emerging adulthood: a theory of development from the late teens through the twenties', *American Psychologist,* 55(5), pp. 469–80; Arnett, J. J. (2003) 'Conceptions of the transition to adulthood among emerging adults in American ethnic groups', *New Directions for Child and Adolescent Development,* 2003(100), pp. 63–76; Arnett J. J. (1998) 'Learning to stand alone: the contemporary American transition to adulthood in cultural and historical context', *Human Development,* 41(5–6), pp. 295–315.

4   Zhong, J., Arnett, J. J. (2014) 'Conceptions of adulthood among migrant women workers in China', *International Journal of Behavioral Development,* 38(3), pp. 255–65.

5   Mintz, S. (2015) *The Prime of Life: a history of modern adulthood.* Cambridge, Mass. USA: Belknap Press of Harvard University Press.

6   Office for National Statistics (ONS) (2019) *Milestones: journeying into adulthood.* Available at: https://www.ons.gov.uk/peoplepopulationandcommunity/ populationandmigration/ppulationestimates/articles/ milestonesjourneyingintoadulthood/2019-02-18 (Accessed: 20 September 2021).

7   Waller-Bridge, P. (Dir.) (2019) 'Episode 1', in *Fleabag,* season 2, Amazon Prime, 17 May.

8   Flood, A. (2020) 'Jacqueline Wilson reveals publicly that she is gay', *The Guardian,* 4 April. Available at: https://www.theguardian.com/books/2020/ apr/04/jacqueline-wilson-reveals-publicly-she-is-a-lesbian-love-frankie (Accessed: 20 September 2021).

9   Freud, S. (1923) 'The ego and the id' in *The Standard Edition of the Complete Psychological Works of Sigmund Freud.* Vol. 19. London, UK: Hogarth Press, 1961, pp. 3–66.

10   Freud, S. (1933) 'New Introductory Lectures on Psycho-Analysis' in *The Standard Edition of the Complete Psychological Works of Sigmud Freud.* Vol 22. London, UK: Vintage, 2001, pp.57-80.

11   Freud, S. (1905) 'Three essays on the theory of sexuality' in *The Standard Edition of the Complete Psychological Works of Sigmund Freud.* Vol. 7. London, UK: Vintage, 2001, pp. 125–245.

12   Hinshelwood, R. D. (2019) 'The good, the bad, and the superego' in Harding, C. (ed.) (2019) *Dissecting the Superego, Moralities Under the Psychoanalytic Microscope.* Oxford, UK: Routledge.

13   Mintz, S. *The Prime of Life.*

14   Carty-Williams, C. (2019) *Queenie.* London, UK: Trapeze.

15   Sandler, P. C. (2005) *The Language of Bion: a dictionary of concepts.* London, UK: Karnac Books.

16 Bion, W. (1962) *Learning from Experience*. London, UK: Heinemann; Bion, W. (1963) *Elements of Psychoanalysis*. London, UK: Heinemann; Bion, W. (1965) *Transformations*. London, UK: Heinemann.

Chapter Three: The ghosts in the nursery

1 Fraiberg, S., Adelson, E., Shapiro, V. (1975) 'Ghosts in the nursery: a psychoanalytic approach to the problems of impaired infant-mother relationships', *Journal of American Academy of Child Psychiatry*, 14(3), pp. 387–421.

2 Freund, A. M., Nikitin, J., Ritter, J. O. (2009) 'Psychological consequences of longevity', *Human Development*, 52, pp. 1–37.

3 Mehta, C., Arnett, J. J., Palmer, C., Nelson, L. (2020) 'Established adulthood: a new conception of ages 30 to 45', *American Psychologist,* 75(4), pp. 431–44.

4 Ibid.

5 Organisation for Economic Cooperation and Development (OECD) (2021) *Family database: age of mothers at childbirth and age-specific fertility.* Available at: https://www.oecd.org/els/soc/SF_2_3_Age_mothers_childbirth.pdf (Accessed: 2 October 2021).

6 Office for National Statistics (ONS) (2019) *Childbearing for Women Born in Different Years, England and Wales: 2018.* Available at: https://www.ons.gov.uk/peoplepopulationandcommunity/ birthsdeathsandmarriages/conceptionandfertilityrates/bulletins/ childbearingforwomenbornindifferentyearsenglandandwales/2018 (Accessed: 20 September 2021).

7 Australian Bureau of statistics (ABS) (2019) *Births, Australia*. Available at: https://www.abs.gov.au/statistics/people/population/births-australia/2019 (Accessed: 20 September 2021).

8 Miller, T. (2005) *Making Sense of Motherhood: a narrative approach.* Cambridge, UK: Cambridge University Press; Miller, T. (2010) *Making Sense of Fatherhood: gender, caring and work.* Cambridge, UK: Cambridge University Press; Miller, T. (2017) *Making Sense of Parenthood: caring, gender and family Lives.* Cambridge, UK: Cambridge University Press.

9 Ramírez-Esparza, N., García-Sierra, A., Kuhl, P. K. (2014) 'Look who's talking: speech style and social context in language input to infants are linked to concurrent and future speech development', *Developmental Science*, 17(6), pp. 880–91; Ramírez-Esparza, N., García-Sierra, A., Kuhl, P. K. (2017) 'The impact of early social interactions on later language development in Spanish-English bilingual infants', *Child Development*, 88(4), pp. 1216–34; Ramírez-Esparza, N., García-Sierra, A., Kuhl, P. K. (2017) 'Look Who's Talking NOW! Parentese speech, social context, and language development across time', *Frontiers in Psychology*, 8, p. 1008.

10 Fraiberg, S., Adelson, E., Shapiro, V. 'Ghosts in the nursery', 14(3), pp. 387-421.

11 King, L. (2015) *Family Men: fatherhood and masculinity in Britain, 1914–1960*. Oxford, UK: Oxford University Press.

12 Zweig, F. (1961) *The Worker in Affluent Society: family life and industry*. London, UK: Heinemann.

13 'End Corporal Punishment' (2020) *Country Report for the United Kingdom*. Available at: https://endcorporalpunishment.org/reports-on-every-state-and-territory/uk/ (Accessed: 20 September 2021).

14 Shakespeare, W. (1978) *As You Like It* in *The Complete Works of William Shakespeare*. London, UK: Abey Library, pp. 220-244.

15 Roth, P. (2001) 'The paranoid-schizoid position' in Bronstein, C. (Ed.), *Kleinian Theory: a contemporary perspective*. London, UK: Whurr.

16 Klein, M. (1957) *Envy and Gratitude and Other Works, 1946–1963*. London, UK: Hogarth Press; Klein M. (1996) 'Notes on some schizoid mechanisms', *The Journal of Psychotherapy Practice and Research*, 5(2), pp. 160–79; Klein, M. (1935) 'A contribution to the psychogenesis of manic-depressive states', *The International Journal of Psychoanalysis*, 16, pp. 145–74; Klein, M. (1940) 'Mourning and its relation to manic-depressive states', *The International Journal of Psychoanalysis*, 21, pp. 125–53; Klein, M. (1945) 'The Oedipus complex in the light of early anxieties', *The International Journal of Psychoanalysis*, 26, pp. 11–33.

17 Blackstone, A. (2019) *Childfree by Choice: the movement redefining family and creating a new age of independence*. N.Y., USA: Dutton.

18 Hoekzema, E., Barba-Müller, E., Pozzobon, C., Picado, M., Lucco, García-García, D. et al. (2017) 'Pregnancy leads to long-lasting changes in human brain structure', *Nature Neuroscience*, 20(2), pp. 287–96.

19 Barba-Müller, E., Craddock, S., Carmona, S., Hoekzema, E., (2019) 'Brain plasticity in pregnancy and the postpartum period: links to maternal caregiving and mental health', *Archives of Women's Mental Health*, 22(2), pp. 289–99.

Chapter Four: *La selva oscura*

1 Alighieri, D. (1472) *La Divina Commedia* [Online]. Urbana, Illinois: Project Gutenberg (1997). Available at https://www.gutenberg.org/files/1012/1012-h/1012-h.htm (Accessed: 9 January 2022).

2 Infurna, F. J., Gerstorf, D., Lachman, M. E. (2020) 'Midlife in the 2020s: Opportunities and challenges', *American Psychologist*, 74(4), pp. 470–85.

3 Alighieri, D. (1472) *La Divina Commedia* [Online]. Urbana, Illinois: Project Gutenberg (1997). Available at https://www.gutenberg.org/files/1012/1012-h/1012-h.htm (Accessed: 9 January 2022).

4   Morgan Brett, B. R. (2010) 'The negotiation of midlife: exploring the subjective experience of ageing'. PhD thesis, University of Essex. Available at: https://ethos.bl.uk/OrderDetails.do?uin=uk.bl.ethos.531545 (Accessed: 21 September 2021).

5   Jaques, E. (1965) 'Death and the midlife crisis', *International Journal of Psychoanalysis*, 46(4), pp. 502–14.

6   Morgan Brett, B. (2013) 'Growing up and Growing Old' in Nicolas, A., Flaherty, I. (Eds) *Growing Up, Growing Old: trajectories of times and lives*. Oxford, UK: Inter-disciplinary Press.

7   Lachman, M. E. (2015) 'Mind the gap in the middle: a call to study midlife', *Research in Human Development*, 12(3–4), pp. 327–34.

8   Bion, W. (1979) *Clinical Seminars and Other Works*. London, UK: Karnac Books, 2000.

9   Sarner, M. (2019) '"You've got to carry on that fight": strangers swap life-changing experiences', *The Guardian*, 19 October. Available at: https://www.theguardian.com/lifeandstyle/2019/oct/19/carry-on-that-fight-strangers-swap-life-changing-experiences (Accessed: 22 September 2021).

10 Infurna, F. J., Gerstorf, D., Lachman, M. E. (2020) 'Midlife in the 2020s: opportunities and challenges', *American Psychologist*, 74(4), pp. 470–85.

11 Robinson, O. (2013) *Development through Adulthood: an integrative sourcebook*. Basingstoke, UK: Palgrave Macmillan.

12 Hollis, J. (1993) *The Middle Passage: from misery to meaning in midlife*. Toronto, Can.: Inner City Books.

13 Jaques, E. (1965) 'Death and the midlife crisis', *International Journal of Psychoanalysis*, 46(4), pp. 502–14.

14 Cohen, J. (2021) *How to Live. What to Do*. London, UK: Ebury.

15 Bion, W. (1970) *Attention and Interpretation*. London, UK: Karnak Books, 1984.

Chapter Five: Young-old rising

1   Frost, E., McClean, S. (2014) *Thinking about the Lifecourse: a psychosocial introduction*. Basingstoke, UK: Palgrave Macmillan.

2   Thane, P. (2005) *The Long History of Old Age*. London, UK: Thames & Hudson.

3   Neugarten, B. (1974) 'Age Groups in American Society and the Rise of the Young-Old', *The Annals of the American Academy of Political and Social Science*, 415(1), pp. 187–98.

4   Neugarten, B. (1978) 'The young-old and the age-irrelevant society', *The young-old ... a new North American phenomenon, the annual winter conference of the Couchiching Institute of Public Affairs*. Ontario, Can.: Couchiching Institute on Public Affairs.

5   O'Connor, A. (2001) 'Dr. Bernice L. Neugarten, 85, early authority on the elderly', *The New York Times*, 30 July. Available at https://www.nytimes.com/2001/07/30/us/dr-bernice-l-neugarten-85-early-authority-on-the-elderly.html (Accessed: 22 September 2021).

6   Culver, V. (2011) 'Dail Neugarten, professor emerita at UC Denver and advocate for the aging, dies at 66', *The Denver Post,* 11 June. Available at: https://www.denverpost.com/2011/06/11/dail-neugarten-professor-emerita-at-uc-denver-and-advocate-for-the-aging-dies-at-66/ (Accessed: 3 October 2021).

7   Binstock, R. H. (2002) 'In Memoriam: Bernice L. Neugarten', *The Gerontologist*, 42(2), pp. 149–51.

8   Thane, P. (2000) *Old Age In English History: Past Experiences, Present Issues.* Oxford, UK: Oxford University Press.

9   Parker, J. (2019) 'The decade of the "young old" begins', *The Economist*, December. Available at: https://theworldin.economist.com/edition/2020/article/17316/decade-young-old-begins (Accessed: 22 September 2021).

10 Ibid.

11 Freund, A. M. (2020) 'The bucket list effect: why leisure goals are often deferred until retirement', *American Psychologist*, 75(4), pp. 499–510.

12 Thane, P. *The Long History of Old Age.*

13 Freund, A. M. (2020) 'The bucket list effect: why leisure goals are often deferred until retirement', *American Psychologist*, 75(4), pp. 499–510.

14 Lamb, S., Robbins-Ruszkowski, J., Corwin, A., Calasanti, T., King, N. (2017) *Successful Aging as a Contemporary Obsession: global perspectives*. New Brunswick, N.J., USA: Rutgers University Press.

15 Murakami, H., trans. Gabriel, P. (2009) *What I Talk About When I Talk About Running*. London, UK: Vintage.

16 Lamb, S., Robbins-Ruszkowski, J., Corwin, A., Calasanti, T., King, N. (2017) *Successful Aging as a Contemporary Obsession: global perspectives*. New Brunswick, N.J., USA: Rutgers University Press.

17 Ibid.

18 Hill, A. (2021) 'Ageing process is unstoppable, finds unprecedented study', *The Guardian*, 17 June. Available at: https://www.theguardian.com/science/2021/jun/17/ageing-process-is-irreversible-finds-unprecedented-study (Accessed: 22 September 2021).

19 Freud, A. (1936) *The Ego and the Mechanisms of Defence*. London, UK: Karnac Books, 1993.

20 Klein, M. 'Mourning and its relation to manic-depressive states' 21, pp. 125–53.

21 Ibid.

22 Ibid.

23 Rowling, J. K. (1997) *Harry Potter and the Philosopher's Stone*. London, UK: Bloomsbury.

24 Murakami, H., trans. Gabriel, P. (2018) *Killing Commendatore*. London, UK: Harvill Secker.

25 Grossmann, I., Karasawa, M., Kan, C., Kitayama, S. (2014) 'A cultural perspective on emotional experiences across the life span', *Emotion*, 14(4), pp. 679–92; Karasawa, M., Curhan, K. B., Markus, H. R., Kitayama, S., Love, G. D., Radler, B. T., Ryff, C. D. (2011) 'Cultural perspectives on aging and well-being: a comparison of Japan and the United States', *International Journal of Aging & Human Development*, 73(1), pp. 73–98; Curhan, K. B., Sims, T., Markus, H. R., Kitayama, S., Karasawa, M., Kawakami, N., Love, G. D., Coe, C. L., Miyamoto, Y., Ryff, C. D. (2014) 'Just how bad negative affect is for your health depends on culture', *Psychological Science*, 25(12), pp. 2277–80.

26 Kitayama, S., Berg, M. K., Chopik, W. J. (2020) 'Culture and well-being in late adulthood: theory and evidence', *American Psychologist,* 75(4), pp. 567–76.

27 Park, J., Kitayama, S., Miyamoto, Y., Coe, C. L. (2020) 'Feeling bad is not always unhealthy: culture moderates the link between negative affect and diurnal cortisol profiles', *Emotion*, 20(5). pp. 721-733.

28 Bion, W. *Elements of Psychoanalysis*.

29 Steiner, J., Bell, D. (2020) 'Maintaining an analytic setting in an NHS context', *The Tavistock and Portman NHS Foundation Trust centenary scientific meeting*. Attended via Zoom on 12 October 2020.

30 Bion, W. (1962) 'A theory of thinking', *International Journal of Psychoanalysis*, 43(4–5), pp. 306–10.

31 Bion, W. *Transformations*.

32 Bion, F. (1995) 'The days of our years', *The Melanie Klein & Object Relations Journal*, 13(1), p. 106.

33 Waddell, M. (1998) *Inside Lives: psychoanalysis and the growth of the personality.* London, UK: Karnac Books, 2005.

Chapter Six: The last chapter

1 Savage, M., Tapper, J. (2021), 'Patients were sent back to care homes without Covid test despite bosses' plea', *The Observer*, 29 May. Available at: https://www.theguardian.com/society/2021/may/29/patients-were-sent-back-to-care-homes-without-covid-test-despite-bosses-plea

2 Rosen, M. (2020) 'Every day, there's a mental struggle, to come to terms with what happened to me, how I feel now and how I was before'. Interviewed by Martha Kearney. *Today*, BBC Radio 4, 15 December.

3 Neugarten, B. 'The young-old and the age-irrelevant society'.

4   Thane, P. *The Long History of Old Age.*
5   Office for National Statistics (ONS) (2020) *Estimates of the Very Old, Including Centenarians, UK: 2002–2019.* Available at: https://www.ons. gov.uk/peoplepopulationandcommunity/birthsdeathsandmarriages/ageing/ bulletins/estimatesoftheveryoldincludingcentenarians/2002to2019 (Accessed: 22 September 2021).
6   Office for National Statistics (ONS) (2018) *Living Longer: how our population is changing and why it matters.* Available at: https://www.ons.gov.uk/ peoplepopulationandcommunity/birthsdeathsandmarriages/ageing/articles/livin glongerhowourpopulationischangingandwhyitmatters/2018-08-13#how-is-the-uk-population-changing (Accessed: 22 September 2021).
7   Office for National Statistics *Estimates of the Very Old.*
8   Administration for Community Living (ACL) (2018) *2017 Profile of Older Americans.* Available at: https://acl.gov/sites/default/files/Aging%20and%20 Disability%20in%20America/2017OlderAmericansProfile.pdf (Accessed: 22 September 2021).
9   Australian Institute of Health and Welfare (AIHW) (2018) *Older Australia at a Glance.* Available at: https://www.aihw.gov.au/reports/older-people/older-australia-at-a-glance/contents/demographics-of-older-australians/australia-s-changing-age-gender-profile (Accessed: 22 September 2021).
10 Brandtstädter, J., Rothermund, K., Kranz, D., Kühn, W. (2010) 'Final decentrations: personal goals, rationality perspectives, and the awareness of life's finitude', *European Psychologist*, 15(2), pp. 152–63.
11 Livingston, G. et al. (2017) 'The Lancet Commissions: dementia prevention, intervention, and care', *The Lancet*, 390(10113), pp. 2673–734. Available at: https://www.thelancet.com/journals/lancet/article/PIIS0140-6736(17)31363-6/fulltext#seccestitle1480 (Accessed: 22 September 2021); Livingston, G. et al. (2020) 'Dementia prevention, intervention, and care: 2020 report of the Lancet Commission, *The Lancet*, 396(10248), pp. 413–46. Available at: https://www. thelancet.com/journals/lancet/article/PIIS0140-6736(20)30367-6/fulltext (Accessed: 22 September 2021).
12 'Miller Reese Hutchison' (2021) *Wikipedia.* Available at: https://en.wikipedia. org/wiki/Miller_Reese_Hutchison (Accessed: 3 October 2021).
13 (1944) 'Miller Hutchison, inventor, 67, Dead; devised acousticon, klaxon horn and the dictograph former Edison executive', *The New York Times.* February 18. Available at: https://www.nytimes.com/1944/02/18/archives/miller-h1jtchison-inventor-67-dead-devised-acousticon-klaxon-horn.html (Accessed: 3 October 2021).
14 The Vicarage by the Sea: https://www.thevicaragebythesea.com/
15 Wigg, J., 'Intimacy among the socially dead' in Nicolas, A., Flaherty, I., *Growing Up, Growing Old.*

16 Office for National Statistics (ONS) (2019) *Life expectancy calculator.* Available at: https://www.ons.gov.uk/peoplepopulationandcommunity/healthandsocialcare/ healthandlifeexpectancies/articles/lifeexpectancycalculator/2019-06-07 (Accessed: 3 October 2021).

Afterword: What's next

1 Alighieri, D. *La Divina Commedia* [Online]. Urbana, Illinois: Project Gutenberg (1997). Available at: https://www.gutenberg.org/files/1012/1012-h/1012-h.htm (Accessed: 9 January 2022).